I BELIEVE IN THE BIBLE

I Believe in
the Bible

David Jackman

Hodder & Stoughton
LONDON SYDNEY AUCKLAND

Copyright © 2000 David Jackman

First published in Great Britain in 2000

10 9 8 7 6 5 4 3 2 1

British Library Cataloguing in Publication Data
A record for this book is available from the British Library

ISBN 0 340 74574 6

Typeset by Avon Dataset Ltd, Bidford-on-Avon, Warks

Printed and bound in Great Britain by
The Guernsey Press Co. Ltd, Channel Isles

Hodder and Stoughton Ltd
A Division of Hodder Headline
338 Euston Road
London NW1 3BH

Contents

Editor's preface

This new series is intended to build on the widely acknowledged success of the original 'I Believe' series, of which several volumes continue to be in print. Now as then, each book sets out to tackle one of the key issues which faces Christians today. The overall aim is to stimulate informed thinking and to encourage living faith by building a bridge between the ever-relevant teaching of the Bible and the complex realities of the modern world.

When I was planning this series, David Jackman was the obvious author to approach with an invitation to tackle the subject of the Bible itself. He exercises a widely appreciated Bible teaching ministry and, as Director of the Cornhill Training Course, is hard at work preparing Bible teachers and preachers for the next generation. He is therefore no stranger to the challenge of helping Christians tackle the questions and controversies that surround the Bible.

As you will soon see from what he has written, David brings a combination of intellectual rigour and passionate enthusiasm to his subject. Here is someone who really does believe in the Bible! I'm delighted at the way his gentle and persuasive manner comes across so clearly as he shows how to make sense of this ancient book and apply it to the issues we face in the modern world. For David Jackman, the Bible is far more than a fascinating book from long ago: it's how we hear God speak today. Keep reading and let him show you how!

David Stone

Acknowledgments

I should like to thank the Proclamation Trust for study leave to enable me to do much of the writing of the text, and the students of the Cornhill Training Course, by whom many of its ideas and examples have been tested and clarified over the years. My warmest thanks are due to Nancy Olsen, whose keyboard skills converted my hieroglyphics into successive drafts of a readable manuscript, and to Annabel Robson and David Moloney for their editorial support and help. To my colleague Doug Johnson and my daughter, Philly Simpkin, who read the first draft, many thanks are due for their helpful suggestions, and to my wife Heather, whose love and support, as always, enabled me to start, continue and complete the project, I owe my deepest thanks and gratitude.

Introduction

'Of making many books there is no end.' The words of the writer of the Bible book of Ecclesiastes certainly have a contemporary ring about them. However, the purpose of this particular book is to encourage the reader to read the greatest book of all, of which God himself is the author. The Bible, still the world's best-seller, is probably found in more copies, editions and translations than any other text which has ever been published, and yet in spite of its availability it remains unknown – a closed book – to so many people today.

Most of my adult working life has centred on this book, ever since I first tried to explain one of its texts, as a raw and somewhat nervous student, to a supportive and hugely tolerant little congregation in a rural chapel, nearly forty years ago now. My great passion is still to understand the contents of this amazing book, so as to seek to live it out and share its truth and light with others. As a Christian pastor and teacher, it has been my privilege to open the Bible and try to explain its meaning, several times a week, in a great variety of contexts, to all sorts of people, believing and sceptical, around the world. I have been able to put the Bible to the test and I have never found it to fail. Wherever you go, whatever the culture, the Bible speaks to the basic needs of the human heart and mind with an immediate relevance and a penetrating power, which can only be explained by its divine origin. 'Men spoke from God as they were carried along by the Holy Spirit' (2 Peter 1:21).

I believe in the Bible because it is God's book, articulating in human language the mind of the God who made us for relationship with himself. It is through the pages of the Bible that we come to know his character and to understand his ways. It is here that we encounter

God in person, as we meet Jesus Christ, the central focus of the whole revelation, and are called to repent of our rebellious autonomy by acknowledging God as God, in our own personal lives. The Bible is not a book about God; it is God speaking to us, in a directly engaging way, teaching, rebuking, correcting, training and equipping us to live rightly in his world now, in preparation for the life of the world to come.

Like all good gifts, the Bible can be abused, and has often been misused by those whose own agenda is to distort its message and destroy its credibility. It is often said that you can make the Bible mean anything you want it to. But that is only true if the basic rules by which we understand and interpret any document are ignored or infringed. Of course, if a sentence is lifted entirely out of its setting and then made to stand on its own as an absolute statement, the Bible can be made to say some strange things. 'There is no God' is a straight quote from Psalm 14:1, but look at it in its context! Playing childish games like that with the Bible is the worst sort of trivialisation. And yet the Bible remains a closed book to millions of people for a variety of reasons which are almost as trivial. The tragedy is that so many of the answers to the dilemmas of our contemporary world are contained within its pages, and yet lie there unknown and ignored. It is as if medical researchers were to discover a cure for cancer, write it up in a widely circulated textbook, distribute it to every hospital and health centre around the world, and then for the precious information to remain unread on the bookshelf, as people continued to die of the disease. If we were told that God was going to make a television broadcast after the evening news tonight, most of us would plan to be in, or at the very least to have the video set. We would be interested to know what he would say. But he has already told us all we need to know to bring us to eternal life, and the book lies unopened and unread.

The purpose of this book is to encourage you into reading the Bible for yourself, whether or not you have tried it before. They say that you can eat an elephant if you tackle it slice by slice. So the aim of these pages is to make the Bible more accessible, by seeing how its great variety keeps returning to, and underlining, its central story. Its goal is to give confidence in handling the Bible well, practising the principles of good understanding and interpretation, so that its message becomes clear and compelling. We may not always like what we discover, because the Bible has a way of getting under the skin, challenging our comfort zones and questioning our dearly held opinions. But that is what we most need if our lives are going to be changed and renewed. However, it is perhaps true that this book should come with a 'health warning', because reading and understanding the Bible is a high-risk activity. What we do with what we discover can have eternal implications, because we never walk away from an encounter with God in the Bible unchanged. Either our hearts are softened, as we accept what he says to us, through faith and practical action in obedience, or they are hardened, as we refuse his revelation and reject his demands. The Bible will not allow anyone who reads it seriously to remain neutral.

'I believe in the Bible' is not just a credal statement; it expresses the passion which motivates my life and ministry. When Martin Luther was accused of being obsessed with the Bible and totally prejudiced in its favour, he didn't deny the fact. Rather, he retorted that it was natural for anyone to be prejudiced in favour of his own mother, affirming that it was through the Bible he was brought to birth – to the new life in Christ, which is being born again. That is the experience of every Bible-believing Christian. The Spirit of God still uses the Word of God to produce the people of God. Those who belong to that community affirm that all they believe comes from God's revelation in the Holy Scriptures. They are supremely those who believe in the Bible.

Chapter 1

The Bible at the Start of the Twenty-First Century

IT WAS AN ordinary afternoon at the school gate, as the cars pulled up and the pushchairs were wheeled across the zebra crossing. But Alison had a mission in the couple of minutes before the children began to stream out. She had got to know Christine quite well during the term and had enjoyed the snatched conversations they often had together. Now was the time to ask her to the Bible study on investigating Christianity which she and some other mums at the Church were planning to start. She grabbed her courage with both hands and launched out into the invitation. Christine's response was hardly enthusiastic. 'The Bible? You mean you actually spend your time reading that old-fashioned stuff? I can only remember bits of it from school in RE lessons — all that fusty, musty language, people slaughtering one another or committing adultery, and those weird, out-of-date explanations about how the world began. Anyway, science disproved it all long ago, and it's all been rewritten and changed down the centuries. I really don't have time to waste on all that rubbish. I'm just too busy with the children.'

The debate round the table in the students' union bar was getting more heated. 'No, Dan, I don't want to come and read the Bible with you and your friends,' Matt was almost shouting. 'I tried to read it once and it didn't make any sense. Anyway, didn't you listen to that lecture this morning? A literary text doesn't have a "meaning". It's just black marks on white paper. It's just a place where the ideas of the author are expressed. I'll relate to it one way, and you another, and Kate another. It's only what you want it to be. You want your Bible to mean something to boost your predetermined religious ideas, and that's fine for you. Sure! You can have your Bible study circle, but don't try to force your ideas on me, because at the end of the day the Bible is just an ancient text from a totally archaic culture. I'm twenty-first-century man, mate, not neolithic!'

Julia and Andy slowly realised that they were facing a dead end. The circles their relationship had been going round in for two years or more had become a downward spiral and they were facing break-up. They had tried so hard and invested so much in one another. They'd had their good times and neither of them really wanted to face the future alone, but they couldn't face it together, either. 'Someone at work today asked whether we'd ever looked at the Bible,' Julia ventured. 'Supposed to give us some uplift, direction even – full of good advice, that sort of thing.' Andy stopped stirring his coffee and looked up. 'Yeah, right! But where would you even start? I tried it once, but it doesn't have a subject index, does it, and none of it seems to make sense or fit together, and what on earth have all those incomprehensible names got to do with us? Anyway, we're not the religious sort, are we? That's not what we need right now!'

Three different, but negative, views of the book that is still, by all the figures, the world's best-seller. We could all multiply the scenarios from our own personal experience, because to most people, at the beginning of the twenty-first century, the Bible is quite simply a closed book. For many it's a black, forbidding book, speaking in a language 'which thou dost no longer use in conversation with thy friends', consigned to the mists of antiquity. To others, it's a slippery collection of mutually contradictory ideas that can be made to mean almost anything, and then be pressed into the service of almost any cause. For some, it's a glorious part of our cultural heritage, along with Shakespeare and Dr Johnson – the flowering of the English language, a profound influence on the minds and imaginations of generations long since forgotten. To most, it has nothing to say to life today, because it deals in certainties and absolutes which no longer command any credibility. Its ethos is more the quill pen than information technology. To a few, it is the living and enduring Word of God, the means by which the eternal creator of the world, everything and everyone in it, continues to reveal his purposes and character to human beings, created to know their deepest fulfilment and satisfaction in a personal relationship with him.

I believe in the Bible. It is a book written in time, unfolding eternity. It could not be more relevant and is never out of date, because it reveals the unchanging character of the God who is there. Its divine truth still transforms human life and experience, and it is available in easy-to-read, accurate, modern translations in every bookshop in the land. But the Bible does need to be unlocked, and all too often we lack the time and patience to unpack its treasures carefully enough. We pick it up and, rather like a lucky-dip at the village fête, hope to pull out something of value with the minimum amount of effort. We are like the eager five-year-old returning from her first day at school, bitterly complaining that she hasn't learned how to read yet. What we need to do is to make a start!

Let's do that by exploding two myths about the Bible, which commonly deter the contemporary explorer at the very outset of the process. The first is that it is an advanced religious textbook, accessible only to the experts after years of study in Semitic languages or the more abstruse areas of philosophy and theology. On the contrary, if you can read a newspaper, you can read the Bible, particularly if it is in one of the excellent contemporary English translations. It has been said that, like the ocean, the Bible is shallow enough for a toddler to paddle in and deep enough for an elephant to drown in. Through its pages, we are introduced to otherwise unimaginable spiritual depths, mysteries which were kept hidden in God's providence but which have now been revealed. But it is neither obscure nor mysterious in its essential contents.

The second myth is that its historical antiquity makes it remote from our everyday, contemporary life. Its historical particularity seems to distance it irretrievably from our world. But the Bible is full of human life. On every page we encounter real people who have the same concerns and struggles, the same problems and opportunities, as we do. Their cultural clothing is different, but we would be blind not to see beyond such superficial distinctives to their essential humanity, which is common to ours. We are not in a fairy-tale world, nor are we bound up in a cultural time-warp, when we read the pages of the Bible. We are among flesh and blood like our own, facing a common experience of what it is to be human, in the real world, and exploring the possibilities of knowing the God of eternity in the midst of time.

The Bible's claims

But why a book, and what is this phenomenon we call 'the Holy Bible'? To answer these initial questions, we need to step outside of the immediate picture in order to pose some issues which are even more fundamental. For example, what is the ultimate ground for believing anything about anything? How do we come to the practical judgments we make in everyday life as to what is true or false, right or wrong, what works or doesn't work? Or, to express the issue more abstractly, what grounds of authority do we look for in making decisions about what we believe or how we behave?

In the practical affairs of everyday life, we recognise the authority of fact, established by proof, which becomes a conditioning factor in every aspect of our lives and experience. The law of gravity is an example of an observable and constant physical phenomenon, which I am powerless to contradict, either by argument or will-power. It is a fact that if I jump from the top of a high-rise building I shall fall to the earth, irrespective of what I may have persuaded myself, in my own mind, as to the likely outcome of the event. If the action takes place, the consequence follows, and both are facts. They can be proved by visible evidence and tangible results. There can be plenty of argument about how and why the event happened, but the fact that it did happen cannot be denied. The radar speed trap, the police cameras, the video clip are all automatically accepted as corroboration of past events. Arguments can and do happen about interpretation, but they only happen because there are facts and events about which to argue. The Bible has many claims to this sort of factual authority.

But there are very many areas of human thought and expression where facts need to be interpreted if their full significance is to be appreciated. Our opinions and subsequent actions will probably be based on the degree of authority, or credibility, we attribute to a particular explanation or interpretation. In such areas, we may utilise a whole range of criteria by which to make our assessment. How *do* we come to our value judgments? It may be on the basis of what the majority think, so that the opinion survey percentages become the arbiter of what is acceptable and what is not. Or we may decide to go with what the experts say, even though different schools of equally well-qualified people may fundamentally contradict one another's findings. Perhaps we revert to what we were taught at school, or by our parents, – 'well, my mum always used to say. . .' – and it becomes a dictum which influences our thinking, almost without our realising it.

The problem with all such criteria is that they are limited in scope and transient in relevance, because they are conditioned by our humanness. For example, in the recent discussion about the lowering of the age of consent for homosexual activity, the percentages of the public approving or disapproving the various proposed changes have swung wildly backwards and forwards over a period of time and according to different polls. But if the 50 per cent who wanted reform at one time have been reduced to 25 per cent a few months later, does that affect the rights or wrongs of the issue either way? It may provide a more or less accurate barometer of public opinion, but it has no authoritative comment to make in the area of morality. Existentialist philosophers throughout the second half of the twentieth century consistently pointed out that right and wrong, truth and error can only be meaningful concepts if they are grounded in a divine being, outside of and distinct from our human relativism. Jean-Paul Sartre's dictum, that finite man is meaningless without an infinite reference point, recognises the reality that human beings cannot attribute meaning in life without an authority external to ourselves, greater than we are, consistent and unchanging, by which moral absolutes can be declared and upheld. This is the authority which the Bible claims to be able to mediate.

Let's spend a short time understanding the logic of the claim. If the only ground for Truth (with a capital 'T') as a given absolute lies in a divine being whose attributes are infinite and eternal, then the most important quest any of us can be involved in is to discover whether such a God actually exists. This is the quest for an ultimate authority. But how could we ever discover such a reality with any certainty? Clearly, such a 'God' could not be expressed as a mathematical formula, however complex, or be available for our examination like the data of a scientific experiment. Such a being must be, by definition, far beyond human analysis and even imagination, because of our finitude. Any 'deity' that could be encompassed within the framework of a human mind, however brilliant, has thereby forfeited the title of 'god'. So the long quest by humankind either to discover God or even to create our own deity is doomed to failure. We have neither the mental nor the spiritual capacities to achieve the goal. Indeed, the Bible recognised the dilemma centuries ago, in one of its earliest books, when it asked the rhetorical questions, 'Can you fathom the mysteries of God? Can you probe the limits of the Almighty? They are higher than the heavens — what can you do? They are deeper than the depths of the grave — what can you know?' (Job 11:7–8).

At this point, we must not miss an important clue in the Bible itself. It is that nowhere in the sixty-six books, which constitute the Bible as we have it, is the existence of God argued or proved on a philosophical basis. The Church has sometimes attempted the task, with arguments about the unmoved Mover, or that just as a watch is inexplicable without a watch-maker, so a complex universe requires an infinite creator. But the Bible's own method is to state God's existence and point to the evidence of his words and actions. In other words, the Bible's claim to ultimate authority lies in its declaration that God has chosen to reveal himself by what he does and what he says, and that its own pages are the authoritative record of that self-disclosure. 'Proofs' will always be inadequate, because God's reality transcends the greatest human intellect. The God of the Bible is not the sum total of our best thoughts and most insightful notions about him. God would remain for ever hidden from human perception and completely unknowable had he not chosen to make himself known, and to do that in terms which his human creation can understand, because they are the same currency of words and actions by which we make ourselves known to one another.

The human parallels are both clear and helpful. We have all had the galling experience of trying to get to know someone only to be met with a brick wall of resistance. Of course, we each have the right to reveal, or conceal, our thoughts, words and actions from others. Indeed, the measure of depth in our interpersonal relationships is largely the extent to which we are happy to disclose ourselves to another person, marriage being the prime example. But while relationships among equals are conducted on the basis of mutual disclosure, the same is not true of relationships with superiors. There the measure of relating is determined by the condescension of the higher to the lower. The first-year schoolboy does not bowl along to the headmaster's office for a chat whenever the whim takes him. The subject cannot demand access to his or her monarch. The greater has to stoop to the lesser, if any relationship between them is to exist at all. How much more, then, must this be the case between the infinite, yet personal, God who is the creator of the universe and his finite, human creatures? To imagine that we could saunter into his presence, with our hands in our pockets, or could put him through our computers and come up with a comprehensive analysis, is simply an indicator of our human arrogance. The only hope that finite human beings have of relating to the infinite is if he condescends to reveal himself to us. The only way that morally flawed people can relate to a God of perfection is if he discloses himself on terms that can bridge the chasm between us. Again, it is the Bible's claim to do just that, which constitutes a unique authority.

Alternative authorities

There are, of course, many rival claims of authority within the broad field of religious belief systems. Even within Christianity itself, different emphases have emerged, and at root these account for the many divisions, along denominational lines, which church history has sadly witnessed. However, all Christians would agree that all authority within creation rightly belongs to the creator. As Daniel told King Nebuchadnezzar, we must 'acknowledge that the Most High is sovereign over the kingdoms of men and gives them to anyone he wishes' and that 'Heaven rules' (Daniel 4:25–6). Again, 'His dominion is an eternal dominion; his kingdom endures from generation to generation . . . He does as he pleases with the powers of heaven and the peoples of the earth' (Daniel 4:34–5). The question is how that authority is mediated to us.

For some, it is through the Church and its traditions. The Bible is seen as the product of the believing community, which is therefore superior to it. The interpretation of a book that would otherwise be dead therefore becomes the primary task, and only then can it become a source of authority. The properly appointed officers of the Church become the custodians and arbiters of truth, by whom the Bible's message is interpreted and applied. The Thirty-Nine Articles of the Church of England recognise an important place for tradition in the life of the Church, but add the rider: so long as it 'be not repugnant to the Word of God', recognising that the Church is subsidiary, as an authority, to the Bible. The authors of the Reformation formularies recalled the charges Jesus himself laid at the door of the traditionalists of his own day, the Pharisees, when he accused them of elevating their traditional practices above the teaching of the Old Testament. 'You have let go of the commands of God and are holding on to the traditions of men' he told them (Mark 7:8). And again, 'You have a fine way of setting aside the commands of God in order to observe your own traditions . . . Thus you nullify the word of God by your tradition that you have handed down' (Mark 7:9, 13). Jesus is criticising tradition as the ultimate authority because it actually takes us back to a human base, which is inevitably flawed and inadequate.

The same weakness must be identified in the exaltation of human reason to the position of ultimate authority. The Bible then becomes *an* authority, but acceptable only in so far as it accords with what seems reasonable. It is argued that, after all, the Bible is a book produced by human authors, who were themselves inevitably conditioned by their culture, language and thought-forms. To give them an authority beyond that of a witness to developing religious experience would be naïve and misleading. Once again, this view internalises the ultimate authority to that of our own wisdom and knowledge, both of which are notoriously subjective and ephemeral. Bible writers claim much more for their writings, though in the relativism of our own times the authority of what seems reasonable is culturally very attractive. In the end, of course, we lose any concept of unchanging truth or absolute standards, so that the Bible itself is relativised and shorn of its divine power and authority.

But perhaps the most popular authority base for twenty-first-century people is that of personal experience. We have become suspicious of being overly dependent on reason and sceptical about the effects of warring schools of rationalism within our world. The experience of the twentieth-century mass murderers such as Hitler, Stalin and Mao, all in the name of rationality, has produced a sense of vulnerability within human beings which has contributed to a headlong retreat from all externally informed authority systems. Whether religious, political, academic or parental, authority *per se* is no longer trusted and now subjected to the most rigorous examination. Indeed, one might argue that the defining characteristic of our post-modern, contemporary culture is the repudiation of the very concept of objective authority, in favour of personal autonomy and individual creativity. 'Just do it!' has become more than a sales pitch; it embodies a culture. If it feels good, it *is* good. If it's OK for you, then do it your way. The only restriction is that it shouldn't inhibit me from enjoying what's OK for me.

In such a context, the message of the Bible takes on authority only when I decide personally to agree with it. Its record of how prophets and apostles met with God in the past may or may not reverberate with my experience, but it is that experience which becomes the ground of my personal being. What I feel and experience emotionally therefore becomes more real, more significant to me, as a living human being, than what I think, or read, of what others have written. There is an immediacy, a 'nowness', to the authority of experience, which becomes all-controlling. The Bible may be a useful foil, or even a plumb-line by which to evaluate experience in a wider, deeper context, but it can also be restrictive and inhibiting. Why should God commit himself to words spoken yesterday, if he is the living God of today? Who is to say that he cannot reveal himself equally through current dreams and visions, trances and altered states of consciousness, prophecies and inspired utterances? The real issue is not so much whether there is an authority that can be imposed upon resistant human minds and consciences. The history of the past century is full of examples of that sort of totalitarianism, the misery it generates and the seeds of its own inevitable decline which it always sows. The new century may well witness a reaction against such structures and a resistance to all sorts of control. The real issue is whether there is an authority which can win the recognition and submission of human beings, voluntarily and gladly. Is there a liberating source of truth and reality which can provide a foundation for life to be fulfilling and a dynamic to transform human nature? That is what the Bible claims to offer, as an objective, gracious and eternal reality.

How the Bible works

Why should we be willing to believe it? The answers relate to both reason and experience, to both the tradition of the past and the daily challenge of the future. We need, at this point, however, to return to the concept of our personal relationships depending on words and actions, by which we reveal ourselves to one another.

Human relationships of trust and confidence can only develop through mutual self-disclosure, which comes through words and actions. Both are needed. We may say that actions speak louder than words, but they do not speak as clearly and informatively. Indeed, the very development of language and the nuances of vocabulary, within different cultures, are evidence of a deep human striving for precision and focus, for communication that is unmistakable and therefore understood. If that is the way human beings relate, why should we not expect an infinite, yet personal, creator to relate to those made in his own image in exactly the same way?

The Bible is the self-revelation of this personal God, in the particularities of time and space, to real people in history, by his actions and his explanatory words. Both are vital. The actions are the necessary proof of the reality of the divine purposes and power. Without them, the words would be merely philosophical and theoretical. But the words are equally vital, to predict or explain the meaning of God's activity, as it reveals his character and purposes, to the recipients of revelation. He is not a miming but a speaking God. Sometimes the actions are on a grand scale, such as Noah's flood, or the exodus of the nation of Israel, or the Babylonian exile. Often, they are very detailed and personal, as when the shepherd-boy David is anointed to be king, or when the prophet Elijah crumbles into depression. But at the heart of every biblical event, God is the prime mover, the chief actor and the divine author, whose script explains the action. The way the Bible works has often been summarised in the form of the following equation:

EVENT + EXPLANATION = REVELATION

One of the clearest Bible passages to explain and illustrate this methodology comes in the short second letter written by the apostle Peter, as he faced imminent martyrdom, to encourage his fellow-Christians to stand firm in their faith, in spite of fierce persecution. He wants them to have confidence in the authenticity and reliability of the message of the good news about Jesus Christ, which he and the other apostles have been faithfully preaching and for which they intend to die, rather than deny its truth. Peter writes:

> So I will always remind you of these things, even though you know them and are firmly established in the truth you now have. I think it is right to refresh your memory as long as I live in the tent of this body, because I know that I will soon put it aside, as our Lord Jesus Christ has made clear to me. And I will make every effort to see that after my departure you will always be able to remember these things. We did not follow cleverly invented stories when we told you about the power and coming of our Lord Jesus Christ, but we were eyewitnesses of his majesty. For he received honour and glory from God the Father when the voice came to him from the Majestic Glory, saying, 'This is my Son, whom I love; with him I am well pleased.' We ourselves heard this voice that came from heaven when we were

with him on the sacred mountain. (2 Peter 1:12–18)

As a Bible writer, Peter claims to have witnessed the truth of God's self-revelation in two striking ways. He is referring to the event described in the gospels as the transfiguration of Christ (Matthew 17:1–8), when, for a brief moment, Peter, James and John were made overwhelmingly aware of the transcendent glory and divine splendour of the Son of God. They were 'eye-witnesses of his majesty' (2 Peter 1:16). It was an event they would never forget, demonstrating to them beyond all doubt the divine character of the master they loved and served. But they were also ear-witnesses of the explanation, equally divine. 'We ourselves heard this voice that came from heaven . . .' (v. 18). The voice explained the meaning of the event, together culminating in the divine revelation, 'This is my Son, whom I love; with him I am well pleased' (v. 17). That is how the Bible always works. God is its hero on every page. He is the one who acts and speaks, to disclose himself to finite, sinful people.

It is one of the great distinctives of the God revealed in the Bible that he is a speaking God, and this helps to explain why the Bible itself, as a written record of God's words, is so central and indispensable to the Christian faith. The God of the Bible stands in stark contrast to the idols of the pagan world, as Psalm 115 so ruthlessly points out. Such idols may be of silver and gold, but they are 'made by the hands of men. They have mouths but cannot speak, eyes, but they cannot see; they have ears but cannot hear, noses, but they cannot smell . . . nor can they utter a sound with their throats' (vv. 4–7). But the God of the Bible does speak and see and hear. Indeed, nothing else would ever have come into existence if he did not. For it is by his word that creation exists and at every point where that created order is least like him, it is the Word of the living God which bridges the gap.

The Bible begins with the creation of the cosmos, according to the will and power of God. But it is no accident that paragraph after paragraph of that majestic overture to the whole Bible begins 'and God said, "Let there be . . ." and there was . . .' (Genesis 1:3, 6, 9, 11, 14, 20, 24, 26). The mind of God is articulated in the Word of God, which becomes the executive agent by which his will is carried out. When God speaks, it is done, and the rest of the Bible never lets us forget it. To quote but two examples, one from each testament: 'By the word of the LORD were the heavens made, their starry host by the breath of his mouth . . . For he spoke, and it came to be; he commanded, and it stood firm' (Psalm 33:6, 9). Or, in the New Testament letter to the Hebrews, 'By faith we understand that the universe was formed at God's command, so that what is seen was not made out of what was visible' (Hebrews 11:3). Because the world is not self-generated, but created by the word of God, the world will never be able to be explained coherently and consistently by its own terms or framework of visible reference, but only by the revelation of God in the words he has spoken. Those words are in themselves our ultimate authority, because they constitute the revelation of the otherwise unknown character and purposes of the invisible, infinite God. We shall deal with this more fully when we explore the Bible's own story in Chapter 3, but all the way through the sixty-six books which make up the whole of the Scriptures, the same principle holds good. Human beings rightly understand and relate to God only through his Word. Often this is a word of promise, which needs to be believed and acted on. Frequently, it is a word of command, to be obeyed, or a warning to be heeded, or a propositional statement to be understood and applied.

The Bible's relevance

But there is one important further link to establish, and that is to us today. When we begin to understand why the Bible has been given to us and how it works, the problem of its alleged 'remoteness' and questions about its relevance to contemporary life start to find their answers. For the God who spoke once in the particular words of every Bible verse is unchanging in his character and settled in his will. What he once said, he is still saying. We do not have to make the Bible relevant (what an absurdly arrogant idea!); it is 'the living and enduring word of God' and 'the word of the Lord stands for ever' (1 Peter 1:23, 25). We have to work hard at understanding its message both within its own context and in our own, but we do not have to discover some elusive interpretative key, because God is interpreting himself to us and the keys to understanding are all within the text, if we will only give ourselves to it. All that God asks of us is a humble spirit, an attentive mind and a willingness to put into action whatever he reveals to us. 'For the word of God is living and active. Sharper than any double-edged sword, it penetrates even to dividing soul and spirit, joints and marrow; it judges the thoughts and attitudes of the heart' (Hebrews 4:12).

So we can see that the answers to our opening scenarios do in fact lie in this much-neglected best-seller. It will introduce Julia and Andy to the God who made them and provide them with the Maker's handbook on personal relationships. That won't be comfortable at first. There will be some harsh realities to face in their own selfishness and ingrained wrong thinking. But the Bible won't moralise, or set them on a course of relational-improvement therapy. It doesn't just deal with alleviating symptoms; it has a much more radical solution, as we shall see. Christine will need to lose her prejudices, founded on half-remembered, immature judgments and half-digested popular excuses for not bothering. Far from finding that science has 'disproved' the Bible, she could discover that God's self-revelation has always been way ahead of our human understanding, and rather than assuming the biblical text to be distorted and unreliable, she might do a little research and find out how reliable the contemporary translations of these well-established ancient documents really are. And if Matt could lay aside his presuppositions for a moment to see that no one can actually live in a world where words are meaningless, he might discover in the Bible the God who gave him his mind, and who is the only one who will be able to satisfy his hunger, which is deeper than the intellect and more enduring than a slick argument. It would be such a tragedy to miss life's greatest adventure, in getting to know God, because of pride or prejudice about a book which has been his channel of communication to countless multitudes of people over two millennia.

To remind you
- The Bible is not a religious textbook, but a book about real people, like us, living in the real world. It communicates (pp. 16–17).
- The Bible claims the authority of factual accuracy, but does not set out to prove it, so much as to demonstrate it by revelation (pp. 18–19).
- If an infinite yet personal God can be known, it must be by self-revelation, since our finite human minds could not discover or comprehend the infinite (pp. 19–23).
- God reveals himself in the Bible by acting in human history and explaining his actions in authoritative interpretation (pp. 23–5).
- The God of the Bible is supremely the speaking God who accomplishes his will through his word (pp. 25–6).
- What God once said, he is still saying, since his nature is eternal. So there is no doubt about the Bible's relevance in the new millennium (pp. 26–7).

Chapter 2

The Bible's Own Story

IT TOOK SOME time for Christine to overcome her prejudice, but eventually, partly because of Alison's gentle persistence and partly out of sheer curiosity, she decided to visit the Bible study and discussion group, 'just this once' as she told herself. She was pleasantly surprised. They seemed a normal enough group of people. Even her husband, Rob, would have had to admit that they were not obviously religious maniacs, or even eccentric. There was no hocus-pocus, no manipulative techniques, no artificial 'atmosphere' – just a bunch of ordinary people, each with a copy of the same book in their hands, talking about what they understood it to mean – and what they didn't, or couldn't, understand. It was intriguing. The Bibles were all in the same contemporary language translation and, mercifully, the pages were numbered, so that even a complete novice like Christine could find her way around. People seemed to speak genuinely and in a down-to-earth way about how what was in the book related to their everyday lives, at work and at home, so that Christine felt much less embarrassed and much more involved than she had ever expected to be.

But one of her most lasting impressions was of the sheer size of the Bible. It was rather like facing the complete works of William Shakespeare. At least that had only one author. But who wrote the Bible? And when? Someone in the group had said its composition spanned a thousand years or more. But when you think how much human knowledge develops during a millennium, doesn't that mean that it must be full of contradictions, that the later must have displaced the earlier? And who was it who pulled all these different authors and topics together and decided to call them 'the Holy Bible'? The group had been discussing from a book called 'John' or 'the gospel of John', as they called it. But who was John? And what was the gospel? And how did he fit in with all the other sixty-five books that made up the Bible library?

Christine's questions will be familiar enough to anyone who has tried seriously to get some grip on the Bible as an entity. Because it is a collection of sixty-six books written over a long period of time, probably as much as 1,600 years, and because these books are not always arranged chronologically, nor do they seem on the surface necessarily to relate to one another, many an explorer of the Bible has quickly got lost in the jungle and given up. Some have begun enthusiastically to read their way through, only to get bogged down irremediably in Leviticus (book three). Others have 'picked 'n' mixed' their way through their own selection of biblical texts, but never seen how the whole fits together, and are therefore conscious of huge 'black holes' of biblical material, into which they have not yet had the courage, or energy, to plunge. All of us who read the Bible need to have some awareness of its organising principles, its unifying themes, so that we develop some map references, or marker-points, by which to plot our passage into its interior. That is the purpose of this chapter.

The Bible library

Opening a Bible in modern English at the page entitled 'Contents', one immediately recognises it to be a book of two halves. Within the longer, first section, known as the Old Testament, there are thirty-nine books, followed by the twenty-seven books which comprise the New Testament. The first documents were written during the time of Moses, the first great leader of the Hebrew people (fifteenth century BC), while the latest date from the end of the first century AD, or as it is increasingly designated, the Common Era. This method of dating in itself presents us with the most significant key to understanding not only the millennia of human history, but also the message of the Bible itself. It centres on Jesus Christ. The Old Testament predates his coming, preparing the way and explaining the focus of God's purposes for all humanity in the 'Messiah', God's specially appointed and unique revealer, ruler and rescuer. The New describes and explains his life, death, resurrection and all that flows from these great events for the potential benefit of all people, in every place, at every time, and indeed throughout eternity. Jesus Christ is the centre and focus of the entire Bible.

However, that may not be immediately obvious to the new reader. Returning to the contents page, we discover that our English translations of the Old Testament follow a simple three-part division, based on the Greek translation of the original Hebrew, known as the Septuagint, which itself dates from at least 200 years before Christ. Broadly speaking, Genesis to Esther are historical books, Job to Song of Songs books of wisdom and poetry, and Isaiah to Malachi books of prophecy. But the original Hebrew order is rather more instructive. Following a three-fold pattern, it divides the material into the law, the prophets and the writings.

Genesis, Exodus, Leviticus, Numbers and Deuteronomy, often called the books of Moses, constitute the first main section of the library. Sometimes also called the Pentateuch ('five scrolls'), the best title is the Hebrew word *Torah*, usually translated 'law', but having the sense not so much of an inflexible and impersonal moral code as of a father giving his children 'teaching' and 'instruction', as a foundation for their living. These are the five foundation stones on which the whole of the rest of the Bible is built, by way of explanation and application.

The next long section (the prophets) is subdivided into two, the former and the latter. The former prophets are the books of Joshua, Judges, 1 and 2 Samuel and 1 and 2 Kings. They are historical books with a great deal of narrative, factual account, concerning the history of the nation of Israel. But they are 'prophets' because the history is explained from God's perspective, and as such it is used to present God's authoritative word to his people. The interest of the authors is never merely historicist, but overtly theological. The latter prophets are equally preachers of God's truth to his people, though they reflect on Israel's past and present experience in the light of God's future plans, including both judgment and rescue. Of these, there are three major, or longer, prophets – Isaiah, Jeremiah and Ezekiel – and twelve minor prophets, so called because they are shorter, not less important – Hosea, Joel, Amos, Obadiah, Jonah, Micah, Nahum, Habakkuk, Zephaniah, Haggai, Zechariah and Malachi.

To class all the remaining Old Testament books as 'the writings' may seem a 'catch-all' solution to the problem of unifying what seem to be quite different books. But, in fact, there are two types of material here which can very legitimately be grouped together. The books of Job, Proverbs, Ecclesiastes, Song of Songs and some of the Psalms constitute what is called the 'wisdom literature', in which the principles of God's self-revelation and will are applied to the circumstances of everyday life. The remaining books largely cover the history of the people of Israel at the time when they were carried into exile in Babylon, their eventual restoration and the rebuilding that followed.

Such divisions provide useful handles for dealing with large amounts of biblical material, through which otherwise we might not easily see our way. But before we turn to the New Testament, it is important to look beyond the classifications and structures, to see the story which progressively unfolds through this first half of the Bible. In doing this, we begin to move from description to understanding. For it is one coherent story. Every Christmas Eve, the service of nine lessons and carols from King's College, Cambridge, is broadcast around the English-speaking world, and marks for many the beginning of Christmas. The 'Bidding Prayer' bids, or invites, the congregation, in these words: 'Let us read and mark in Holy Scripture the tale of the loving purposes of God from the first days of our disobedience unto the glorious redemption brought us by this holy child.' And the lessons begin in Genesis chapter 3. For the story of the Old Testament is the story of God's grace, reaching out in rescue to a lost humanity. Let me explain.

The seed-bed of the Bible

It has sometimes been said that the Bible's division into two could be best expressed as Genesis chapters 1 to 11, and the rest! The point which is being rightly made is that the first eleven chapters are the seed-bed of the whole Bible. They act as a sort of spring-board for all that follows. The story starts with God. 'In the beginning God created the heavens and the earth' (Genesis 1:1). That creation expresses not only God's unfathomable wisdom and incalculable power, but also reflects his essential nature of perfection: 'It was very good' (Genesis 1:31). At its climax is a creature, made for a personal relationship with God, to act as God's agent in governing and tending the whole created order – a human being, or, to be precise, two human beings. 'Male and female he created them' (Genesis 1:26–8).

What is created on the grandest scale in Genesis 1 seems almost domestic by comparison in Genesis 2, where the focus shifts to the relationship with God for which Adam and Eve are designed. It is a relationship of great fulfilment and freedom and yet there is a necessary structure, within which alone the freedom can be enjoyed and continue. God has to be recognised and honoured as God. That is the fundamental 'given' of the world as he has made it. What he says has to be obeyed. So although human beings are created in God's image, with the amazing potential to be able to love, worship and serve him, they are not to usurp God's authority, or seek to dethrone God by using their own very considerable autonomy to rebel against his rightful rule. Yet, that is exactly what happens. God's one prohibition, 'You must not eat from the tree of the knowledge of good and evil' (Genesis 2:17), is ignored. The meaning clearly is that to seek the knowledge of good and evil would be an attempt to be 'like God' (Genesis 3:5), no longer dependent on him, no longer recognising him as creator, but exalting oneself as a God-substitute. So the disobedience of Adam and Eve begins the long unending trail of human rebellion against God and consequent alienation from him. 'Sin' (a word the Bible will use many times) enters the scene, the relationship of loving trust and dependence is shattered and God acts in righteous judgment against the offenders by expelling them from his presence in Eden, and so from the tree of life. Death, not immediate in the physical sense but nonetheless real and inevitable, becomes the lot of humankind. Disintegration of human relationships swiftly follows, so that by chapter 4 the first murder has taken place, as Cain kills his brother, Abel (vv. 1–8). Work becomes toil, as human beings struggle with an environment which has become hostile because its creator has been rejected.

> To Adam he said, 'Because you listened to your wife and ate from the tree about which I commanded you, "You must not eat of it," Cursed is the ground because of you; through painful toil you will eat of it all the days of your life. It will produce thorns and thistles for you, and you will eat the plants of the field. By the sweat of your brow you will eat your food until you return to the ground, since from it you were taken; for dust you are and to dust you will return.' (Genesis 3:17–19)

Here, then, is the seed-bed of the rest of the Bible's story. By chapter 6, when Noah is introduced, the situation has reached the point of desperation.

The LORD saw how great man's wickedness on the earth had become, and that every inclination of the thoughts of his heart was only evil all the time. The LORD was grieved that he had made man on the earth, and his heart was filled with pain. So the LORD said, 'I will wipe mankind, whom I have created, from the face of the earth – men and animals, and creatures that move along the ground, and birds of the air – for I am grieved that I have made them.' (Genesis 6:5–7)

Everything seems bleak and hopeless, but at that very point God steps in, and a new sequence begins. He selects a man, called Noah, not in the first place because he was inherently more righteous than his rebellious contemporaries, but in order to show his grace to him. A new biblical concept is introduced – that of 'grace', which is God's unmerited favour and goodness to those who do not deserve it in the least. God's grace found Noah and made of him a righteous man (Genesis 6:8–9). The point is made in the text by the Hebrew term often translated in English as 'generations'. It is inserted at the beginning of verse 9 and could be translated literally 'This is what was generated by that'. So, to paraphrase, God's grace found Noah and this is what was generated by that – Noah became a righteous man. That was God's doing, not Noah's, and it becomes a paradigm of the way God will go on dealing with his fallen, rebellious human creatures throughout the whole Bible story.

Another new concept, also introduced at this point, is that of 'covenant'. 'I am going to bring floodwaters on the earth to destroy all life under the heavens, every creature that has the breath of life in it. Everything on earth will perish. But I will establish my covenant with you, and you will enter the ark – you and your sons and your wife and your sons' wives with you' (Genesis 6:17–18). God determines freely, out of sheer mercy, to rescue Noah and his family from the judgment of the flood which is about to destroy that entire generation. It is as though he will start again with Noah. The covenant is the free promise of God to carry out what he has said he will do, rescuing the recipient of his mercy, by his own initiative and power. Noah has to build the ark, but God shuts (and eventually opens) the door, so that the God who sends his judgment to consume evil also preserves his chosen one, by covenant grace. Nor is this unjust in any way. Noah is not rescued because he is righteous, or else the Bible's pattern would mean that we have by our own works and efforts somehow to attempt to make ourselves acceptable to God. Noah is a sinner like all the rest, and he undergoes the experience of the flood like all the rest, but the grace of God provides him and his family with a protection from God's righteous wrath in the form of the ark, and this means of salvation carries him through the judgment, into the new world beyond.

When the waters recede, God formalises his covenant with Noah, his family and all living creatures. 'Never again will all life be cut off by the waters of a flood; never again will there be a flood to destroy the earth' (Genesis 9:11). Moreover, he gives Noah a sign as proof of his covenant promises, 'my rainbow in the clouds', investing it with the covenant significance that the promise will never be broken. It looks like a wonderful new beginning, and it is a great step forward in understanding God's plan for humanity, but the infection of sin and rebellion has not been expunged from human nature. Noah and his sons may father a new human race, but all the old signs of rebellion reappear too soon and culminate in the ultimate act of human defiance we call the tower of Babel, recorded in Genesis 11.

> Now the whole world had one language and a common speech. As men moved eastward, they found a plain in Shinar and settled there. They said to each other, 'Come, let's make bricks and bake them thoroughly.' They used brick instead of stone, and bitumen for mortar. Then they said, 'Come, let us build ourselves a city, with a tower that reaches to the heavens, so that we may make a name for ourselves and not be scattered over the face of the whole earth.' But the LORD came down to see the city and the tower that the men were building. The LORD said, 'If as one people speaking the same language they have begun to do this, then nothing they plan to do will be impossible for them. Come, let us go down and confuse their language so they will not understand each other.' So the LORD scattered them from there over all the earth, and they stopped building the city. That is why it was called Babel – because there the LORD confused the language of the whole world. From there the LORD scattered them over the face of the whole earth. (Genesis 11:1–9)

Once again, the motivation is human pride and self-assertion.

Building technology has developed. We can preserve ourselves by our own techniques and skills. We will climb up to the heavens. Not only do we not need God, we can challenge his very right to rule. So the fall and the flood are followed by the third great judgment – the scattering, with its confusion of languages, its destruction of relationships and fragmentation of human society. Human beings cannot set up their own independent kingdom, because they remain God's creatures living in God's world, and that inescapable bottom-line means that all our rebellion will ultimately blow up in our faces.

This, then, is the dilemma which the first eleven chapters of the Bible articulate so clearly and pose so challengingly. If human nature is corrupted by sin and rebellion, so that any relationship with a holy and righteous God becomes an impossibility, is there any hope for the human race? Can the effects of sin ever be undone? Can a just God ever accept an unjust person into relationship with himself? Could life shared with God, in an environment of perfection such as Eden had been, ever be on the agenda again? By way of answer, chapter 12 begins, 'The LORD had said to Abram, "Leave your country, your people and your father's household and go to the land I will show you" ' (v. 1). It is in Abraham that the solution begins to take shape. And the shape it takes is that of promise and fulfilment – covenant grace.

Covenant community

The Abraham story revolves entirely around the covenant promises and becomes the pattern on which the whole of the biblical enterprise operates. So what did God promise? First, that Abraham's descendants will become a great nation.

I will make you into a great nation and I will bless you; I will make your name great, and you will be a blessing. (Genesis 12:2)

I will make your offspring like the dust of the earth, so that if anyone could count the dust, then your offspring could be counted. (Genesis 13:16)

He took him outside and said, 'Look at the heavens and count the stars – if indeed you can count them.' Then he said to him, 'So shall your offspring be.' (Genesis 15:5)

The angel added, 'I will so increase your descendants that they will be too numerous to count.' (Genesis 16:10)

Abraham will surely become a great and powerful nation, and all nations on earth will be blessed through him. (Genesis 18:18)

Here we have the beginnings of the nation of Israel, which becomes such a key actor in the drama that is the unfolding of God's purposes. It was because of God's direct promises to Abraham that Israel existed, as the focus of his blessing. In the place of the curse, so graphically worked out in chapters 1–11, God now promises its opposite, and the call of Abraham and his family to a new beginning is integral to the plan. Second, the great nation will be given a land, Canaan, the land of promise, in which to live.

The LORD appeared to Abram and said, 'To your offspring I will give this land.' So he built an altar there to the LORD, who had appeared to him. (Genesis 12:7)

The LORD said to Abram after Lot had parted from him, 'Lift up your eyes from where you are and look north and south, east and west. All the land that you see I will give to you and your offspring for ever. (Genesis 13:14–15)

On that day the LORD made a covenant with Abram and said, 'To your descendants I give this land, from the river of Egypt to the great river, the Euphrates.' (Genesis 15:18)

The whole land of Canaan, where you are now an alien, I will give as an everlasting possession to you and your descendants after you; and I will be their God. (Genesis 17:8)

While this will not be Eden restored, nevertheless the land will be a place of rest where God's blessing will be enjoyed in prosperity and security. This good and pleasant land will be given to God's people as a tangible manifestation of his grace towards them. But this is no narrowly nationalistic blessing, reserved merely for the children of Abraham. 'All peoples on earth' are to enter into God's blessing through Abraham and his descendants. The universal problem of humanity will find a universal solution, but it begins with the particularity of the one man, to whom God gives both a command ('leave your country') and a promise ('go to the land I will show you'). That becomes the pattern for the story which the rest of the Bible is written to tell.

In the course of the rest of Genesis, the family becomes the nation. The promised son of Abraham and Sarah, Isaac, is eventually born, by supernatural intervention, when both parents are in old age, as though to confirm that with God nothing is impossible, especially when the fulfilment of his promise is involved. Of Isaac's twin sons, Jacob (renamed Israel), the younger and the heir of the promised blessing, himself becomes the father of twelve sons, who become the clan-heads of the emerging nation. But though the nation is being formed, they as yet have no land; indeed, they are in Egypt as slave labourers for the Pharaoh. Their present land is a place of suffering and slavery, but God has not forgotten his covenant promise. At the start of the Exodus narrative, he affirms, 'I have come down to rescue them from the hand of the Egyptians and to bring them up out of that land into a good and spacious land, a land flowing with milk and honey' (Exodus 3:8). Raising up Moses as his chosen leader, God delivers the children of Israel, through plagues and passover, bringing them out of Egypt, through the sea, into the desert and eventually on to the land of Canaan. Central to this part of the story is their meeting with God the deliverer at Mount Sinai, where the ten commandments are given as a summary of God's character and a charter, along with many other laws, of their developing relationship with him. The people enter into covenant with God to be his obedient children. 'We will do everything the LORD has said; we will obey' (Exodus 24:7). They have already been designated by God as 'my firstborn son' (4:22), 'my treasured possession . . . a kingdom of priests and a holy nation' (19:5–6). Now they are to live in the enjoyment of God's rescuing grace and travel to the land of promise to receive the fulness of God's covenant blessings.

It seems as though the answer may have been found in the newly redeemed and constituted covenant community that is Israel. Perhaps this will be God's master-plan to bring rebellious humanity back into a right relationship with him. But the optimism is very short-lived. Only days after God has appeared to them on Mount Sinai they are fashioning a golden calf and worshipping man-made idols. Their progress through the desert is sustained on God's part by daily food and drink, protection from enemies, guidance and direction, but on Israel's part it is characterised by grumbling and discontent, fear, disobedience and downright unbelief. Because they are unwilling to trust God to bring them into the land and rather complain to him that he has brought them out of Egypt to kill them in the desert, they are condemned to remain out of the land for forty years, until that generation which had experienced so much of God's deliverance, but failed to trust his grace, has died. The tragedy is that while God is patiently and persistently fulfilling his promises, Israel is equally persistently unfaithful and unbelieving. The old pattern has reasserted itself. Whatever the blessings God's covenant mercy has brought, men and women still seem to respond with sin and rebellion.

And for the rest of the Old Testament there is no real change. From generation to generation, the same dilemma is presented. Under Joshua the people enter and occupy the promised land, but the book of Judges records the recurring downward spirals of rebellion against God and his covenant.

Then the Israelites did evil in the eyes of the LORD and served the Baals. They forsook the LORD, the God of their fathers, who had brought them out of Egypt. They followed and worshipped various gods of the peoples around them. They provoked the LORD to anger because they forsook him and served Baal and the Ashtoreths. In his anger against Israel the LORD handed them over to raiders who plundered them. He sold them to their enemies all around, whom they were no longer able to resist. Whenever Israel went out to fight, the hand of the LORD was against them to defeat them, just as he had sworn to them. They were in great distress. Then the LORD raised up judges, who saved them out of the hands of these raiders. Yet they would not listen to their judges but prostituted themselves to other gods and worshipped them. Unlike their fathers, they quickly turned from the way in which their fathers had walked, the way of obedience to the LORD's commands. Whenever the LORD raised up a judge for them, he was with the judge and saved them out of the hands of their enemies as long as the judge lived; for the LORD had compassion on them as they groaned under those who oppressed and afflicted them. But when the judge died, the people returned to ways even more corrupt than those of their fathers, following other gods and serving and worshipping them. They refused to give up their evil practices and stubborn ways. (Judges 2:11–19)

As the nation was degenerating into civil war and facing break-up, the cry arose for a king who would unify them, 'such as all the other nations have' (1 Samuel 8:5). This was in itself a confession of their failure and persistent unfaithfulness. God had marked them out as different from all the other nations in that he was their king, but the people's idolatry and disobedience to his Torah were effectively a rejection of the LORD as their ruler. And yet the amazing motif running through the whole Old Testament story is that God never gave up on Israel. When they were faithless, he was always faithful. None of his covenant promises were forgotten or unfulfilled. Constantly, in situations of great need, God intervened on behalf of his disobedient people. During their early centuries in the land he raised up a succession of deliverers ('judges') who defeated their enemies and provided times of stability and prosperity. Yet the story of Judges is that each human rescuer seems more flawed than the one before, and no one is able to arrest the downward spiral. The establishment of the monarchy seems to offer a better hope. The creation of a dynastic succession should provide security and strong able government, but because it is actually the old Adam pattern of refusing to let God be God, it is inevitably doomed. The very first king, Saul, begins his reign by disobediently taking to himself the function of priest as well as ruler, and almost before his rule has commenced, the prophet Samuel is telling him, 'Your kingdom will not endure . . . because you have not kept the LORD's command' (1 Samuel 13:14).

The hope of a king

Yet God continues to be gracious. Saul is succeeded by David and then by his son, Solomon, and from many standpoints a new golden age seems to have begun. David captures the city of Jerusalem and makes it his capital (2 Samuel 5). He begins to conquer his enemies, and Israel grows in prosperity and security. In many ways he is the deliverer of his people, a ruler of military prowess, but a man 'after God's own heart', with a deep dependence on God and awareness of his promises and commands. David's psalms reveal just how deep and intimate his relationship with God was. But this is not only a relationship with great benefits for the king, as an individual. 'David knew that the LORD had established him as king over Israel and had exalted his kingdom for the sake of his people Israel' (2 Samuel 5:12).

Another key development in David's reign centres on his desire to build a temple in Jerusalem, to house the ark of the covenant, the tangible symbol of God's presence among his people. 'Here I am, living in a palace of cedar, while the ark of God remains in a tent' (2 Samuel 7:2). But God refuses the warrior-king permission to do this. That will be the role of his son. Instead, God promises to build David a house, a royal dynasty, but with the most amazing addition that this throne will be 'for ever'.

> I declare to you that the LORD will build a house for you: When your days are over and you go to be with your fathers, I will raise up your offspring to succeed you, one of your own sons, and I will establish his kingdom. He is the one who will build a house for me, and I will establish his throne for ever. I will be his father, and he will be my son. I will never take my love away from him, as I took it away from your predecessor. I will set him over my house and my kingdom for ever; his throne will be established for ever. (1 Chronicles 17:10b–14)

Here is another major milestone in the Old Testament story, comparable in importance to those initial covenant promises made to Abraham. Through David's dynasty, God's people will find rest and peace, they will enjoy God's land and live in relationship with him. From this new covenanted promise there developed the recognition of the king as God's 'son' (v. 13), in a sense replacing the failed firstborn son, Israel, and summing up in his own person all that God had intended the nation to be. Coupled to this unseen personal relationship between the king and God was the visible, objective recognition of the ruler in his 'anointing'. In Psalm 2, for example, the king is referred to as God's 'Anointed One' (v. 2) who is his 'Son' (v. 7). The significance of this for the whole Bible is that the Hebrew term for 'anointed one' is *Messiah*, which translates, in Greek, to the word *Christos* – Christ. As the monarchy is established, something of the larger long-term purposes of God is coming into focus.

But even here, as before, the human protagonists are severely flawed. David, the anointed one, becomes an adulterer and a murderer.

His son, Solomon, universally famous for his God-given wisdom, saw his kingdom expand in size and prosperity beyond Israel's wildest dreams in the opening years of his reign. The temple was built and magnificently furnished, not only to provide Israel with a focus of God's presence and a means by which they might make atonement for their sins so as to experience his forgiveness, but also to be a blessing to all the nations of the world. Solomon's consecration prayer at the temple's completion asks that as foreigners come to observe its splendour 'all the peoples of the earth may know your name [that is, God's character] and fear you' (1 Kings 8:43). But Solomon's serial adultery with 'many foreign women' led him away from the exclusive worship of the God whose temple he had built, into all sorts of idolatry, which, as ever, generated God's righteous judgment (1 Kings 11).

As a direct result, on Solomon's death the kingdom was divided. His son, Rehoboam, ruled only over the tribe of Judah, known from now on as the southern kingdom. The rest of the tribes appointed Jeroboam as their king and developed an alternative nation-state, based in Samaria, ignoring the temple in Jerusalem and setting up their own 'shrines' in Dan and Bethel. Such forbidden, idolatrous worship could only bring about disaster (1 Kings 13:33–4), and the rest of the history of the northern kingdom, Israel, is full of the evidence. Kings are replaced by violent usurpers, the worship of pagan idols increases, until gradually the kingdom of Israel slides away from any recognisable identity as God's covenant nation, virtually indistinguishable from its idolatrous neighbours.

Yet still God was merciful. He sent the prophets, most notably Amos and Hosea, to proclaim and apply his covenant instructions to a faithless renegade nation. Their preaching made it abundantly clear that a cataclysmic judgment of God was about to fall on this rebellion and that the northern kingdom would be destroyed and its people scattered. In time this event happened, with the fall of Samaria to the Assyrian army after a three-year siege, and the deportation of many of the Israelites to Nineveh. 'All this took place because the Israelites had sinned against the LORD their God . . . they worshipped other gods and followed the practices of the nations . . .' (2 Kings 17:7–8). The remaining tribe of Judah proved ultimately to be no better. Though the record of their kings was not the unbroken disaster-line that the north suffered, the southern kingdom was mainly governed by idolatrous successors to David. Eventually, after sending more prophets, such as Micah and Isaiah, God's decree of judgment was activated against Judah, and after a long campaign which devastated the country, the city of Jerusalem fell to the Babylonian army and many of her citizens were exiled.

Is that to be the end of the story? What about the promises to Abraham and to David? What, especially, about the Davidic dynasty and the kingdom that would be 'for ever'? Just as Adam and Eve had broken God's laws and forfeited God's place, so now Israel, Abraham's descendants, 'my firstborn son', has trampled on God's word and forfeited the land. Even her kings, anointed for a special role and relationship with God, have proved to be tarnished, sinful individuals, sharing the common disease of a heart that turns away from God's will to do its own. So the monarchy, which had seemed it might be the answer and had offered so much, lies shattered and the kingdom is destroyed. Is there no way forward? Is the whole human race always to be bound in to the same depressing pattern of wonderful promises ultimately unfulfilled, because of wilful rebellion?

New beginnings

But God is still merciful. Even as the prophets thunder their message of inescapable judgment, they also affirm the continuation of God's covenant promises and purposes. Israel has certainly suffered for her faithlessness, but God will not go back on his word. Their enjoyment of God's covenant blessings depended on their faithful fulfilment of their covenant obligations, in obedience to his instructions. But the failure of Israel to be the people he intended did not signal the failure of God's purposes. Beyond the exile there will be restoration. The people will be restored to the land and the structures of the theocracy will be rebuilt. There will be a new temple and a rebuilding of Jerusalem. The theme rings with unmistakable clarity through Isaiah, Jeremiah and Ezekiel. But there is an additional ingredient of huge significance. The root problem of human nature and its wretched propensity to sinful rebellion will be dealt with by God. Just listen to his promises.

'The time is coming,' declares the LORD, 'when I will make a new covenant with the house of Israel and with the house of Judah. It will not be like the covenant I made with their forefathers when I took them by the hand to lead them out of Egypt, because they broke my covenant, though I was a husband to them,' declares the LORD. 'This is the covenant that I will make with the house of Israel after that time,' declares the LORD. 'I will put my law in their minds and write it on their hearts. I will be their God, and they will be my people. No longer will a man teach his neighbour, or a man his brother, saying, "Know the LORD," because they will all know me, from the least of them to the greatest,' declares the LORD. 'For I will forgive their wickedness and will remember their sins no more.' (Jeremiah 31:31–4)

For I will take you out of the nations; I will gather you from all the countries and bring you back into your own land. I will sprinkle clean water on you, and you will be clean; I will cleanse you from all your impurities and from all your idols. I will give you a new heart and put a new spirit in you; I will remove from you your heart of stone and give you a heart of flesh. And I will put my Spirit in you and move you to follow my decrees and be careful to keep my laws. You will live in the land I gave to your forefathers; you will be my people, and I will be your God. (Ezekiel 36:24–8)

My servant David will be king over them, and they will all have one shepherd. They will follow my laws and be careful to keep my decrees. They will live in the land I gave to my servant Jacob, the land where your fathers lived. They and their children and their children's children will live there for ever, and David my servant will be their prince for ever. I will make a covenant of peace with them; it will be an everlasting covenant. I will establish them and increase their numbers, and I will put my sanctuary among them for ever. My dwelling-place will be with them; I will be their God, and they will be my people. (Ezekiel 37:24–7)

Clearly, the best is yet to be! But when, and how? In time, the Babylonian empire fell to the Persians whose leader, Cyrus, decreed the return of all exiled people to their homelands. Though many of the Jews had thoroughly assimilated into Babylonian culture, a large number did return, and over the century that followed they struggled to rebuild the temple, the city of Jerusalem and its defences. The books of Ezra and Nehemiah tell the story, and the prophecies of

Haggai, Zechariah and Malachi date from this period. But these were clearly not the great days which the major prophets had promised. The mere physical restoration of Israel to the land could not deal with the spiritual problems, which were the root of all their troubles. So, when the Old Testament ends, we are still left looking forward, with increasing longing. When will God activate his plan to deal with human sinfulness and its effects? When will the Messiah come, who will truly fulfil the qualities of 'anointed one' and 'son of God'? Where will the eternal kingdom, foreshadowed in the Davidic monarchy come to fruition? All these great Old Testament ideals are still crying out for fulfilment at the end of Malachi, and then for four centuries, as far as God's self-revelation is concerned, there is silence. Successive armies invade and conquer. The 'remnant' of Israelites who continue to believe God's word and obey his commands seems to shrink from generation to generation. But the hope of 'Messiah' is kept alive, and from time to time the tide of expectation runs high, until one day a young man, dressed like the prophet Elijah, in clothes of camel's hair, begins to preach by the Jordan river, 'Repent, for the kingdom of heaven [God's kingly rule] is near' (Matthew 3:1–6). The new day has dawned. The new testament is beginning.

As we turn to the New Testament, one point is now abundantly clear, namely that the page which the translators and publishers customarily place between the Old and the New has no business to be there. At least, that is so if ever it misleads us into separating the two halves of the Bible, to the extent of forgetting that they constitute one integrated whole. The Bible is one book in its great story-line, from Genesis to Revelation. Sadly, that has often been ignored, and specialists in Old and New Testaments have pursued their studies in separation if not mistrust of one another. But our brief survey of the Old Testament has surely prepared us to see the New as its completion and fulfilment, just as the New's own unique message is down-sized and almost trivialised, without relating it to the Old.

The coming of Jesus

So it is not by accident that the New Testament begins with four gospels (Matthew, Mark, Luke and John) or four presentations of one and the same gospel, or 'good news', in the birth, life, death and resurrection of Jesus Christ. Here are eye-witness accounts, carefully researched and brought together with theological coherence, committing to writing what would have been the orally preserved and proclaimed truths of who Jesus was, what he said and did, and what it all meant. John defines his purpose 'that you may believe that Jesus is the Christ, the Son of God, and that by believing you may have life in his name' (John 20:31). Luke writes 'an orderly account', based on his own careful research and investigation, 'of the things that have been fulfilled among us, just as they were handed down to us by those who from the first were eye-witnesses . . . so that you may know the certainty of the things you have been taught (Luke 1:1–4). Here are the events and their explanations which constitute the unique and perfect self-revelation of God in his Son, Jesus Christ. Indeed, the agenda of the four evangelists is to demonstrate for ever, beyond all doubt or contradiction, how the person and the work of Jesus are the fulfilment of all that the Old Testament promised.

The gospels are not primarily biographies, at least in the contemporary meaning of the term, though they have a good deal of biographical detail. Rather, a seemingly disproportionate amount of their time is taken up with the events of the last week of Jesus' life, in his death and resurrection. It is easy for us to pass over the uniqueness of this approach. There is no description of his physical appearance. Huge tracts of his short life (about thirty-three years) are omitted. The focus is clearly on the events by which God's long-awaited promises were being fulfilled and particularly on the specific patterns of the Old Testament Scriptures coming to completion in Christ. Listen to Jesus' own testimony.

Do not think that I have come to abolish the Law or the Prophets; I have not come to abolish them but to fulfil them. (Matthew 5:17)

He said to them, 'How foolish you are, and how slow of heart to believe all that the prophets have spoken! Did not the Christ have to suffer these things and then enter his glory?' And beginning with Moses and all the Prophets, he explained to them what was said in all the Scriptures concerning himself . . . He said to them, 'This is what I told you while I was still with you: Everything must be fulfilled that is written about me in the Law of Moses, the Prophets and the Psalms.' Then he opened their minds so they could understand the Scriptures. He told them, 'This is what is written: The Christ will suffer and rise from the dead on the third day, and repentance and forgiveness of sins will be preached in his name to all nations, beginning at Jerusalem.' (Luke 24:25–7, 44–7)

'My sheep listen to my voice; I know them, and they follow me. I give them eternal life, and they shall never perish; no-one can snatch them out of my hand. My Father, who has given them to me, is greater than all; no-one can snatch them out of my Father's hand. I and the Father are one.' (John 10:27–30)

It is the characteristic of the good shepherd that he 'lays down his life for the sheep' (John 10:11) and it is to his death on the cross that each of the four gospels inexorably moves us. Again, Jesus' own testimony is striking. Take, for example, his saying in Mark 10:45, 'For even the Son of Man did not come to be served, but to serve, and to give his life as a ransom for many.' In context, he is clearly claiming to be the Son of Man, an Old Testament title, dating from Daniel's vision of a human figure led into God's presence and given 'authority, glory and sovereign power; all peoples, nations and men of every language worshipped him. His dominion is an everlasting dominion that will not pass away, and his kingdom is one that will never be destroyed' (Daniel 7:14). Jesus is claiming to be that figure of eternal and universal regal authority. But look at the way in which the authority is to be exercised. This king conquers by serving his subjects, even to the point of offering up his own life as a ransom price, in order to set them free from their captivity. The cross is the means by which this freedom will be achieved, just as the mysterious figure of the 'suffering servant' in Isaiah's prophecy was 'pierced for our transgressions, he was crushed for our iniquities; the punishment that brought us peace was upon him, and by his wounds we are healed' (Isaiah 53:5). To bring the universal king and the suffering servant together was God's master-stroke through the cross of Jesus. It was a voluntary death – 'No one takes it from me but I lay it down of my own accord' (John 10:18). In this way God's immeasurable love for humanity was revealed. But it was supremely an atoning death – 'This is my blood of the [new] covenant, which is poured out for many for the forgiveness of sins' (Matthew 26:28). Because through Christ's sacrifice God's reconciling purposes finally found their fulfilment, he was able to die with a shout of triumph, 'Finished!' (John 19:30). The acceptance of his substitutionary death in the place of the sins of the world is vividly highlighted by the gospel writers when they tell us that the curtain in the Jerusalem temple, a huge heavily woven barrier which prevented the worshipper from entering into the presence of God, symbolised by the 'holy of holies', was torn in two, from the top to the bottom. This was so manifestly a divine action and so deeply significant that it became a visual enactment of what Christ's death had just achieved. It was the means by which God had removed the barrier separating himself, in all his holiness, from sinful human beings, so that in the death of his Son he was declaring to all the world, 'You can come in now.' This is the gospel of Christ.

The other great sign of the efficacy of Jesus' death and consequently the beginning of a new creation is, of course, his resurrection from the tomb on Easter morning. Good Friday and Easter Day for ever belong together. A dead Messiah would be no guarantee of an effective work, but as his followers were soon proclaiming, 'God raised him from the dead, freeing him from the agony of death, because it was impossible for death to keep its hold on him' (Acts 2:24). Jesus and the resurrection became the focus and content of the earliest Christian proclamation, and that unique historical event has marked out the 'gospel' as distinctive from all other religious beliefs and ideologies ever since. The gospel writers are very specific in their accounts of the empty tomb and the many encounters of his disciples with the risen Christ, in person, so that on these two great factual foundations our own understanding and personal relationship with the living Lord Jesus can be solidly grounded. For, as Paul expressed it, 'if Christ has not been raised, our preaching is useless and so is your faith' (1 Corinthians 15:14).

The spreading gospel

Such world-changing events had not only to be believed and entered into through a personal response to God of repentance and faith, but also proclaimed to all the nations. Now at last they all could experience the blessing promised so long ago to Abraham. Through his seed Jesus, Jews and Gentiles can alike enter into peace with God, know the forgiveness of sins, enjoy a deep personal relationship with their creator and begin to realise their destiny as God's own people. This is the agenda which the rest of the New Testament books are dedicated to pursuing. Apart from the Acts of the Apostles, written as a sequel to his gospel by Luke, and the book of Revelation, with which the

Bible ends, all the rest are in the form of letters (epistles) dealing with the life and problems of the early Churches, groups of Christians meeting in a particular locality. Often the area or city of those being addressed provides the title for the letter, to the Romans, to the Galatians, and so on. Sometimes an individual addressee gives his name to the book – Timothy or Titus – and sometimes the author, James, Peter, John.

Many of the epistles divide clearly into doctrinal and practical issues, theology and ethics, or what Christians believe and how they should then live. These two strands are always much more carefully interwoven than such a generalisation might suggest. However, it remains true that the practical issues raised both by the developing theological understanding of the gospel and by the invasion of un-orthodox and distorting teaching from both Judaistic and Gentile sources, largely generated and therefore govern the content of the apostolic writings. Monumental in scale among them is the work of the apostle Paul, once Saul of Tarsus, 'a Hebrew of Hebrews', arrested by the risen Christ as he travelled to Damascus to persecute Christ-ians, and reshaped as Christ's bondslave, commissioned to be his apostle, the evangelist to the nations. Not only is the scope of Paul's missionary endeavours mind-boggling, but the breadth and depth of his theological understanding and reflection are magisterial. To Paul, Peter and John particularly we owe our informed understanding of who Christ really is, what he accomplished, his present provision in the gift of the Holy Spirit to all his people and his future plans and purposes. The outworking of these realities in godly living now is always stressed, not least in the light of the fact that there is still one last stage of the cosmic drama to be completed.

For the Christ who rose from the dead and ascended to heaven will come again, in power and great glory, in the fulness of his divine majesty, to bring in his eternal kingdom. This is expressed by the familiar New Testament term 'the last days', used to describe the period of time, in which the Church has always had to live, between Christ's ascension and his return. 'This same Jesus, who has been taken from you into heaven, will come back in the same way you have seen him go into heaven' (Acts 1:11). These are the last days, because the whole of God's covenant plan is now complete, except for Christ's return to wind up human history. This reflects the tension expressed in Jesus' own teaching when he spoke of the kingdom of God, or of the heavens, having broken into the world of time and space history, in his incarnation; the kingdom is already here because Jesus is, but not yet in its fulness, because Christ is not yet revealed as universal judge and king. Similarly, the blessings of Christ's kingly rule belong to his disciples here and now, but only in a measure, since we do not yet in this world know the full release from sin, suffering or death, which will be fully ours in the life of the world to come. Rather like Old Testament believers waiting for the Messiah to appear, Christians are also a waiting people, but for Jesus' return. It is to that focus that the book of Revelation directs us, with its analysis of human history and its motivational visions of the heavenly kingdom, the destruction of all evil and the permanence of Christ's eternal reign. In that sense, contemporary Christians are still in the uncompleted chapter of the Bible's story, waiting for all that we have already begun to experience in Christ to become fully and eternally our own.

That, in all too brief summary, is the Bible's 'big picture', its meta-narrative, as we might call it today. But only a moment's reflection is needed to underscore that the story is not presented as a textbook of historical information, to be remembered or memorised, but as an invitation to enter into a relationship of faith with its central character, the present-tense God, our ruler, rescuer and judge, who has promised and fulfilled his great plan to bring men and women back to himself, through Jesus. Biblical truth is never merely propositional, but relational. It requires a response. When God came, in the person of Jesus Christ, he came as a preacher, summoning his hearers to repent and believe the good news of his kingly rule (Mark 1:14–15). How do we rightly relate to the promises of God and the God who makes the promises? By believing the promises and building our lives on his trustworthy, unchanging character. That was how it all started with the covenant man, Abraham, who 'believed the LORD and he credited it to him as righteousness' (Genesis 15:6). That is how the New Testament apostles expect us to respond to the word of the gospel, for it is only that content which can generate true belief. But where you have the Biblical word producing faith in God, through his Son, Jesus Christ, there you have the essence of Biblical Christianity and the continuing outworking of the Bible's own story.

To remind you

- The Bible is itself a library of sixty–six books, divided into several 'genres' or types of literature, written over many centuries (pp. 28–31).
- Its first eleven chapters (Genesis 1–11) are a 'seed–bed' for all that follows, showing human rebellion and God's reaction in both righteous wrath and delivering grace (pp. 31–3).
- A key concept introduced is that of 'covenant' – God makes and keeps his promises (pp. 33–5).
- Beginning with a man (Abraham) he creates a family and eventually a nation as the focus of his grace, but human rebellion persists (pp. 35–9).
- The provision of a king cannot solve the problem of rebellion and eventually the prophets predict the loss of land and nationhood (pp. 39–42).
- Beyond the exile, God promises a new start that will deal with the problem of sin, in the person of the Messiah (pp. 42–4).
- With the coming of Christ the exile ends and the kingdom of God breaks in on human history. By his death on the cross and his resurrection from the dead, Christ provides forgiveness for sins and eternal life for all who trust in him. This is the good news (pp. 44–7).
- This gospel has spread throughout the world and down through history. Just one event remains for the completion of God's purposes, which is the second coming of Christ (pp. 47–9).

Chapter 3

The Bible's Own Testimony

'YOU SEE, ONE of the biggest problems you Christians have is that you're all so incredibly gullible.' Matt was warming to a favourite theme. 'Take this commitment to the Bible, for example. You base your whole life on a book that's as old as the hills, but when you're asked why, you don't have any real evidence. It's like a journey on the Circle line. You assume there is a God, that he is wanting to speak to us in words and that the Bible is the true and reliable record of what he has revealed. Why? Because the Bible says it is. Well, it would, wouldn't it?'

'Yes, but hold on a minute,' Dan butted in. 'All arguments are going to be circular in that sense whenever they deal with the ultimate meaning of life, the universe and everything, because they are bound to go beyond the limits of what you can see or prove. Your starting point, Matt, is to try to explain the world without any reference to the "God-hypothesis", but that ties into your *own* circle. So, by assuming there is no God, you interpret your data to "prove" that he doesn't exist. After all, if the word "God" does have any meaning, any reality behind it, then, by definition, only God can demonstrate his true nature to human beings, because we are finite in our understanding and so vastly inferior to him. Only God can break into our little circles of human logic and show us something of the infinite. Ultimately, the only way that can be done must involve words, and the only person who could tell us they are his words is God.'

'Well, I see what you're driving at,' Matt grudgingly admitted, 'but I'd still want some hard evidence before I waste my time reading the Bible.'

'OK. So where shall we start? Archaeology has proved the Bible's historical accuracy over and over again. Or what about the Bible's principles of behaviour which have been the solid foundation of our civilisation for centuries? Then, you can't discount millions of Christians, down the centuries and from all over the world, who have put the Bible's claims to the test and found them to be true. It's not lack of evidence that is the problem, so much as our own unwillingness to submit to any authority other than ourselves. You can go on asking for more evidence until the cows come home. Your danger, Matt, is that you don't want to go into the water until you've learned to swim. But it doesn't work like that. There's a lot of truth in what G. K. Chesterton said, that it was not that Christianity had been tried and found wanting, but that, for most people, it had been found difficult and not tried. Why don't you try the Bible for yourself? All you have to lose is your prejudice!'

'No,' Matt shook his head, and then with a grin, 'you never know, I might be convinced!'

The question of the Bible's authority is of central importance to the whole issue of believing its message. At one level, it is true that the Bible is a book like any other. If you can read a newspaper, you can read the Bible. But at the level of process, something additional is going on, because in the Bible we hear God speaking to us, which is what it consistently claims for itself. When reading a paper or a book, we have been trained to read critically. We look for coherence, logic, evidence, argument. The same approach is entirely appropriate for the Bible, and Christians should never advocate a switch-off of their critical faculties. If the Bible is God's unchanging truth then it must be able to stand up to the most rigorous critical analysis, provided presuppositions from outside the Bible are not being employed to produce a destructive circular argument. But Bible readers of any consistency and application soon discover another process in operation. We may begin by applying our critical faculties to the biblical text, making our judgments as to its credibility or acceptability. Yet it is not long before we find the text itself sitting in judgment on us and our categories, exposing our weaknesses and shortcomings, facing us with our sin and rebellion, posing pressing issues about our relationship with God which are ultimately inescapable. Such a book hardly needs to be defended. As Charles Spurgeon, one of the greatest British preachers of the nineteenth century, commented, you might as well defend a lion. All you do is let it loose!

In his stimulating book, *Working the Angles* (1987, published by

W. M. Eerdmans, Grand Rapids, USA), Eugene Peterson has a chapter on learning to listen to God, through the Bible. His thesis is that we are in danger of being turned, by our culture, into 'cool analysts' rather than 'passionate hearers', because reading is a much less demanding activity than listening. We are in charge of the text; we can pull out whenever we want to. The book can be shut, the newspaper discarded. But a conversation has a much higher level of demand. It requires a response, often in actions as well as words. What makes Bible reading so challenging is the personal address of the voice of God, to which we need to tune in and listen, for that is how its authority and truth are conveyed. The Bible is not a religious treasury of memorable quotations or purple passages, to be used for our delectation or to select what we want out of them. It is the urgent, conversational voice of the living God, inviting us into relationship, probing our innermost thoughts and values, prompting us to stop and reflect, to consider our ways, to learn to live in the light of eternity. Our danger is that because all this is in book form for us, printed and bound like any other on our shelves, we treat it merely as we would any other book. We pick it up, look at it, use it even, for our comfort or inspiration, but we do not listen long enough, or hard enough, to meet the person who is speaking through its pages, or to enter the relationship of love to which we are being invited. We need to let the Bible speak for itself, for what Scripture is saying, God is saying.

What then is the Bible's testimony about itself? A number of semi-technical terms are commonly used to summarise this and it will be best to explore each of them in turn, since they do constitute a logical progression.

Let the Bible speak

It is usual to begin by speaking about the *authority* of the Bible. In a post-modern culture, the word will inevitably convey negative content and be liable to rejection before it has been examined. But separating the idea from any sub-biblical concept of authoritarianism, we can see that we are talking about a 'givenness' which the Bible both discloses and has within itself, by virtue of its origin. There is an 'authority' to the way things are in the created order, which we may rebel against, but cannot overturn. As I write, considerable parts of the world are about to witness a major eclipse of the sun, total in some areas. The newspapers are full of warnings about the danger of looking at the sun's eclipse even through special lenses, let alone with the naked eye, supported by tragic cases of those who have been blinded in very few seconds. That is a 'given', an authority. I may not like it. I can choose to ignore it, but I will blind myself. In an age like ours, so dedicated to pushing back the boundaries of individual freedom as far as we possibly can, it may appear irksome, but nothing changes the reality. Natural laws (as we call them) covering the use of electricity, or gravity, or food hygiene are simply the observed, inevitable properties of the world as we have it. We learn to live our lives within the parameters of the physical order. Why should the creator not build the same patterns of 'givenness' into the spiritual and eternal realities he has chosen to reveal?

It is just that sort of *spiritual* authority which is inherent in the Bible's claim to be the Word of God. Here is one of its clearest, most classic statements.

> The holy Scriptures . . . are able to make you wise for salvation through faith in Christ Jesus. All Scripture is God-breathed and is useful for teaching, rebuking, correcting and training in righteousness, so that the man of God may be thoroughly equipped for every good work. (2 Timothy 3:15–17)

Paul, writing to Timothy, is, of course, thinking of the Old Testament which his young colleague had been taught from childhood, but what he says is equally true of the New. How his writings were recognised as having similar authority we shall examine in Chapter 4. However, orthodox Christian belief has always held to the view that the whole Bible is 'God's Word written' (Article 20 of the Thirty-Nine Articles – the credal statement of the Church of England at the time of the Reformation). Perhaps the clearest contemporary statement of this position is made in 'The Chicago Statement on Biblical Hermeneutics', emanating from the consultations of leading evangelical church leaders and theologians in North America. Article I states, 'We affirm that the normative authority of Holy Scripture is the authority of God Himself, and is attested by Jesus Christ, the Lord of the Church. We deny the legitimacy of separating the authority of Christ from the authority of Scripture or of opposing the one to the other.'

Closely linked to the idea of authority is that of *inspiration*, a term used in older translations of this passage to translate 'God-breathed', which is preferable as it is the literal rendering of the Greek. The words of Scripture carry authority, the right to rule our lives, because they are the expression of the mind and will of God, 'breathed out' in human vocabulary. Paul has no small-print exclusion clauses. He speaks of 'all Scripture'. Everything that God says is true, and the mark of being a Christian is submitting to that truth and so recognising his authority as creator and Lord. Obedience to the word of Scripture is therefore a hallmark of discipleship. However, it is common to want to reduce this element of biblical authority by drawing attention to the fallibility of the human channels through which it is mediated, whether authors or interpreters. How can an infallible divine word be conveyed by human beings who are themselves morally flawed, intellectually limited and the prisoners of a language and culture that are time-bound? The danger of such an attitude is that it will inevitably exalt human reason above the Bible's own words, so that we end up with a subjective assessment as to what we can bring ourselves to believe. In practice this often seems to work out as acceptance that God is loving but not our judge, that heaven exists but not hell, and Jesus was a fine moral example and an inspirational teacher, but not God in human form, fully human and fully divine. This last denial reflects the inability of its proponents to believe that the Bible could be God's words through human writers, at one and the same time. But why should that not be so? In his penetrating little book, *God Has Spoken* (1965, Hodder & Stoughton), Dr J. I. Packer makes the point this way.

> The Bible is not only man's word, but God's also; not merely a record of revelation, but a written revelation in its own right, God's own witness to Himself in the form of human witnesses to Him. Accordingly, the authority of the Scriptures rests, not simply on their worth as an historical source, a testament of religion, and a means of uplift, real though this is, but primarily and essentially on the fact that they came to us from the mouth of God. (p. 72)

To believe in the Bible in this way is clearly to affirm one's faith in the supernatural. But that is neither irrational nor unreasonable. Nor is it to capitulate to subjectivism, which is actually what the critics of this conviction tend to do. Because much of what the Bible teaches confronts and challenges our culture, it is tempting for the critic to decide what cannot be accepted, and then go looking for internal textual 'evidence' that will enable the plain meaning of the Bible to be changed. Usually its new 'meaning' will correspond with the critic's subjective contemporary views, and in this way the voice of God is silenced. We know that in the area of scientific investigation, careful observation and experimentation are the essential foundations of any hypothesis. Wishful thinking and subjective preferences have no place in scientific endeavour. But biblical theology, once the 'queen of the sciences', is no more governed by subjective wish than is chemistry. The difference is that in science the investigator moves towards the object of knowledge, whereas in theology the religious 'object' (God himself) moves towards us, determining the character and expression of the revelation of truth which is inherent in his own nature. We are back to the concept of self-disclosure and the subsequent invitation to a personal response in terms of a relationship with him. The authority principle of the Bible is the living God in self-revelation, which is neither subjectively determined nor authoritarian, but infinite and personal. So, a Christian is subject to the final authority of God himself, revealed supremely in Jesus Christ, and mediated by 'all Scripture'. This prevents us from thinking of 'inspiration' as merely a heightening of human consciousness within the Bible authors, as we might refer to a great composer or artist generally as 'inspired'. If that were so, we would have to sort the more inspired from the less, and we would be back to the limited human authorities of reason, emotion, or even prejudice. The apostle Peter makes the point with trenchant clarity.

> Above all, you must understand that no prophecy of Scripture came about by the prophet's own interpretation. For prophecy never had its origin in the will of man, but men spoke from God as they were carried along by the Holy Spirit. (2 Peter 1:20–1)

In summary, we have seen that without self-revelation God would be unknowable. Having created humankind in his own image, able to think abstractly and with highly developed language skills, God determined to convey his self-revelation through a variety of human channels over a period of years. But his revelatory work is always related to his redemptive plan (see Chapter 2) since the human dilemma is not so much one of finite ignorance as of moral guilt. God's revelation centres then on what human beings need to know of his character and their need, and how the one has met the other, in his great rescue plan to undo the effects of sinful rebellion and bring men and women back into a loving, personal relationship with their creator. Both the key to the plan and its fulfilment lie in Jesus Christ, 'the radiance of God's glory and the exact representation of his being' (Hebrews 1:3). The Bible is the record of this self-revelatory message from God, with his one integrated plan being pursued throughout the one revelation. Because this is so central to God's purposes and activated by supernatural power, the resulting testimony is undistorted, reliable truth for all people, at all times, and reveals, in comprehensible human language, as much of the knowledge of God as we can understand or need to know.

It is a derivative of this high view of Scripture to describe the Bible further as *inerrant*, though this has been an area of prolonged and sometimes acrimonious debate over the last several decades. There is an extensive literature on the whole subject and this is not the place to attempt to do justice to all the arguments. Discussion has often centred on so-called contradictions or apparently conflicting records of events in the Bible. How can both be true? And if the Bible is found to err in its historical or cosmological details, how can it maintain its divine authority? One way of dealing with the issue is to reduce the scope of the Bible's authority range. Thus the Lausanne Declaration in the 1970s spoke of the Bible as 'reliable in all that it genuinely affirms and authoritative for guidance in doctrine and behaviour', while earlier Vatican II had pronounced that the Bible teaches 'firmly, faithfully and without error that truth which God wanted put into the sacred writings for the sake of our salvation'. Such statements allow room for mistakes to have occurred in areas which do not have an impact on the major doctrines of the faith. If it is agreed, however, that God's providential and supernatural over-ruling has prevented the distortion of his message in such essential areas, why could such care not also extend to its entire contents? Indeed, if it does not, what guarantees of its veracity can we claim?

Frequently, it is assumed that the Bible is 'full of contradictions' but they become notoriously difficult to find and generally come down to such issues as whether one or two angels were present at Christ's tomb, or whether a blind beggar was healed by Jesus on his way in or out of Jericho. In these and similar cases harmonisation of the accounts is perfectly possible and even reasonable. An error is a false statement which is presented as true, yet to prove that such exists would require us to be certain that we have a correct understanding, that we possess all the knowledge needed to come to a judgment and that no further light can possibly be thrown on the issue by further research or discovery. But it is precisely the incompleteness of our knowledge and the inadequacies of our interpretations which constitute the problem. To prejudge unsolved difficulties as errors is equivalent to insisting that the current absence of a solution means that no solution is possible. The discussion then lies more in the area of presuppositions. We cannot understand how Jesus could be both God and man: we rightly speak of the great mystery of the incarnation. But if we accept its reality we have no problem in accepting also his life of moral perfection and sinless righteousness. We do not charge the Bible writers with error or exaggeration because the one is the corollary of the other. In the same way, if the Bible is the Word of God, how can it be anything other than true and inerrant in every word? And, indeed, every word does matter. For meaning does not exist in isolated words, but in their grouping together in phrases, sentences and paragraphs. We all know how the addition or removal of one word, or its relocation in a different position in a sentence, can substantially change the meaning of that sentence. So, when we speak of the 'verbal inspiration' of Scripture, we mean that every word is 'God-breathed', that each word has a vital, constituent part to play in its own unit of meaning, and that God's sovereign control extends as much to the details of each verse as to the grand themes of the Bible's books. To return to the Chicago Statement, we find at Article XX the following, helpful summary. 'We affirm that since God is the author of all truth, all truths, biblical and extra-biblical, are consistent and cohere, and that the Bible speaks truth when it touches on matters pertaining to nature, history, or anything else.'

These general affirmations we have been considering are, however, all derived from the Bible's own testimony about itself, and to that we must return. In Chapter 2 we saw how Christ is himself the centre and pivot of the whole story. It is not for nothing that John describes him as 'the Word made flesh' (John 1:14). So it is to the infallible Christ that we must turn for a true understanding of the nature of the Scriptures. Indeed, it is in the light of my allegiance to Jesus Christ as Lord that I believe in the inspiration, infallibility and inerrancy of the Scriptures. Yet I have been brought to that conviction through their own self-authenticating power and through the gracious illumination of the Holy Spirit. Bible readers come to Bible convictions as they experience Bible truth.

Jesus and the Old Testament

There is no doubt that Jesus fully accepted the Old Testament's claim, which occurs hundreds of times throughout its pages, 'This is what the LORD says . . .' He had a comprehensive knowledge of those Scriptures, quoting and referring to them constantly and with ease. For Jesus, whatever the Scriptures said settled the argument. The gospels include direct reference by Jesus to Genesis, Exodus, Leviticus, Numbers, Deuteronomy, Samuel, Kings, Chronicles, Psalms, Isaiah, Jeremiah, Daniel, Hosea, Joel, Micah, Zechariah and Malachi – at least! Each time the message is clear. Scripture is totally authoritative because what it says God says. Constantly, he recognised Old Testament Scripture as the 'Word of God'. A key and representative passage occurs in Mark 7 (paralleled in Matthew 15).

The Pharisees and some of the teachers of the law who had come from Jerusalem gathered round Jesus and saw some of his disciples eating food with hands that were 'unclean', that is, unwashed. (The Pharisees and all the Jews do not eat unless they give their hands a ceremonial washing, holding to the tradition of the elders. When they come from the market-place they do not eat unless they wash. And they observe many other traditions, such as the washing of cups, pitchers and kettles.) So the Pharisees and teachers of the law asked Jesus, 'Why don't your disciples live according to the tradition of the elders instead of eating their food with "unclean" hands?' He replied, 'Isaiah was right when he prophesied about you hypocrites; as it is written: "These people honour me with their lips, but their hearts are far from me. They worship me in vain; their teachings are but rules taught by men." You have let go of the commands of God and are holding on to the traditions of men.' And he said to them: 'You have a fine way of setting aside the commands of God in order to observe your own traditions! For Moses said, "Honour your father and your mother," and, "Anyone who curses his father or mother must be put to death." But you say that if a man says to his father or mother: "Whatever help you might otherwise have received from me is Corban" (that is, a gift devoted to God), then you no longer let him do anything for his father or mother. Thus you nullify the word of God by your tradition that you have handed down. And you do many things like that.' (Mark 7:1–13)

Jesus is in dialogue with the religious leaders of Israel, as so often in the gospels. This time the issue under discussion is that of ritual purification before meals. His disciples have been accused of less than satisfactory practices of holiness, but Jesus turns the tables on his opponents by scrutinising their lives for a much deeper, internal sanctity. They imagine that they have the right to set aside one of God's commands (the fifth of his ten 'words' or commandments in Exodus 20) and find a way around its demands (vv. 9–13). For Jesus, the words of Moses are the commands of God. The written Scriptures must therefore constitute the supreme authority over all religious traditions, however important or impressive their proponents may seem to be, and however venerable a pedigree they may be able to present. Similarly, using Isaiah's prophecy (29:13), Jesus elevates God's Word over all human teaching and all the structures of institutionalised religion. Without submission to that authority, religious teachers are 'blind guides', whose work cannot be authorised by the heavenly Father (Matthew 15:13–14). Without detailed obedience to his written instructions in Scripture, any professed worship of God is in fact 'in vain' (v. 7).

Nor is this merely an isolated instance. In John 10:34, in another argument with the Jews, Jesus bases his case on one word used in Psalm 82:6 which he refers to both as 'your Law' and 'the word of God'. For Jesus there was no problem with dual authorship, for he was convinced of their divine inspiration and consequent authority and infallibility. Either we must dismiss his attitude as being conditioned by the prevailing fashions of his day and so fallible, which in effect is to deny his full deity, or we recognise that above every other man who ever lived he alone knew how that word was given and its true authority. If Jesus Christ is truly Lord, then his attitude to the Old Testament Scriptures must be followed by his contemporary disciples. It is significant too that for Jesus those Scriptures are to be reverenced in their entirety. We are not at liberty to pick and choose, or to base our beliefs on single proof texts without setting them in the context of the whole revelation. This brief quotation from the closing days of Jesus' earthly life provides an excellent example of this very important principle.

While the Pharisees were gathered together, Jesus asked them, 'What do you think about the Christ? Whose son is he?' 'The son of David,' they replied. He said to them, 'How is it then that David, speaking by the Spirit, calls him "Lord"? For he says, "The Lord said to my Lord: Sit at my right hand until I put your enemies under your feet." If then David calls him "Lord", how can he be his son?' No-one could say a word in reply, and from that day on no-one dared to ask him any more questions. (Matthew 22:41–6)

The Pharisees are only partly right. In all the discussion about Jesus' identity and whether or not he might be the promised Messiah, the Pharisees, who greatly revered the Scriptures, made the point that he would be David's son, born into the tribe of Judah, as Jesus was in Bethlehem, David's home town. But what they had not come to terms with was the reference from Psalm 110:1 to the Messiah as also being David's 'lord', that is having a divine nature. One Scripture is not to be set against another, but Scripture is to be used to interpret Scripture since its single divine authorship predisposes the careful reader to harmonising what seem to be contradictions, or at least to holding both together with equal conviction. Had they done so they would not have been so keen to dismiss his claims and hound him to the cross.

Similarly in Mark 12:18–27, Jesus is dialoguing with the Sadducees on the subject of the resurrection, in which they did not believe.

Then the Sadducees, who say there is no resurrection, came to him with a question. 'Teacher,' they said, 'Moses wrote for us that if a man's brother dies and leaves a wife but no children, the man must marry the widow and have children for his brother. Now there were seven brothers. The first one married and died without leaving any children. The second one married the widow, but he also died, leaving no child. It was the same with the third. In fact, none of the seven left any children. Last of all, the woman died too. At the resurrection whose wife will she be, since the seven were married to her?' Jesus replied, 'Are you not in error because you do not know the Scriptures or the power of God? When the dead rise, they will neither marry nor be given in marriage; they will be like the angels in heaven. Now about the dead rising – have you not read in the book of Moses, in the account of the bush, how God said to him, "I am the God of Abraham, the God of Isaac, and the God of Jacob"? He is not the God of the dead, but of the living. You are badly mistaken!'

They take as their text Deuteronomy 25:5–6.

> If brothers are living together and one of them dies without a son, his widow must not marry outside the family. Her husband's brother shall take her and marry her and fulfil the duty of a brother-in-law to her. The first son she bears shall carry on the name of the dead brother so that his name will not be blotted out from Israel.

Their point, that in theory a man might have married a number of wives, is being used to rubbish the idea of a resurrection. But Jesus rounds on them with a stinging rebuke for their facetious confidence. 'Are you not in error, because you do not know the Scriptures or the power of God?' (Mark 12:24). The Scripture concerned is Exodus 3:6, in which God declares himself to be the God of Abraham, Isaac and Jacob, who must therefore be living beyond this world, proving that there is life beyond death. Jesus argues that *all* the biblical evidence must be weighed and considered, and that as this is done it will be found to be coherent and increasingly illuminating, which is actually the experience of every serious Bible student.

In his personal earthly life, the human Jesus used the Old Testament Scriptures to discover God's purpose and to determine his conduct. As he faced the cross he saw the details of his coming betrayal, passion, death and resurrection as the fulfilment of Old Testament prophecy (Matthew 26:24, 31, 53–6). Indeed, these events are in themselves a demonstration of the Old Testament's reliability since their fulfilment was beyond Christ's 'engineering'. So much that others did to him, over which he had no human influence, had already been predicted. Evidence of the way in which Old Testament principles controlled his whole thinking and subsequent life-style often comes almost incidentally, as when, in response to the Pharisees' criticism of his 'eating with sinners', he quotes Hosea 6:6, 'I desire mercy, not sacrifice', going beyond the narrow, more precise meaning of the words in their original context to a broader, more basic truth, which they clearly illustrate.

But perhaps the strongest and most impressive way in which Jesus confirms the authority and infallibility of the Old Testament Scriptures is his constant linking of himself to them, since it is through knowing them that we can come to know him. We can take one example from the many cited during his ministry. Much of the debate in John's gospel settles on the issue of Christ's personal identity, but Jesus again accuses his religious opponents of blindness because they do not recognise how he fulfils the prophecies and promises. 'You diligently study the Scriptures,' Jesus says, 'because you think that by them you possess eternal life. These are the Scriptures that testify about me, yet you refuse to come to me to have life' (John 5:39–40). Again, he challenges them. 'If you [really] believed Moses, you would believe me, for he wrote about me. But since you do not believe what he wrote, how are you going to believe what I say?' (John 5:46–7). Theoretically their belief in the truth of the Old Testament was impeccable, but they refused to see its fulfilment in Christ and so they revealed a practical unbelief. Frequently Jesus drew attention to the testimony of the Old Testament as to his identity and its explanation of his mission. He is the fulfilment of the Passover lamb by whose death God's people are liberated (Exodus 12), and the brass serpent bringing healing and life to all who obeyed Moses to look and live (Numbers 21). Most profoundly of all, he is the suffering servant of the Lord (Isaiah 53) by whose wounds we are healed. We cannot therefore separate Jesus from the Old Testament witness to him. We shall not worship him as we ought if we do not accept its authoritative divinely-given testimony to his person and work.

Moreover, the risen Christ goes out of his way to make exactly this point to his disciples before his ascension. The Scriptures are to remain as the authoritative rule and guide of the new community, the Church, he came to build. What could have been more 'natural', or supernatural, than for the risen Christ to demonstrate his continuing identity to his, at first, agnostic disciples by power displays of miraculous energy and effect? But the final chapter of Luke's gospel goes out of its way to show the opposite. How does Jesus convince his doubting disciples that he really has conquered death, has risen in power and is Lord of the universe? Luke tells us twice. To the two travelling from Jerusalem to Emmaus, the stranger who joined them seemed to demonstrate no supernatural appearance or character, but he explained his resurrection, demonstrating its inevitability from the Scriptures. ' "How foolish you are, and how slow of heart to believe all that the prophets have spoken! Did not the Christ have to suffer these things and then enter his glory?" And beginning with Moses and all the Prophets, he explained to them what was said in all the Scriptures concerning himself' (Luke 24:25–7). It may seem at first that he was taking them on a 'loop-line', when he might have revealed himself directly to them, but that is to miss his purpose. For all the future centuries of the Church, the pattern was being set. We meet the Lord Jesus in the written Word, and without the Book we shall never understand him. Unless the Scriptures determine the real character of the true Christ, and unless we humbly allow the Holy Spirit to be our teacher through them, we shall always be vulnerable to re-creating a false Christ of our own imagination, and being deluded by the echo of our own thoughts, rather than knowing the certainty of his self-revelation. The scholar George Tyrell said of the nineteenth-century critics who embarked on a quest for the 'Jesus of history' that they looked into the well of history and came up with a Jesus who was but a reflection of themselves. It is only by submitting to the Jesus of Scripture that we can enter into the true experience of his rescue and rule. Luke makes the point a second time when Jesus appears on Easter evening, to his bewildered disciples in the upper room. 'He said to them, "This is what I told you while I was still with you: Everything must be fulfilled that is written about me in the Law of Moses, the Prophets, and the Psalms." Then he opened their minds so they could understand the Scriptures. He told them, "This is what is written . . ." ' (Luke 24:44–6). It may sound more immediately convincing and impressive when someone says, 'I don't need to go back to the Bible, I have an encounter with the living Christ. My authority is that dynamic personal relationship with God, into which Jesus has brought me, not an impersonal book.' But the inescapable biblical truth is that the risen Christ taught his disciples to understand and proclaim the good news of all that he had achieved only through the written Scripture, since that is his chosen channel of self-revelation.

Jesus and the New Testament

But what about the New Testament? We have just been quoting extensively from the gospels to establish Christ's own attitude to the Old Testament. What about their own authenticity? Did Jesus have anything to say about that? Again, the answer is strongly positive. We saw earlier that the New Testament was written in order to guarantee continuing accurate records of the events of Jesus' life, death and resurrection, for succeeding generations, as the apostles began to die. What had been oral testimony was committed to writing, and with the events ran the explanations of them, as the apostolic theology deepened and strengthened, both by reflection and through experience of the gospel impacting alien cultures. But Jesus had already made provision for all this. John records his words to the disciples.

> I have much more to say to you, more than you can now bear. But when he, the Spirit of truth, comes, he will guide you into all truth. He will not speak on his own; he will speak only what he hears, and he will tell you what is yet to come. He will bring glory to me by taking from what is mine and making it known to you. All that belongs to the Father is mine. That is why I said the Spirit will take from what is mine and make it known to you. (John 16:12–15)

Clearly, this is a very wonderful promise, but limited to the apostolic circle. It is not to be understood that Christians in any succeeding generation will be miraculously led into understanding everything about everything through the Holy Spirit. Nor does it mean that in our day we receive direct, authoritative revelation which should be preserved and bound into the covers of the Bible, because it is universally and infallibly true, as Scripture is. But it is a great promise that the Holy Spirit, given to all Christians from the day of Pentecost onwards (Acts 2:1–4, 38–9), would inspire the closest followers of Jesus to understand and apply the benefits of Christ's teaching and work and so to be able to preach the gospel authoritatively and with confidence throughout the world. The same supernatural activity, which inspired and empowered the prophets of the Old, would be active in the writing of the New Testament, as a divine gift. That is what John 14:26 clearly promises. 'But the Counsellor, the Holy Spirit, whom the Father will send in my name, will teach you all things and will remind you of everything I have said to you.' Again, it is a promise to the apostles, who were the personally commissioned witnesses of the risen Christ, and the result is the sure and certain testimony, which is our New Testament. It explains why apostolic authority was such an important touchstone in the early Church and how this affected the recognition of individual books of the New Testament as holy Scripture. But more of that in the next chapter. What is significant to note is that by the time the apostle Peter wrote his second letter (probably in the 60s AD), the apostle Paul's letters were already circulating with Scriptural authority. 'Our dear brother Paul also wrote to you with the wisdom that God gave him . . . His letters contain some things that are hard to understand, which ignorant and unstable people distort, as they do the other Scriptures, to their own destruction' (2 Peter 3:15–16). If Paul, who had not been one of the original twelve, was already recognised as writing Scripture, it is hardly surprising that Peter, John or Matthew and others within their immediate circle should be acknowledged as having been divinely inspired in their writings.

This special status of the apostles in the early Church, undergirding the authority of the New Testament writings, can be traced back to Christ's own commission. 'Apostle' (*apostolos*) simply means someone who is sent. 'Missionary' is the English term derived from the equivalent Latin. As early as Mark 3:14, we are told that Jesus appointed twelve, 'designating them apostles that they might be with him and that he might send them out to preach and to have authority to drive out demons'. Though Judas Iscariot was removed from their number by his suicide, following Christ's betrayal, Matthias was added in his place (Acts 1:15–26). But a further apostle, Paul, commissioned and sent by the risen Lord to the Gentile world, in a sense eclipsed them all. From time to time in his letters, particularly in Galatians and 1 and 2 Corinthians, there is a discussion and major defence of his apostleship. Clearly it was under considerable criticism, since as Paul himself admits he was not part of the original group. But he argues fervently that his apostleship is no less authoritative or divinely commissioned. 'For I am the least of the apostles and do not even deserve to be called an apostle because I persecuted the Church of God. But by the grace of God I am what I am, and his grace to me was not without effect' (1 Corinthians 15:9–10). If the mark of the apostle is a direct meeting with the risen Christ and a personal commissioning, then Paul's credentials are impeccable. 'Am I not an apostle? Have I not seen Jesus our Lord? Are you not the result of my work in the Lord? . . . For you are the seal of my apostleship in the Lord,' he tells the Corinthian Church he founded (1 Corinthians 9:1–2). Again, speaking of the evidences for his claim in his ministry among them at Corinth, he affirmed, 'The things that mark an apostle – signs, wonders and miracles – were done among you with great perseverance' (2 Corinthians 12:12).

The reason it all matters so much is because, in Christ's purposes, the apostles were to be the foundation of the whole future Church. They became this, Paul explains, by being the custodians of the revelation of the gospel, through the Holy Spirit's revelation, as we saw Jesus promise in John's gospel. They are therefore the first gift of the ascended Christ to his Church (Ephesians 2:20, 3:5, 4:11) and, as such, their testimony becomes the foundation for the future building, with Christ himself as the chief cornerstone. They are the eyewitnesses who became the authoritative preachers and, for some, writers of the gospel word. This view was not a later accommodation to Paul, but a central ingredient of early church life from the beginning. It is already clearly established in Peter's thinking when he preaches the gospel for the first time to Gentiles, in the house of Cornelius, the Roman centurion, at Caesarea. The apostles see themselves as specially chosen and accredited witnesses, whose responsibility is to proclaim that in Christ all the promises of forgiveness made by the prophets have been fulfilled, and since he is also the judge of all, the rescue he offers is certain and sure.

> God raised him from the dead on the third day and caused him to be seen. He was not seen by all the people, but by witnesses whom God had already chosen – by us who ate and drank with him after he rose from the dead. He commanded us to preach to the people and to testify that he is the one whom God appointed as judge of the living and the dead. All the prophets testify about him that everyone who believes in him receives forgiveness of sins through his name. (Acts 10:40–3)

Not surprisingly, therefore, the apostles regarded their teaching as having Christ's authority in the Church, not by virtue of their office or any kind of label, but because of their inspiration by the Holy Spirit. Paul reminds the Corinthians of 'the gospel I preached to you' and affirms, 'by this gospel you are saved . . . for what I received I passed on to you' (1 Corinthians 15:1–3). For him it was of primary importance that this was the special gift of God to him. 'I want you to know, brothers, that the gospel I preached is not something that man made up. I did not receive it from any man, nor was I taught it; rather, I received it by revelation from Jesus Christ' (Galatians 1:11–12). When he eventually visited the Jerusalem church, 'they saw that I had been entrusted with the task of preaching the gospel to the Gentiles, just as Peter had been to the Jews' (Galatians 2:7). It was the same gospel, with the same Christ-given authority.

The logical inference is that they expected this authoritative teaching to be read aloud when the groups of Christians met together, just as the Old Testament Scriptures were read aloud in the Jewish synagogue. 'After this letter has been read to you, see that it is also read in the church of the Laodiceans' (Colossians 4:16). 'I charge you before the Lord to have this letter read to all the brothers' (1 Thessalonians 5:27). So, it came about that what we know as the Old and New Testaments were immediately placed together as having the same divine authority. This was not something which the Church gave to the Bible, rather it was the Bible, the word of God's truth in the gospel, which gave birth and life to the Church. Peter joins the two together when he writes, 'I want you to recall the words spoken in the past by the holy prophets and the command given by our Lord and Saviour through your apostles' (2 Peter 3:2). Paul makes the same conjunction when he quotes the law (Deuteronomy 25:4) and the gospel (Luke 10:7) in the same verse. 'For the Scripture says, "Do not muzzle the ox while it is treading out the grain" and "The worker deserves his wages" ' (1 Timothy 5:18). Both are equally designated 'Scripture', so that both are equally authoritative.

Modern views of the Bible

This, then, is the Bible's self-testimony, which represented original, orthodox Christian belief down the centuries, and still does. Rediscovered during the Protestant reformation of the sixteenth century, the watchword '*Sola Scriptura*' swept across much of Europe and on into the New World. It was ironic, however, that the fruit of this new understanding, in terms of scientific investigation and the consequent exaltation of the faculty of human reason in the Enlightenment, was to provide its greatest challenge over the last four centuries. If Psalm 111:2 was true, 'Great are the works of the LORD; they are pondered by all who delight in them', then the Christian motivation to modern science was rooted in revelation. But what if the human 'pondering' took on a greater authority and delight than the 'works of the Lord', and what if it developed its own autonomy and rival authority to the word written? It was only a small step for the Cambridge Platonists to affirm, 'To follow reason is to follow God', for in all our investigations humankind would simply be thinking God's thoughts after him. Certainly God had revealed himself and his truth to the apostles, but would he not do so to anyone who lived according to reason? The Bible could illuminate and confirm new discoveries of truth, but the apostles no longer had a monopoly on revelation.

From there, it was only another small enough step to affirm that Reason (now capitalised and personified) is the undoubted Word of God, or that the spiritual understanding of the reasonable (enlightened) man is a more sure guide to truth than Scripture. Evidence that the apostles were mistaken was produced. Had they not wrongly expected Christ's imminent return? Were they not children of their times, with all the limitations that implied? Were there not serious differences between Peter and Paul, between Jewish and Gentile Christianity? Such questions as these have clear internal answers within the Bible. We are to live every day ready for Christ's coming and eagerly awaiting the fulness of his kingdom. The supernatural works of the Holy Spirit over-ruled the inevitable human fallibility of the biblical writers. The New Testament demonstrates a wonderful unity in the authentic gospel, so that no one author needs to be set against another.

But by now theology was the 'queen of the sciences', whose purpose was to discover the historical process by which the religious ideas of the Bible were formed, and as a result the reconstruction of the history of New Testament Christianity became the arbiter of what is true and what could therefore be believed. Apostolic theology was accounted for in terms of a cultural expression of a particular religious faith, which borrowed from, and reacted to, the surrounding climate of religious ideas and beliefs. Anti-supernatural assumptions became more blatant. The miracles were superstition, myths designed to teach religious truth, but without any historical foundation. The resurrection was not a literal event. It would no longer do to proclaim unequivocally the deity of the Lord Jesus Christ. Relentlessly, as these expressions of doubt and unbelief dominated higher theological education, based on a culturally fashionable denial of the supernatural (as an unsubstantiated presupposition), it became only too clear that the so-called 'higher criticism' inevitably undermined the theological and moral value of the Bible.

As the critics saw the implicit destruction of Christian culture in their denigration of the Bible, an existential methodology was developed to hold on to what was regarded as religiously important, even though in their understanding it no longer had any basis in objective, historical fact. Jesus may not have fed the multitude miraculously with bread and fish, but the eternal truth remained that compassion and active charity towards the under-privileged is a godlike quality. In such a scheme we have an explanation without any event. Of course, it is a nonsense. If the events did not occur, then there is not the slightest guarantee that what they are alleged to teach has any lasting objective validity either. Not surprisingly, the history of the twentieth century was of the churches of the Western world being emptied because the supernatural Christ of the New Testament was rejected. Not destroyed – for none of these arguments was unanswerable, and indeed throughout the long process, Bible-believing scholars have developed their skills of understanding and interpretation to give an even greater confidence than ever before in God's written Word – but despised and rejected, as being out of tune with the intellectual fashions of the age, and the process continues. As with the religious leaders of his day, Jesus 'came to that which was his own, but his own did not receive him. Yet to all who received him, to those who believed in his name, he gave the right to become children of God' (John 1:11–12).

Of course, this is not to say that the development of close, analytical critical studies of the Bible has been entirely negative. There is much of immense value that has been learned from exploring how the Bible writers put their work together, their sources and the forms used. These are well-developed tools which have their usefulness. What is dangerous is the unproven presuppositions which insist on approaching the Bible, scissors in hand, to reduce and ultimately destroy. Then we are left with conscience, or more often personal opinion, as the final arbiter of belief, and truth no longer exists. The Bible becomes a closed book, the province of the critical expert alone, and the voice of the living God is silenced. Instead we have the voice of our own subjective reaction, a notoriously fickle and unreliable guide, since we are usually the prisoners of the spirit of the age to a much greater extent than we are prepared to admit. 'This is what the Lord says . . .' has been transmuted into 'I like to believe that . . .'

Most of us in the Western world are familiar with the 'Bible minus' approach I have just been describing, but it is less common to realise that there is an equally dangerous virus attacking healthy orthodox Christian faith, which we might identify as the 'Bible plus'. Subtracting from the Bible is only one way of denying its authority. Certainly the history of the last hundred years, with its bewildering multiplication of cults and sects, confirms that the Bible can be distorted and ultimately rejected by adding another parallel authority alongside it, to which equal credence is given. So the Bible *plus* the Book of Mormon, or the teachings of Mary Baker Eddy, or the words of some new contemporary prophet, such as a David Koresh, become the new base of authority.

At first, it all sounds so reasonable. It is simply an attempt to bring the application up to date, to make the Bible more relevant to a new cultural context. But very soon the new authority begins to re-interpret the plain teaching of Scripture by adding so-called 'fresh revelation' direct from God, and the written Word, having been considered insufficient, is quickly undermined. 'You may go to the Bible for what God was saying yesterday,' we are told, 'but the prophet is needed to hear what God is saying today.' That is the quick route to disaster. Once another human authority is added to Scripture, its unique truth claims will soon be reinterpreted, redefined and ultimately dismissed.

For this reason, I think it is right to express concern about the contemporary emphasis on 'prophecy' in some Christian circles. At root, it is the sufficiency of the Bible which is at stake. The Church has rarely been without those who have claimed to speak directly from God, but such claims are not to be accepted uncritically. When Christians say, 'the Lord told me', with regard to decisions being made, what do they actually mean? In practice, they are often speaking of an inner conviction about a course of action, formed through study of the Scriptures, prayer and consultation with others. But it would be unwise to assume that all such convictions are automatically the work of the Holy Spirit. Sincerity is not in itself a proof of reality, since the smallest amount of self-knowledge tells us that we can all be sincere, but sincerely wrong!

The sufficiency of the Bible

The only truly objective test we have is the word which God has already spoken in the Scriptures. Any Christian who claims a word, insight or vision from God must be willing for it to be submitted to the primary revelation of the Bible, for what God has once said he is still saying. His Word is eternal, and because it is Truth it is obviously non-contradictory. So, if any so-called 'prophecy' is truly from God it will be able to be confirmed by the message of Scripture. If that is so, then we could have derived its content from Scripture anyway, so that what is happening is in no sense the receiving of fresh revelation, but a new focus on, or better comprehension of, the specific revelation already given. In my own view, the appropriate biblical description of this ministry is exhortation or teaching, rather than prophecy. Indeed, once we accept the sufficiency of the written Scriptures, it follows that the gift of prophecy, in its narrow biblical sense of direct revelation, will no longer function. We still need to be guided in all our decision-making by the Holy Spirit, but the tool he uses is the Word he has already inspired, of which Christ is the great centre and theme. He is *the* Word of God to man, totally sufficient in every way, and any other words must be assessed by the standard of whether they exalt the Lord Jesus and reflect his glorious character. But the only way we know about him, with divinely revealed certainty, is through the written record of revelation, the Bible.

This is what is meant when Bible commentators refer to the 'sufficiency' of Scripture. Biblical Christianity affirms not only that God *can* speak to man, whom he has made in his own image, but that he has so spoken. This word has been committed to writing, because it has continuing application and binding authority for every generation and because God's intention is that his message should be preserved and proclaimed. It is a complete word, coming to its fulness and culmination in the 'Word made flesh', who is God's last word to man – Jesus Christ (Hebrews 1:1–2). Beyond Christ, God has nothing more to say. The apostolic record of that revelation forms the authoritative and inspired New Testament. So the God who reveals himself in nature by his works reveals those same truths in Scripture by his written Word.

Therefore, we have in the Bible the total revelation which God has designed to provide the rule of faith and practice in the Church, until Christ returns and human history ends. Its sufficiency means that nothing can be added to it or subtracted from it. It is God's truth, the whole truth and nothing but the truth! Accordingly, nothing is to be imposed on the consciences of God's people, whether as truth or duty, if it is not taught in the Bible. The people of God are bound by nothing but the Word of God.

A corollary of this is what the Reformers called the 'perspicuity' of Scripture. By this they meant that the Bible is a plain book, intelligible to all. It is not the preserve of a priestly or scholarly caste. Every Christian must therefore study the Word of God, in dependence on the illumination and guidance of the Spirit of God. All that is needed for salvation and godly living is sufficiently plain in the Scripture to be understood by all (2 Peter 1:3–4). The teaching of gifted leaders in the churches, in matters of interpretation, is of course to be heeded, but the principle of individual judgment, under the sovereign rule of the Holy Spirit, is central to biblical Christianity. It is because ultimately we all have to answer to God for ourselves that we are commanded to search the Scriptures. They are addressed not to a special clan of church leaders, but to all believers ('the saints'). Always the apostles appeal to the authority of the inspired word, not that of individual teachers, however good or godly. We are to weigh our understanding and interpretation of Scripture with others, and not to lean on our own wisdom. But, in the end, we all have to believe and act on what we have discovered. That is why we need, and have, a sufficient Bible.

To remind you

- When we let the Bible speak, we discover it claims a spiritual authority, deriving from divine inspiration and leading to its inerrancy (pp. 52–9).
- The witness of the gospels to Jesus' own view of the Old Testament is that he gave it supreme authority as the Word of God. Further, he claimed the fulfilment of its prophecies and promises in his own person and ministry (pp. 59–64).
- The authority of the New Testament derives from Christ's commissioning of the apostles as the authoritative communicators of the gospel (pp. 64–8).
- Views of the Bible's authority have changed since the Reformation due to the elevation of the principle of reason over that of revelation (pp. 68–71).
- The Bible is therefore the sufficient Word of God to the Church in all generations and we must neither subtract from it nor add to it. What we need to do is to understand it and apply it (pp. 71–3).

Chapter 4

Can We Trust the Bible's Reliability?

JULIA AND ANDY travelled home from the supper party in silence. They had responded to Julia's work colleague's invitation to go round to her home for a special evening, 'just looking' at the Christian faith. Assured that it wouldn't be a pressurised sales-pitch, they had agreed, with a good deal of reluctance. After all, they had never thought seriously about Christianity, or imagined it could have any relevance whatever to their lives. They knew they needed some help, but from *that* source? It was all very unlikely. It had been an intriguing experience. The food had been good and the other guests seemed friendly enough. There had been a short talk in which basically it became clear that the Bible was the key source to understanding the whole thing. Andy's memories of hearing it read at school assemblies and never being able to make much of it came flooding back. But now here they were, driving back, with Julia clutching a Bible which her friend had pressed into her hand as they left. 'Do read it,' she'd said, 'it will really help you to understand.'

Andy had been fielding all the objections to the whole bizarre process which had been filling his mind, as he drove. Eventually, he broke the silence. 'But, I mean it's just not that easy, is it? It's all very well saying "do read it", but it's not like any other book, is it? Is it really going to be worthwhile taking time to understand it? I mean, where did it come from? Who wrote it? How did it all get put together? And how do we know it hasn't been altered and changed beyond recognition from its original format? You know, it's not like just dipping into some ancient document, out of interest, just to see what people thought in those days. Those people tonight, they really take it seriously; even base their lives on it, don't they? I mean that can't be normal, can it?'

Julia sighed. 'Well, they all looked pretty normal to me,' she replied. 'Perhaps there are perfectly good answers to those questions, only we just haven't ever thought about it. Surely it's worth finding out, isn't it? We don't want to walk away from it all, just because it's different, do we?'

Any serious reader of the Bible is going to come up with questions similar to those Andy was grappling with. We are dealing, after all, with very ancient documents of which the original manuscripts have long since disappeared. Those documents are being read in translation, but nearly two millennia stretch between us and the latest of the originals. The reliability of both the text and the translation is of paramount importance. Moreover, given the wide range of authorship, how did these sixty-six books and no others come to be regarded as the authoritative 'word of God written'? They are important issues for us to tackle.

At first sight, a new explorer of the Bible, in English, might decide that the nearest equivalent to it in his experience is a literary anthology. In fact, the Bible has sometimes been marketed as 'designed to be read as literature'. The older English translations, with their rich vocabulary, majestic sentences and vivid turns of phrase, represent some of the most memorable images of the emerging English language and in turn had a major formative influence on its development. But as we have seen, the quality of literary composition is not the criterion by which the Bible was assembled. In fact, it was not compiled by any anthologist, although it is the most remarkable collection of writings. The late Professor F. F. Bruce put the point well in his title *The Books and the Parchments* (1950, Pickering & Inglis).

If we enquire into the circumstances under which the various Biblical documents were written, we find that they were written at intervals over a span of nearly 1500 years . . . The writers themselves were a heterogeneous number of people, not only separated from each other by hundreds of years and hundreds of miles, but belonging to the most diverse walks of life. In their ranks we have kings, herdsmen, soldiers, legislators, fishermen, statesmen, courtiers, priests and prophets, a tentmaking Rabbi and a Gentile physician . . . The writings themselves belong to a great variety of literary types. They include history, law (civil, criminal, ethical, ritual, sanitary), religious poetry, didactic treatises, lyric poetry, parable and allegory, biography, personal correspondence, personal memoirs and diaries, in addition to the distinctively Biblical types of prophecy and apocalyptic. (p. 87)

Yet the amazing and unique quality of the Bible's composition is that it simply grew. No one ever compiled it; no committee ever decreed its contents. Councils of the Church later affirmed its divine origin and accepted contents, but they did not compile it, or decide on it. Perhaps Paul's comment to the Corinthians, in a slightly different context, is the best explanation of this supernatural gift we call the Bible. 'So neither he who plants nor he who waters is anything, but only God, who makes things grow' (1 Corinthians 3:7). Neither the author nor the interpreter is the secret of the Bible's composition, but the fact that God gave the living Word and he alone made it grow.

New Testament manuscripts

The process of that growth we can, however, explore. Let's begin with the documents. It is an obvious principle of documentary research that older documents taking us back as near in time to the original as possible are likely to provide a more authoritative text than later ones. Our oldest biblical documents, before the discovery of the Dead Sea Scrolls about fifty years ago, were actually New Testament passages, written in Greek, their original language. Dating from the first century of the Christian era, the New Testament books were likely to have been written on paper (papyrus) with ink (see 2 John 12). In the case of the largest books, a papyrus roll or scroll would have been used, while the shorter would have been accommodated on papyrus sheets. The life expectancy of papyrus is not great, so it was sensible, as well as providential, that the documents associated with apostolic authority should be often copied and widely circulated. There is evidence from the early church fathers, such as Clement of Rome writing in 95 AD, that already copies of the gospels and apostolic letters were available in the churches. Until the invention of the printing press in the fifteenth century that was how the Bible spread and was preserved. It has always been recognised that such copying of a detailed text, by hand, was bound to have the potential to produce errors in any particular manuscript. No copy, let alone translation, can carry the same implicit authority as the original autograph. Even the most careful and reverent copyist may miss a word or jump a line, so that it might be presumed that the original text has become changed and distorted down the centuries. But that is precisely why so much scholarly energy has been expended on the quest to produce the most accurate text possible. Some statements of belief recognise this when they speak of the authority of the Scriptures 'as originally given'. Far from being some sort of 'get out', this phrase quite properly recognises the need for detailed textual scholarship. We can be grateful that so much excellent work of this sort has been done that Professor Bruce can assert that no other body of ancient literature in the world has such a strong and reliable text as the New Testament.

There are good reasons for this. The sheer number of early Greek manuscripts which have survived, in whole or in part, constitute the primary evidence. Perhaps the oldest of all is a papyrus fragment of John 18, discovered in Egypt and dated about 120 AD, held by the John Rylands Library in Manchester. It represents a remarkably short time-gap between copy and original. It also indicates the wide circulation of John's gospel in the early second century, as strong evidence towards the confirmation of its apostolic authorship. In 1931, the discovery was announced of what have become known as the Chester Beatty papyri, dating from the first half of the third century, containing the four gospels and Acts, Paul's nine letters to the churches and the epistle to the Hebrews, and from the second half of that century a copy of the book of Revelation. But it is to the fourth century and the following two that we look for our fullest Greek New Testament texts.

Throughout the twentieth century the science of textual criticism developed and research multiplied. The number of early New Testament manuscripts, in whole or part, is estimated as about four thousand, so there is a vast resource of material by which to check potential scribal error and to explore the reasons for any textual changes or apparent discrepancies. Even considerably later manuscripts are not automatically of less significance, since they may be copies of much earlier versions. If it is argued that a larger number of manuscripts may produce a larger number of possible errors, it also provides a much surer safeguard by which to identify them. By contrast, it is often not realised how comparatively meagre is the manuscript evidence for the classical Greek and Latin authors of the equivalent historical period. There is a fascinating account of this in F. F. Bruce's popular treatment *Are the New Testament Documents*

Reliable? first published in 1943 and still in print today (Inter-Varsity Press). Surveying Caesar's *Gallic Wars*, the histories of Livy and Tacitus, Theucydides and Herodotus, Bruce points out that in almost every case our best manuscripts date only from the tenth century AD, but affirms that there is no question about their authenticity among classical scholars, even though 'the earliest manuscripts of their works which are of any use to us are over 1,300 years later than the originals'. Even the Old Testament texts are 'astonishingly well attested' when compared with these authors, in terms of manuscript evidence.

There are other factors we need to recognise, as well. The New Testament manuscripts multiplied due to demand. The gospel was spreading rapidly throughout the Mediterranean world. This meant also that translations of the text into other languages began to be made early in the life of the Church, and these too multiplied. The continuing existence of these early translations today means that scholars have been able to cross-check and compare texts and subsequently come to a clearer understanding of the underlying Greek, when manuscripts vary. A further source of information and authentication of the original biblical text occurs in the many quotations from the New Testament to be found in the writings of the early church fathers. In Greek, there is a direct relation back to the original, but many such documents occur in Latin, Syriac, Coptic and Armenian, so that the sort of cross-checking mentioned above is able to be carried out, but from a non-biblical source. All of this means that when Andy and Julia sit down to read the Bible in a contemporary English translation, they can have confidence that they are reading an accurate, scholarly rendering of a remarkably well-attested first-century text. Far from the Bible having been changed or distorted down the centuries, it has been amazingly preserved, and with all the textual scholarship of the past hundred or more years, our generation is in the favoured position of the easiest and most reliable access to the biblical text since its first readers. That doesn't make the Bible true, but it does mean that to read its text carefully and study its implications is to approach as nearly as possible to genuine, original Christian testimony and belief.

Old Testament documents

But what of the Old Testament, which is even older? What manuscript evidence do we have for its textual authenticity? When the Revised Version of the Bible was published in the late nineteenth century (it was a revision of the 1611 Authorised or King James Version) the translators commented that the earliest Old Testament manuscript which could be dated with certainty belonged to 916 AD. The reason for this relates to the extreme reverence in which the Scriptures were (and are) held by the orthodox Jewish rabbis. Rather than use old or threadbare copies of the Scriptures, these texts were withdrawn, stored away or even buried, so that new copies were continually needed. In order to guard the accuracy of these, Jewish scholars worked hard to establish and safeguard the purity of the text, becoming known as 'Masoretes', a title derived from the Hebrew word for 'tradition'. At the beginning of the tenth century AD a final authoritative version was produced, with vowel sounds added by 'pointing' since the Hebrew alphabet is composed only of consonants. However, we know that nine centuries earlier, a 'standard text' of the consonantal version had appeared and that great efforts were made to transmit this, with total accuracy, in the copying of the intervening centuries. All the evidence points to the success of this policy, since quotations from the Old Testament in other sources down the centuries, and not least Jerome's Latin translation of the Hebrew text, the Vulgate (about 400 AD), indicate little change or variation over the period. Other means of cross-checking include the Syriac Old Testament, translated from the Hebrew in the first century AD, the Samaritan Pentateuch (a text of the Bible's first five books preserved by transmission that is independent of the Masoretic tradition) dating from about 400 BC, and supremely the Greek translation of the Old Testament, known as the Septuagint.

The title of this important source is taken from the Latin word *septuaginta*, meaning seventy, often represented by the Roman numerals LXX. Under King Ptolemy of Egypt, a great library was founded at Alexandria, in the third century before Christ. Considerable numbers of Jews had been living in Egypt since the time of the Babylonian exile (587 BC), but it was in Alexandria, founded by Alexander the Great in 332 BC, that they exercised their greatest influence and lived in greatest numbers. It was, of course, a Greek-speaking city and the Jews were soon speaking the local language and needing a translation of their Hebrew Scriptures. Tradition has it that seventy translators did the work and presented the final version for Ptolemy's library. F. F. Bruce comments, 'The language suggests that the translators were Egyptian Jews, and quotations from the Septuagint text of Genesis and Exodus appear in Greek literature before 200 BC' (op. cit. p. 143). It seems well established that a standard Greek translation of at least the Pentateuch was available in the second century BC and that additions and revisions were probably being made over the next centuries, not least when the Christian gospel began to spread so widely and rapidly. Not surprisingly, many of the versions of the Septuagint which have survived seem to have been produced in Christian circles. Ultimately, Origen (the Christian scholar of the early third century), an Alexandrian himself, produced his own version of the Septuagint alongside the Hebrew text, and although only fragments of that have been preserved it became the basis of what soon became the standard Greek version of the Old Testament. Although scholarly opinion is that as a translation it is variable in quality, the Pentateuch being the most accurate, nevertheless the Septuagint takes us back a thousand years beyond the Masoretic text. It also had a profound influence on the Greek New Testament, providing a ready-made vocabulary by which to express predominantly Hebrew ideas and concepts, fulfilled by Christ in the gospel. It was the means by which the apostolic preachers were able to declare the Old Testament and what became the New as one book, by one divine author, bringing one story of the good news of God's rescue for all the world.

In the last fifty years, the 'hot' issue has been that of the Dead Sea Scrolls. The story of their discovery, in and around the Wadi Qumran on the northwestern shore of the Dead Sea in the spring of 1947, has often been told. The sound of breaking pottery as a result of a stone he had thrown into a cave attracted a young local shepherd and his friends to explore further. They discovered seven leather scrolls, the beginning of a massive find of some 500 documents, eventually gathered from eleven caves. Over one hundred of the scrolls are books of the Old Testament, in Hebrew, and every book is covered, with the exception of Esther. The oldest text, dated to 250 BC or even earlier, is a fragment of Exodus. The other scrolls are regarded as later, up to the middle of the first century AD. They were in effect the community library of a group of devout Jews, probably a branch of the Essenes, who withdrew to the Judean wilderness to study and practise God's law. They wanted to prepare themselves for God to bring in his new kingdom of righteousness to end the present darkness, and to be ready to be used as his agents of judgment on the ungodly. In fact, the Essene community was destroyed by the Romans in 68 AD as part of their brutal suppression of the First Jewish Revolt. A full scholarly account can be found in Professor F. M. Cross's essay in *Understanding the Dead Sea Scrolls* (ed. Hershel Shanks, 1993, Vintage Books, New York). But for our purposes, their great significance lies in the Hebrew texts now available, predating the Masoretic text by nearly a thousand years. Professor Edwin Yamauchi of Miami University explained the significance in this way: 'Thanks to Qumran we know that the Masoretic Text goes back to a Proto–Masoretic edition antedating the Christian Era, and we are assured that this recension was copied with remarkable accuracy. This means that the consonantal text of the Hebrew Bible must be treated with respect and not freely emended' (in *The Stones and the Scriptures*, 1973, Inter-Varsity Press, London). One of the earliest scrolls found in Cave 1 was a complete copy of a prophecy of Isaiah. There were differences from the Masoretic text in spelling and grammar, but no significantly major changes (only thirteen new readings in sixty-six chapters) in meaning or substance. We can best sum up the impact of the scrolls by quoting the considered judgment of another academic authority, Dr David W. Gooding, sometime Professor of Old Testament Greek at The Queen's University, Belfast.

> The great significance of these manuscripts is that they constitute an independent witness to the reliability of the transmission of our accepted text. There is no reason whatever to believe that the Qumran community would collaborate with the leaders in Jerusalem in adhering to any particular recension. They carry us back to an earlier point on the line of transmission, to the common ancestor of the great Temple scrolls and the unsophisticated scrolls from Qumran. (Quoted from 'Texts and Versions', article in *The Illustrated Bible Dictionary Part 3*, published by Inter-Varsity Press, 1980.)

How the Bible was put together

We must now turn to another of Andy's dilemmas. How did the Bible come together? Who decided what was to be included and on what criteria? This is the area of biblical study known as the canon of Scripture. The term originally meant a 'reed' or 'cane', from the Greek *kanon*. Derivative from this root came the idea of a reed or rod by which to measure, and so a standard, or rule. In that Scripture is to be the rule of our belief and practice as Christians, it is an appropriate quality to assign to the Bible. But it also meant an index or list of contents, perhaps derived from the marks on a measuring rod. Either way, the term is used to denote the agreed authorised contents of the rule or standard of God's self-revelation. But how did it happen?

It is important to realise that the books of the Bible were listed in this way not because some religious leaders decided that an anthology of inspired writing was needed and that sixty-six ingredients might be a good number to have. Each of the books was included in the canon because its divine authority had already been recognised. The practical logic of the situation is readily understandable. When Moses descended from Mount Sinai with the 'words' which God had spoken to him as his unchanging commands to his people, he presented what Exodus 24:7 calls 'the Book of the Covenant' to the Israelites. They, in turn, recognised its divine authority by responding, 'We will do everything the LORD has said; we will obey.' The existence and acceptance of such a 'book' indicates that what is contained in it is recognised as having an authority, which any other commands outside of it do not have. If other books are written and recognised, at later dates, as having the same divine origin and subsequent authority, together they constitute a 'canon', automatically excluding other claimants which are not recognised as authoritative.

With regard to the Old Testament canon, we need to remember that the process of revelation through its thirty-nine books stretches back over a long period of time, beyond a thousand years. The Pentateuch (law), the prophets and the psalms made up the three divisions of the Hebrew Scriptures to which Jesus referred in Luke 24:44. This was the usual method of sub-division and it was probably customary to refer to the 'writings' (the third section) as the 'psalms' because of the position of that book as the first and largest in the whole unit. As we have seen, Jesus regarded them as being 'written about me' and not only having divine authorship, but being 'canonical', since they had been gathered into a recognised collection, from which everything else was automatically excluded. There is another interesting insight into the status of the Hebrew canon in the time of Jesus, earlier on in Luke's gospel. In the midst of a series of 'woe' pronouncements to the Pharisees, Jesus affirms, 'Therefore this generation will be held responsible for the blood of all the prophets that has been shed since the beginning of the world, from the blood of

Abel to the blood of Zechariah, who was killed between the altar and the sanctuary' (11:50). Abel was clearly the first victim of such a murder (Genesis 4:8) and Zechariah is intended to stand as the last, probably because the books of Chronicles are the last books of the last section (the 'writings') in the Hebrew Scriptures, and Zechariah's story occurs in 2 Chronicles 24:17–22, almost at the end of that unit. So it is very likely that the three-fold division, itself defining and delimiting the canon, was already well established in the first century AD. For the Christians, the dominical authority given to these Scriptures and continued by the apostles is decisive. Professor F. F. Bruce expresses it so well.

> The apostles, no doubt, found in their Master's attitude to these writings sufficient warrant for theirs, and He accepts them, not because their canonicity had been handed down by tradition, but because He recognized their divine quality. In many points He condemned the Jewish tradition, but not with respect to the canonicity of Scripture. His complaint, indeed, was that by other traditions they had invalidated in practice the word of God recorded in canonical Scripture. But in point of the canonicity of Scripture, He confirmed their tradition, not because it was tradition, but because He knew on independent grounds that it was right. And in this as in all else we are safe when we follow Him. (*The Books and The Parchments*, p. 102)

But can we go back further beyond the first century to determine with any clarity how the process of such recognition developed? There is a detailed and fascinating discussion in Dr David Dunbar's essay 'The Biblical Canon' in *Hermeneutics, Authority and Canon*, edited by D. A. Carson and J. D. Woodbridge, published in 1986 by Inter-Varsity Press. Yet his conclusions are that lack of evidence prevents us from dating the completion of the Old Testament with any certainty. Two important points must always be borne in mind. To quote Dunbar, 'With regard to Scriptural status, there is no historical evidence for the biblical books "acquiring" such a position. The earliest references to biblical books (or to portions of them) treat them as authoritative' (p. 314). The other is that at some point following the ministry of Malachi, the last of the post-exilic prophets, the Jewish religious leaders recognised that prophecy in its classical (biblical) form was now a thing of the past. This made the fixation of the Old Testament canon much more likely, scholarly estimates of the date varying from 300 to 100 BC. Discussion certainly continued about certain books, in Jewish rabbinical circles, well into the Christian era. Most famous among them are discussions held at Jamnia, in the years following the fall of Jerusalem in AD 70, which were ultimately recorded in writing. The debate centred on the canonical status of four books included in the 'writings' – Proverbs, Ecclesiastes, Song of Songs and Esther. Yet the outcome was to affirm each one and to reject other candidates, probably of a Jewish–Christian origin. No new books were admitted; no old ones rejected. By this date, at the very latest, the Old Testament canon was firmly established.

In turning to the New Testament, we find the same process in operation by which writings are first accepted as having divine authority and therefore included in later listings of such documents. The churches at the end of the first century had twenty-seven books of the New Testament in their possession, reading and valuing them as the authoritative teaching of Jesus and the apostles, but they were not yet a formal collection or canon. The need for such a development became clear in the second century but only came to its formal conclusion at the end of the fourth, when in 397 AD the Council of Carthage defined the twenty-seven books as canonical Scripture. This was the rule of faith, believed and taught throughout the orthodox churches and the touchstone of that orthodoxy, described in Jude verse 3 as 'the faith that was once for all entrusted to the saints'.

The criterion for accepting these writings as having divine authority was apostolic attestation, since it was through the apostles that the Master's own authority was delegated and exercised. This became an increasingly vital issue as alternative versions of Christianity began to appear and false teachers multiplied. One of the most famous challenges, from the second century, came from the new teaching introduced by Marcion to the church at Rome, which began to exercise considerable influence in the early decades of the century. Marcion was a dualist, based on his distinction between the merciful God and Father, revealed in Jesus Christ, and the just but cruel law-giver of the Old Testament. He therefore rejected the whole Old Testament Scriptures and accepted only one gospel (an edited version of Luke, whose author was a Gentile) and the letters of Paul, who was the only faithful follower of Jesus among the apostles, in his view. What

Marcion effectively introduced, as the basis of his challenge to Christian orthodoxy, was his own 'canon'. This related to what the churches had already accepted as their working 'canon', usually called the 'gospel' and the 'apostle', each gospel distinguished by its author and each letter distinguished by the sub-headings 'To the Romans', 'To the Corinthians' and so on. But it also forced the churches to begin to articulate more clearly a canon of orthodoxy.

The four gospels were never in doubt, since Mark was widely known to be Peter's interpreter, while Matthew and John had apostolic authorship, and Luke, although not an apostle, was a close associate of Paul, who had carried out his own detailed research. Luke's second volume, the Acts of the Apostles, contained a great deal of apostolic testimony, as did the thirteen letters of Paul and the first letters of Peter and John. It was the remaining seven books – Hebrews, James, 2 Peter, 2 and 3 John, Jude and Revelation, which were the disputed titles. Sometimes the disputes mirrored the geographical division in the early churches, as the eastern churches focused on Alexandria, while those in the west looked increasingly to Rome. Most often, the debate ranged around the apostolicity of the document concerned, since apostolic authorship was freely claimed for a variety of heretical productions, so that the mere ascription of a work to an apostle or the apostolic circle was not in itself proof of its authoritative origin.

The letter to the Hebrews is an interesting example. The authenticity of the letter's teaching was never questioned and there is evidence that it was known to Clement of Rome before the end of the first century. The question was over its authorship, not its orthodoxy. Could an anonymous letter be given 'biblical' authority? Vigorous claims were made for its Pauline authorship, but never with any generally persuasive conviction. What convinced successive generations of Christians of its inspiration and authority was its contents, what Donald Robinson has called 'the spiritual quality of the epistle as it spoke to their hearts' (in *Faith's Framework*, 1985, published by the Paternoster Press).

This important strand has been further developed by contemporary scholars, such as Herman Ridderbos and Oscar Cullmann, who stress that the criterion for authority must be related to the gospel, God's intervention in Christ's mighty works and revelatory words, and in their proclamation (both oral and written) by his appointed and authorised apostolic messengers. This is in keeping with the *purpose* for which the New Testament Scriptures were originally given and also explains why the canon is in principle closed. Having completed his great work of salvation in Christ, and spoken his last words in Christ, God has nothing more to reveal of his purposes and nothing more to say. Jesus *is*, in fact, God's final word to humankind (Hebrews 1:1–3). Just as it was the gospel which produced the Church, not the Church which created the gospel, so the work of Christ for the world's redemption (the fulfilment of salvation in history) proclaimed and explained became the canon or rule of the churches. This was not a subjective test by which authority would only be attributed to texts which 'resonated' with the readers. It was robustly objective, in that it was grounded in the historical facts of the gospel message, and in their direct experience as truth in the lives of every Christian believer. 'Faith comes from hearing the message, and the message is heard through the word of Christ' (Romans 10:17). That same understanding and acceptance of biblical authority is of course equally the experience of the contemporary reader. Many of us came to 'believe in the Bible', not primarily because of intellectual arguments regarding its inspiration, infallibility and authority, or about the composition of the canon. Rather, coming with a reasonably open mind, we found the Bible imposing its authority on our thinking, exposing our innermost thoughts, convicting us of our sin and leading us to put our faith in Jesus Christ. We began to read the Bible deciding what we were, or were not, willing to accept, and sitting in judgment on its contents, only to find the process being subtly reversed, and the Bible now imprinting its authority on us and sitting in judgment on our arrogant independence from God. We began by asking whether there was any way we could bring ourselves to accept the God whose self-revelation it claims to be, but soon began to ask whether there was any way that God could be brought to accept us, and found that, in Christ, indeed there is. David Dunbar's conclusion sums up this brief discussion of the New Testament canonicity.

The church regarded apostolicity as the qualifying factor for canonical recognition; however, this apostolicity should be understood not strictly in terms of authorship but in terms of content and chronology. That which was canon must embody the apostolic tradition, and this tradition was to be discerned in the most primitive documents. (op. cit. p. 358)

But in all this, it is highly significant that the New Testament canon was never dictated or settled by any council or synod issuing an authoritative and binding decree. Such statements merely articulated the inner witness of the Holy Spirit and the objective evidence of gospel history, in both the individual Christian and in the believing community across the world, that the New Testament documents were indeed God's written Word. That conviction already existed; the canon formalised it.

The Word and the Spirit

Throughout our discussion of the issues surrounding the reliability and authority of the sixty-six books, which constitute the phenomenon we call 'the Bible', we have seen the interweaving of two equally important ingredients. We might identify them by a series of contrasts – the objective and the subjective, truth and experience, the human and the divine, the Word and the Spirit. Precision of language is particularly difficult when we attempt to describe what will always be something of a mystery to finite human beings – the mind and purposes of almighty God. Bible teachers often speak of the dual authorship of Scripture, by which they mean to draw attention to the essentially supernatural process which produced it. For the 'word of God written' was originally committed to papyrus or parchment by human hands, as the product of an intelligent human mind, written in a linguistic style and vocabulary peculiar to that author, and reflective of his own social and literary environment. Such a product very clearly requires a human author, but the claim of Scripture writers and readers is that the ideas, propositions, descriptions, speech, even the individual words of each chapter of every book were governed and over-ruled by God the Holy Spirit, so that in the words of the human writer we encounter the words of the living God. 'All Scripture is God-breathed', we read in 2 Timothy 3:16, but in what sense and how?

Here, the ministry of the Holy Spirit is of central importance. First, we need to recognise that the words translated 'spirit' in our English Bibles – *ruach* in Hebrew and *pneuma* in Greek – also carry the meaning of breath, or wind. As Dr Leon Morris once remarked, 'After all, what is wind but a lot of breath, in a hurry?' However, the analogy of breath with words may help us to delve a little deeper into the mystery of the Bible's origins. In Genesis 1:2–3, the Spirit (breath) of

God is pictured hovering over the waters of an empty, formless earth. Immediately, God speaks, 'Let there be light,' and light exists. The breath of God enables the articulation of God's will, in the word of his creative command. Reflecting on this in Psalm 33:6, the writer expresses the same truth in typical Hebrew poetic parallelism. 'By the *word* of the LORD were the heavens made, their starry host by the *breath* of his mouth' (italics mine). Just as 'heavens' parallel the 'starry host', so 'word' parallels 'breath'. The two are inseparable.

We are familiar with this as a fact of everyday experience. Take preaching, or any sort of public speaking, as an example. Thoughts are formed in the mind of the speaker, which he wants to communicate as accurately and effectively as possible to his hearers. Expressed in words, those unseen, and otherwise unknown, thoughts in the mind of the speaker are carried on his breath in the form of articulate sounds making up intelligible words. Without the breath there would be no communication. Without the communication, there could be no development of understanding, relationship or subsequent action. So the Spirit of God carried the otherwise unknown and unknowable thoughts of God into articulate verbal form in the minds of the inspired biblical writers, without error or distortion, but with individual particularity and focus. This is unashamedly supernatural in character. In this procedure we call 'inspiration', God the Holy Spirit initiates the process and so controls the human author throughout that he speaks or writes with a quality, insight, accuracy and consequent authority that is possible in no other form of human communication. In Peter's memorable and illuminating comment, 'men spoke from God as they were carried along by the Holy Spirit' (2 Peter 1:21).

While we can never, of course, fully understand the mystery of this divine process, any more than we shall ever be able fully to explain how the divine and human natures of the Lord Jesus Christ are united in the one person, nevertheless the Bible clearly indicates certain guidelines which help us to keep this concept of dual authorship in a proper balance. For example, God clearly chose a wide variety of different human personalities as the human authors of Scripture and these personal characteristics were neither superseded nor overridden. The lyricism of David's poetry, the logic of Paul's well-honed arguments, the meticulous investigations of Dr Luke are all indications of gifted and prepared individuals whose natural abilities and skills are being channelled and employed for the fulfilment of God's providential purposes. It seems very likely, then, that the varied backgrounds, temperaments, training, skills and life-experiences of the Bible writers are an integral part of God's plan, so that the authors might represent as diverse a range of individuals as the variety of circumstances experienced in God's world.

This same principle of variety led them to communicate in a wide diversity of literary styles or 'genres', each with its own conventions and methodologies, to which we shall need to give attention in later chapters. So there is nothing flat or depersonalised about the process of inspiration. Their writing was never mechanical. We must never think of the Bible writers as though they were merely word-processors into which God typed his messages. But neither should we imagine that they always saw the full implications of what they were expressing. There is a sense in which no writer can. Peter tells us, for example, that the prophets 'searched intently and with the greatest care, trying to find out the time and circumstances to which the Spirit of Christ in them was pointing when he predicted the sufferings of Christ and the glories that would follow'. He continues, 'It was revealed to them that they were not serving themselves but you' (1 Peter 1:10–12). So they were consciously writing God's inspired Word for their own and succeeding generations. But as they wrote, they used their own distinctive vocabularies and favourite stylistic devices, as every author must. So Paul is not like John, who is not like Peter or James. They also built on the past revelation that had already been given in earlier books and undoubtedly used such resources as source documents, oral testimony, extant genealogies and histories. Yet the divine control was such that God permitted no inaccuracy, misguided opinion or falsity to impair the truth and authority of his revelation.

To speak, then, of the whole Bible as the inspired Word of God is not to adopt a flattened, 'fundamentalist' reading of Scripture which irons out all metaphor or pictorial language. Sometimes I am 'pinned to the wall' by enquirers about the Christian faith who want to know, 'Do you believe the Bible literally?' To this my only possible reply is, 'Yes, I believe the Bible literally, when it is being literal. But I believe it metaphorically, when it is being metaphorical.' So when Isaiah 55:12 tells me, 'the mountains and hills will burst into song before you, and all the trees of the field will clap their hands', I am not committed to a view of the end of all things, in which 'the hills are alive with the sound of music'! But I do believe it is true that when God's kingdom comes in all its completeness, at the end of time, that the whole created order will be renewed and rejoice in the glorious freedom of the new world (see Romans 8:19–21). The truth of Isaiah 55 is no less truth because it is expressed metaphorically rather than literally.

In a similar vein, God has clearly caused the erroneous thoughts of misguided, fallible human beings to be recorded in Scripture. Job's 'comforters' spend many chapters in that book putting Job right, only to be contradicted by God himself and to see their arguments completely overthrown at the book's climax. Moreover, particular texts must be interpreted within their contexts, if we are not to fall into the critic's trap that the Bible can be made to mean anything. After all, the Bible actually says, in so many words, in black and white, 'There is no God.' It is in Psalm 14:1. But the context reads, 'The fool says in his heart, "There is no God"'! The Bible is not a book with which to play games. Each author described in his own language what he understood God's message to be, consciously applying his mind to its descriptions, propositions and applications. And the Holy Spirit, as the revealer and inspirer, provided adequate and accurate words and structures, for the expression of the mind of God.

By way of reflection here, it is important to note that the Spirit of God and the Word of God are therefore indissolubly united in the revelation of God in holy Scripture. There is no opposition between the Word and the Spirit. Christians today need to remember that and to draw the inference, 'What God has joined together let not man divide.' Sadly, the history of the last few decades in Western Christianity has all too often been soured by such divisions, caused by polarisations which the Bible writers would find it difficult to comprehend. The root of the divisions has often been over the ministry of the Holy Spirit and how that might be experienced today. 'Charismatic' Christians have stressed the ministry of the Spirit, with a strong emphasis on his fruit of love, producing a heart-centred, experiential faith. 'Conservative' Christians have sometimes defined themselves, or allowed themselves to be defined, in opposite terms, over against their charismatic brothers and sisters. Their stress has been on the ministry of the Word, with a strong emphasis on unchanging truth, on the mind being full-engaged in a doctrinally focused faith. Either side has become practised at drawing its caricatures of the other, as when 'cerebral' is pitched against 'emotional'. The net result has often seemed to be the separation of the Word and the Spirit, to the great disadvantage of both groups, and the bewilderment of many.

To assume that an individual, or a local church, might be governed by the Spirit without the Word, or the Word without the Spirit, is to betray a fundamental misunderstanding of basic Christianity. How do we know what the Christian faith, the gospel and its resultant life-style are? Only by the Word of God. As we have already argued, we are entirely dependent upon the Scriptures for the knowledge of God's truth. But those Scriptures would not exist had not the Holy Spirit inspired them, and we shall never be able rightly to understand and apply them if the same Spirit is not also our illuminator and teacher. Without the enabling power of the Spirit, we would not have faith in Christ or be able to live the Christian life for one moment. Without his new life and equipping power the Church would be powerless, impoverished and moribund. But the great ministry of the Spirit is to exalt Christ, to lead us to trust and obey him, to live consistent and godly lives as we love God and love our neighbours. And the only sure content as to what God requires of us, as well as the resources of his grace which are freely available to us, is found in the written Word. It is in the sixty-six books alone that the revelation of God is reliably, infallibly and sufficiently expounded, so that whatever I may think the Spirit may be saying to me must be tested against what God has already said in Scripture, and is therefore still saying. And whatever is not read in Scripture, or provable from it, cannot therefore have any binding authority on an individual or a church. The Word of Scripture will never be by-passed, much less contradicted, by the Holy Spirit. But its message cannot be received, believed and obeyed without the enabling ministry of the Holy Spirit. The two are inextricably bound together, for the Word of God is the expression of the mind of the Spirit. What a great step forward it will be when Christians on both sides of the divide realise this!

The Bible for today

As we conclude this chapter, it will be clear that the reliability of the Bible, understood and applied under the illumination of the Holy Spirit, is the indispensable requirement for all true Christian belief and practice. This is not just an optional extra, but the bed-rock foundation on which everything else is built. If it is true that God has spoken, and that what he has said is available in written form today, meticulously preserved and accurately translated, and if those words reveal the means by which I can be brought back into a right relationship with my creator, here in time, but with fulfilments on into eternity, then the reason for such a book being the world's best-seller of all time is not difficult to understand. The stakes are very high. Our happiness and fulfilment in the world, not to mention our hopes for the world to come, ride on this foundational claim. The reliability of the Bible is therefore of crucial importance.

If we know that the Bible is the source of heavenly wisdom, 'a lamp to my feet and a light for my path' (Psalm 119:105), then to study that resource, to understand and apply it rightly to our lives, becomes our greatest privilege and responsibility. When we think of the vast wealth of divine revelation contained in the Bible, the grace of God in inspiring its existence and preserving its integrity and the huge labours which human authors, scribes and translators have exerted to bring it to us today, we must surely take seriously the words of the British coronation service when the new sovereign is presented with the Bible and told that it is 'the most precious thing that this world affords'. Yet we can buy it in a variety of translations and bindings from any bookshop for just a few pounds. To give it an occasional cursory glance, or to ignore its wealth except for a few very familiar passages, or to keep it unopened, is surely a statement of ingratitude at best, and perhaps at worst, of practical atheism. If we knew that God would be speaking with us on the phone in an hour's time most of us would be ready to take the call. If he summoned us to an audience, we would probably make sure we were there. Yet both these possibilities – meeting personally the God who speaks in Scripture – are the daily opportunities given us by the Bible on our bookshelf at home, or in the hotel bedside cabinet, or the hospital room, or the school desk.

The problem is that it all seems so ordinary. 'Why doesn't God speak today?' people ask, unaware that he is speaking all the time. In the beauty and majesty of creation, 'his eternal power and divine nature have been clearly seen, being understood from what has been made' (Romans 1:20). In history, as he dealt with his people, Israel, he spoke of his righteousness and mercy, his covenant love and justice. Supremely he spoke through his Son, Jesus Christ, the living Word. And it is all in the pages of the Bible, waiting to be explored. But as with most worthwhile things in this life, the Bible demands time and application to understand it properly and live in the benefit of its instruction. Whether it is learning a practical skill, or an academic subject, or a sporting technique, or developing a friendship, it takes time and practice. The Bible is no exception. Some of its jewels lie on the surface, but much more lies buried, awaiting those who set aside time prayerfully to explore its highways and byways and who are prepared to give regular amounts of quality time to its study. If you have ever read that great English classic *The Pilgrim's Progress*, by John Bunyan, you will probably have been amazed at how much biblical quotation and allusion it contains. How did the Bedford tinker acquire such a knowledge of Scripture that it could be said of him that his blood was 'Bibline', that if you cut him the Bible would flow out of his veins? The answer is probably to be found in his long period of imprisonment in Bedford gaol, as a dissenter. Here he not only read the Bible but studied, memorised and meditated on it, until it became the dominant and controlling influence of all his thinking, speaking and writing.

That sort of understanding of God, through his Word, does not come 'on the back stroke', or in a few hastily reserved minutes of superficial reading from time to time. It depends upon a determination to make time for what matters most in time, with eternity in view, and that is to get to know God more deeply and intimately, so as to love him more worthily, obey him more completely and glorify him more passionately. That is what we can rely on the Bible to do for us, if we submit ourselves to the ministry of the Holy Spirit as our instructor and give time to study and live out its message. It's a personal choice we all make, because we all find time to do what we think is really important and what we really want to do. That is why it is worthwhile for Andy and Julia to persist through the unfamiliarity of the text, recognising that in their hands they have the chief means by which God has determined to reveal himself to men and women like them, and like us. It is time to consider now how that sort of serious commitment to Bible study might work out.

To remind you

- As we explore how the Bible has come down to us, the number and quality of the manuscripts of the New Testament are amazing (pp. 75–8).
- The stories of the Septuagint (Greek version) and the Dead Sea Scrolls

indicate the equivalent reliability of the text of the Old Testament (pp. 78–81).

- The canon of Scripture gradually emerged through the testimony of faithful readers and was never a committee decision (pp. 81–6).
- The ministry of the Holy Spirit generated the inspiration of Bible writers and illuminates the understanding of humble Bible readers (pp. 87–91).
- To hear God speak with certainty to us today we need to go to the Bible, and that requires reverence, attention and hard work (pp. 91–3).

Chapter 5

And What Does It Really Mean?

DAN AND RACHEL made themselves a cup of coffee and sat down to do a 'post-mortem' on the evening's Bible study session. They had to admit that it seemed as though a 'death' had actually occurred! The group had run into such problems in deciding what the Bible text actually meant that it had virtually ground to a halt. But worst of all, Matt had been there and all that had happened had only served to support his theories. He had held forth famously at the end. 'There you are; you've proved it!' he crowed. 'I always said you could make the Bible, or any other text come to that, mean exactly what you want it to mean, and that's what you've been doing all evening. You haven't been listening to yourselves, have you? How many times did I hear one or other of you say, "Well, to me, it seems as though what it's saying is this . . ." And within a minute or two somebody else is not wanting to be argumentative or offensive in any way, but, "Well, I take it another way and think something quite different."' Of course, Matt was right, but it all became rather embarrassing, especially when he said that no one could ever really work out the meaning of the Bible, because it didn't have one. 'Don't think I'm saying that what you're doing is a waste of time,' he had said. 'It's a perfectly valid activity to sit round in a group and share what a particular text is saying to each person. Isn't that what literature tutorials are all about? But why do you people have to insist that the words of the Bible have divine authority and then try to force other people to accept them as "gospel truth"? That's just not on! What right have you got to say what it should mean to me, or anybody else? What are you – a bunch of control freaks, or do you just enjoy trying to brainwash other people?'

The need for interpretation

When I was a sixth-former studying history, there was a question that seemed to crop up year after year, in different guises but in almost all of the exam papers. It was on the lines of 'Is it ever possible for the writing of history to be impartial?' or 'What objectivity can the historian reasonably hope to achieve?' Each of us, inevitably, sees the world through a pair of personal prescription spectacles. They are as unique to each of us as we are unique people. Genetic inheritance, upbringing, training, education, life-experience, all have a part to play in producing the framework of convictions and questions, prejudices and presuppositions with which we view the universe and our single, solitary lives in it. This is commonly referred to as our 'pre-understanding' and we cannot entirely escape it. One of the aims of education is to remove ignorance and prejudice as far as is possible from our mind-sets. Nevertheless, when we open the Bible to read it, we inevitably bring our prior understanding with us. Take even a simple statement, such as John 3:16, 'God so loved the world that he gave his one and only Son', and it immediately becomes clear how much we automatically begin to interpret in order to understand. What content do we give to the word 'God'? How can he 'love' and in what way does 'giving his Son' relate to that? What is the 'world' – the planet, the people? How can God have a son? Some questions may have more obvious or clearer answers than others, but all of them will give rise to others, as we begin to think through the meaning and implications of even quite a straightforward sentence.

But for much of the time we are unaware that the process is happening. Good communication happens when a message is conveyed with such clarity and precision that its hearer or reader receives the meaning which the originator intended. But that has to happen via a medium, such as speech or print. We are not able to read one another's minds. All we can work with are the words which make up the written or spoken message. It is possible that the author may not have expressed his meaning clearly enough, or that the reader has not understood it fully, but there are realities hidden in their minds. They might meet each other and be able to discuss the issues concerned to come to a greater clarity, but whatever the author intended or the reader perceived, all we have to work with are the words on the page, and so our aim must always be to understand the meaning of that text. I imagine that is why you bought this book and (hopefully!) have persevered to this point in reading it. For my part there are things I want to say, convictions I want to share, enthusiasms I want to explain about the Bible. In writing the book, my endeavour is to be as clear, accurate and motivational as I can be, since my overall purpose is to encourage you to study the Bible for yourself, with enthusiasm and confidence. To that end I try to choose my words carefully and structure my sentences clearly, so as to make it as easy as possible to receive the message I am trying to communicate. If my style is cryptic and obscure, or vague and imprecise, the reader will find the experience unrewarding and give up. How many times have we walked away from a book (or sermon) with the comment, 'I really didn't see what he was trying to say'? But the unspoken agenda in writing and publishing a book is that it contains something worthwhile and informative to say and invites the reader to respond to the message which is perceived in the text. It is as though the author is saying 'This is so, isn't it?', to which the reader may reply 'Yes, indeed', or 'Yes, but . . .', or 'No, not at all.' The significance of the text will vary greatly from reader to reader, but we cannot begin to discuss it at that level until we have established its meaning. Let's see how it might work out.

Dan and Rachel's study group ran into the sands because they started asking the wrong sort of first questions. It's a common error. Faced with a complex passage, a heterogeneous group of readers and above all an awareness of the need to be 'relevant', Bible study leaders often plunge into the question which seems to pull them all together. 'So, Matt, what do you think this verse (paragraph) means to you?' It is the 'to you' bit that causes all our problems, because it fatally confuses the meaning of the passage for us all with its significance for an individual. In an article entitled 'What it means to me' (printed in *Christianity Today*, 26 October 1992), Dr Walt Russell, a Californian New Testament professor, tackles the issue with great insight and penetration. He asserts, 'The meaning of a text never changes. Our first goal is to discover this fixed thing. In contrast, the significance of that text to me and to others is very fluid and flexible.' In support of this view Dr Russell quotes the literary critic E. D. Hirsch Jr in his book *Validity in Interpretation* (1967, Yale University Press), distinguishing the two strands from each other. '*Meaning* is that which is represented by a text: it is what the author meant,' Hirsch writes. '*Significance*, on the other hand, names a relationship between that meaning and a person, or a conception, or a situation, or indeed anything imaginable.' If these two ingredients of biblical interpretation are fused or confused, all our reading of Scripture will be condemned to a relativism, which will never be able to establish or validate any interpretation as the real meaning of the text. That is why so many people give up reading the Bible. It all becomes too slippery, too difficult to pin down or have any degree of certainty about. If the author is located in a remote and very different culture from our own and if the meaning of the words on the page appears complex or ambiguous, then we shall turn to the only other available source of significance, which is ourselves, and consequently invest in the 'What it is saying to me' syndrome.

Such an approach has been the prevailing fashion in academic, literary and critical circles over the past two or three decades. It argues that the reader's response determines the only valid meaning that a text can be said to have. So the text does not exist as a repository of the author's intended meaning, since that meaning can never exist as predetermined or required. Rather, each reader brings his or her own prior understandings into reaction with the text and in that process a whole spectrum of possible meanings can be revealed. To speak of 'the' meaning would be to miss the point. So, it is possible to take a novel, say, and give it a feminist reading, or a Marxist reading, or an African reading. Each one will produce a different range of meanings, but each will be equally valid, because each is generated by interaction with the text. The focus of meaning has shifted through the text to the reader, so that any concept of a normative or given meaning is rejected. To deal with the Bible in this way is, of course, radically destructive of its authority. Instead of God speaking words of unchanging truth, which reveal his eternal nature and dependable purposes, we are left with a religious document, with which we may 'resonate' or 'react', but which has no ultimate authority to shape our thinking or judge our actions. To those wanting to escape from the searchlight of God's Word that may provide an attractive option, but it is true neither to the Bible's self-testimony, nor to the daily experience of millions of Bible readers, down the centuries and across the world.

Looking for the meaning

Our quest for the original, intended meaning of a biblical text is neither irrational nor forlorn. Later generations may have seen the fulfilment of biblical prophecies, for example, in much more detail and with greater understanding than the original authors themselves received, but that in no way changes the intended and foundational meaning to the original hearers, or readers, and that is what we must discover first. The textbook *Introduction to Biblical Interpretation* by W. W. Klein, C. L. Blomberg and R. L. Hubbard (1993, Word, USA) makes the point cogently.

> We assume that the writers or editors of the Bible intended to communicate to all people in the same way. Thus, for the most part, they intended their words to have only one sense. They may have encoded their message in metaphor, poetry, allegory or apocalypse, in addition to more straightforward techniques, but they selected appropriate ways to convey their intended meaning. The historical meaning of these texts remains the central objective of hermeneutics. (op. cit. p. 132)

But, of course, such an objective has to be pursued by fallible human beings, who bring their own pre-understandings to the text. That 'framework' of theological understanding inevitably colours what we see in the text, but if we do our best to let the Bible speak, we shall soon discover our own thinking being challenged, refined and even re-shaped by the authoritative text.

How then should we proceed? Let's go back to our example from John 3:16. The essential unit of communication in written prose is the sentence, which in its most basic and simple form consists of a subject and a verb, an actor and an action. Our text provides an example of a one-sentence verse: 'For God so loved the world that he gave his one and only Son, that whoever believes in him shall not perish but have eternal life.' Incidentally, the verse and chapter divisions of the English Bibles, while being very useful as reference points, must not be allowed to dictate our understanding, since they were not, of course, part of the original manuscripts. We are safer to work with the grammatical marker-points which are built into the text, in the form of sentences and subordinate clauses. Here we have a single sentence, in which the meaning or content of each word and its position and inter-relationship with each of the other words in the whole determines the message it conveys. This is a matter of simple vocabulary and grammar to which we have grown accustomed over many years of reading, and the principles of which we operate automatically whenever we read anything. But the sentence does not exist in a vacuum. Just as 'no man is an island, entire of itself', so is no sentence. It relates to what goes before and what follows. Usually, its own function is to relate as a bridge between the two, as it makes its own unique contribution to the advancement of the argument, the telling of the story, the development of the poem, or whatever the literary form may be. The text exists only in its context, and to ignore that would be to ignore one of the most important aids we have to help us understand its meaning.

> Just as Moses lifted up the snake in the desert, so the Son of Man must be lifted up, that everyone who believes in him may have eternal life. For God so loved the world that he gave his one and only Son, that whoever believes in him shall not perish but have eternal life. For God did not send his Son into the world to condemn the world, but to save the world through him. (John 3:14–17)

In our example, verses 14 and 15 have just related the Son who must be 'believed in', in order to receive 'eternal life', to an Old Testament story, from Numbers 21:4–9. Here the Israelites' sin in grumbling against God and being ungrateful for all his provision and protection brought upon them the judgment of a plague of venomous snakes, from which many of the people perished. However, God provided a rescue, so that they might not perish, but live. He commanded Moses to make a bronze snake, put it up on a pole, 'then when anyone was bitten by a snake and looked at the bronze snake, he lived'. The 'lifting up' of the Son of Man to provide a universal salvation is now explained in v. 16 as God 'giving' his Son, to rescue humankind, and the following verse 17 further explains Christ's mission (in Christ's own words here) as not to condemn but to save the world. It is this immediate context, then, which gives definitive meaning to God's love, the gift of his Son, the necessity for faith and the rescue from death (perishing) and condemnation to eternal life. All this is to be accomplished at the 'lifting up' of Jesus, which is the characteristic way in which John describes Christ's death on the cross.

But while the immediate context is very instructive and formative for our understanding, the verses we have examined are also part of a larger unit, John 3:1–21, where Jesus is in dialogue with Nicodemus, a Pharisee and a member of the Sanhedrin, the Jewish ruling council of seventy elders. Nicodemus has come at night, probably for secrecy, to meet Jesus personally and determine whether or not he is the Messiah, God's chosen and anointed one. He seems to have been genuine in his enquiries and the text relates the dialogue during which Jesus expounds who he is and what he has come to do, of which verse 16 is the famous climax. This is one of a number of such conversations in John's gospel, where individuals are confronted with both the claims of Jesus and the evidence that he is the Christ the Son of God. In the next chapter, he is in dialogue with the exact opposite of the highly respected, wealthy Jewish ruler. Now it is with a woman, a Samaritan not a Jew, and a woman whose moral notoriety has made her an outcast in her own community. All this is clearly part of John's big picture in his gospel, as he accumulates the evidence which should convince his readers that Jesus is the Christ. So the Nicodemus story sits in the broader context of the whole gospel, and though at this point we are not told of his reactions to Jesus after their interview, he later reappears twice. In chapter 7 verses 50–1, he is arguing in the Sanhedrin against the Jewish leaders' determination to do away with Jesus, asking 'Does our law condemn a man without first hearing him to find out what he is doing?' He is summarily dismissed for his pains. 'Look into it, and you will find that a prophet does not come out of Galilee.' Finally, when Jesus has been 'lifted up' on the cross, it is Joseph of Arimathea who secures Pilate's permission to bury the body in his garden-tomb 'accompanied by Nicodemus, the man who earlier had visited Jesus at night. [He] brought a mixture of myrrh and aloes, about seventy-five pounds' (John 19:39). This was a very large amount, equivalent to a very lavish expenditure, such as a royal burial might have demanded. Clearly, Nicodemus greatly revered Jesus and perhaps saw him by the end of the gospel, as Nathanael did at the beginning, as the Son of God and the King of Israel (cf. John 1:49).

The wider context also decides for us the meaning of the 'lifting up' by which God gave his Son for the world's rescue. For in 12:32–3 Jesus affirms, 'But I, when I am lifted up from the earth, will draw all men to myself' and John immediately comments, 'He said this to show the kind of death he was going to die.'

In these comments, we have been looking at two sorts of context without which we are unable properly to understand the meaning of the text under examination. Every text resides in its literary context. The sentence relates to other sentences on either side of it which constitute a paragraph. The paragraph is surrounded by other paragraphs which make up the narrative unit that is chapter 3 of John. Yet the chapter has its own context in the message of the whole book, and the book has its own unique truth contribution to the whole Bible. Just think how immeasurably poorer our understanding of Christ and the gospel would be if we did not have John's gospel! Then, as you think of its unique contribution (as, for example, in this story of Nicodemus) you begin to see how its main themes and distinctive teaching not only fit into, but also illuminate, the whole Bible. Every text also resides in its own distinctive historical, cultural context. This will relate not only to the internal ingredients of the text – the ruler of the Sanhedrin, the snake on the pole and so on – where historical information from elsewhere in the Bible informs our understanding, but also to the big picture of the book as a whole. This addresses the key question as to why the author wrote it and to whom. All the necessary evidence for these deductions is contained within the text, or other biblical texts, and it is by careful reading, meditation and re-reading that we begin to understand the author's predominant concerns and the applications of his message, so that we can better set a particular text within the controlling purposes of the book of which it is a part.

It is in the light of these two analyses of context, both literary and historical, that we can focus on the meaning of words and the structure of sentences. Of course, neither of these processes of understanding is watertight in itself. We cannot work at the contexts without examining the words, and vice versa. So each process is being worked through simultaneously, even though our particular focus will be on one particular aspect, at one particular time. In dealing with the words, we need to look for their normal meaning within the sentence, not the obscure or exceptional. It is important also to remember that the Oxford English Dictionary is not the final authority. The meaning of words is fluid over a period of time and a dictionary will always have to generalise. Remember, too, that we are dealing with a text in translation. This is where our reflection on the contexts can be really helpful. Seeing how a particular author uses the word in another, more straightforward context can often provide just the insight needed to make better sense of its use in a more difficult verse. It is a good test of whether or not we have really understood the meaning of the individual key words in a passage to try to express them in our own equivalents, not necessarily individual synonyms, but usually in phrases that explain their meaning.

The other important aid to understanding is to pay careful attention to the grammatical relationships between the different thought ingredients which make up the passage. Just as every sentence has a main verb and a subject, so every paragraph has a main idea, or point, usually expressed in a topic sentence, around which all the other ingredients are built. Each of these extra clauses, or phrases, is included in order to extend our understanding in some particular way and is connected to the main sentence by one of a whole series of linking words. When we come across them we need to stop and see what is being connected to what, and for what purpose. It is often said that when you come to a 'therefore' you should stop and see what it is there for. The same applies to a list of conjunctions and relative pronouns, too long to quote but containing many familiar friends such as 'and', 'but', 'although', 'so that', 'because', 'as if', 'since'. They are all ways of connecting ideas together, and they help us to analyse and examine the structure of a sentence or paragraph, so as better to appreciate its essential meaning.

Learning to listen

Expressed in these ways, it may appear that studying the Bible is a complex and demanding intellectual task. There is no doubt that it does involve hard work when we come to *study* Scripture in this way and that in our busy lives and the frantic rush of our culture, serious Bible study can appear to be a luxury available only to the professional or the retired. But I want to convince you that such thinking is misguided and potentially disastrous. I have little doubt that the weakness of the Christian cause today is largely due to the degree of biblical ignorance and illiteracy, both within the Church and outside it. At least some of our hesitations and reluctance to take studying the Bible seriously, as a central element of Christian discipleship, stem from our categorising it as an academic pursuit. It takes us back to the comprehension exercises we used to do in English classes at school, which for many will trigger memories of difficulty and boredom. I am not advocating that we come to the Bible in that frame of mind! We need, rather, to remind ourselves that instead of studying an impersonal text for information purposes, we are entering into a dialogue by which to deepen a relationship – with God himself. In fact, the same process of listening and understanding is going on, but it is in an interactive context, where response is required at a personal level.

That is why Christians always link their study of the Bible with prayer. It is our reactive side of the conversation. Of course, we need to bring our minds to the reading of Scripture, to be attentive, switched on and ready to think through what God says to us and its implications. But that is only the first, albeit vital, stage of the process. The aim of our study is not simply to be able to understand and express the meaning of a biblical text. That is only a means to a much more profound end, which is that we should respond appropriately in thought and action to what we have understood, in prayer, faith and obedience. Just as we are dependent on the illuminating power of the Holy Spirit to teach us the meaning of God's written Word, so we are dependent on his energy and power to put whatever we have learned into action in our lives, as faithfully and fully as possible. That is why all our study of the Bible and all our use of helpful methods and techniques to understand its message must be preceded by prayer, in which we consciously open our minds and hearts to the Holy Spirit's teaching, express our dependence on him for all spiritual understanding and ask for his enabling to put what we discover into practice.

The real test of any Bible study, then, is not an intellectual 'buzz' or a warm feeling inside, but a life of joyful discipleship, in which God's love is reciprocated by our personal devotion to him and shared in our care for others. This priority derives from our understanding of the uniqueness of the Bible as God's personal self-disclosure. Biblical revelation is not just a body of information to be understood and assimilated mentally, but an invitation (we might even call it a summons) from the living God to enter into a covenant relationship of loving obedience with him. In order to know biblical truth, we must live it. The Bible's knowledge of God is never merely theoretical, but experiential; never content with theological correctness alone, but rejoicing in personal relationship. In biblical terms, therefore, knowing

God's truth and doing it are mutually interdependent. You cannot have one without the other.

But their connectedness is often not appreciated. We study the Bible not to fill our minds with historical or theological information, as if we were swotting for a *Mastermind* interrogation or 'Bible trivia' contest. You may know the sort of thing – 'Who killed a lion in a pit on a snowy day?' – as though that was Bible knowledge. (See 2 Samuel 23:20, if you can't resist it!) Such a view does indeed 'trivialise' the Bible. No, we need the knowledge of God's truth in Scripture in order to act, in the recognition that it is only as we put it into practice that we are able to learn more. On our wedding day, my wife and I thought we had got to know each other pretty well over a period of three or more years, and we knew that we loved each other. That was why we got married. But thirty years on, we know each other so well and love each other so much more that the reality of that day seems but the faintest outline of the picture painted down the years. Putting our commitment to one another into practice, on a daily basis, through all the ups and downs of life, has meant that we know each other and love each other far more deeply than we could have imagined on our wedding day, though what we knew then was equally real. We have a factual, legal document to prove the historical reality of our wedding, but that is simply the foundation on which the practice of our vows and promises has been based. It is the living out of those verbal affirmations that has given substance and solidity to our marriage. The parallels between marriage and God's relationship with his people are developed by Paul in Ephesians 5:22–33, where the husband's love for his wife, modelled on Christ, and the wife's respect for her husband, modelled on the Church, highlight for us the relationship into which God has called all his believing people. That can only be entered into and developed by listening to God in his Word and putting it into action in our lives, as Jesus himself constantly emphasised.

> Not everyone who says to me, 'Lord, Lord,' will enter the kingdom of heaven, but only he who does the will of my Father who is in heaven. (Matthew 7:21)

> Therefore everyone who hears these words of mine and puts them into practice is like a wise man who built his house on the rock.

The rain came down, the streams rose, and the winds blew and beat against that house; yet it did not fall, because it had its foundations on the rock. (Matthew 7:24–5)

My mother and brothers are those who hear God's word and put it into practice. (Luke 8:21)

A woman in the crowd called out, 'Blessed is the mother who gave you birth and nursed you.' Jesus replied, 'Blessed rather are those who hear the word of God and obey it. (Luke 11:27–8)

If anyone chooses to do God's will, he will find out whether my teaching comes from God or whether I speak on my own. (John 7:17)

Plain for all to see

What we have been advocating as the basic template for interpreting the Bible is usually referred to as the 'grammatico–historical' method. Its aim is to discover the intended original meaning of the text by close attention to the meaning of words, to the grammatical structure of the writing, to the historical occasion that produced it and to the internal contents of the book providing the necessary clues as to its purpose. It may seem to us at our point in history to be the obvious way to approach the Bible, as indeed it did to the apostles of the early Church. But it was not always so, down the centuries of church history, nor indeed is it obviously so to all contemporary Bible readers. The principles of biblical interpretation, which we shall go on to explore in more detail in later chapters, were not invented at the time of the Protestant Reformation in sixteenth-century Europe, but they were re-discovered and powerfully articulated then, as a result of that movement of God's Spirit in spiritual re-awakening. If the Bible was to be the supreme authority over the Church in all matters of faith and conduct (*Sola Scriptura*), then it was vital to define very clearly the principles on which it was to be interpreted. The Reformers were especially conscious of this as they were battling against the obscurantist and sometimes bizarre uses, or abuses, of the Bible, which had become an entrenched feature of medieval religion. The scholars of the Middle Ages had become bogged down in apparently unchangeable traditions, more concerned about their own theological games than about nurturing spiritual devotion and faith. Significantly, the only irresistible force which could move the immovable object was the rediscovery of the Scriptures and their study in the original languages, in order to translate them into the languages of Europe. As the weaknesses of the Church's Latin text, the Vulgate, were exposed, so the quest for a more accurate Bible led to the desire for a more authentic interpretative method, generated by the Bible itself rather than arbitrarily imposed on it by the scholars from the outside.

There is an excellent detailed essay on the history of interpretation in Klein, Blomberg and Hubbard's *Introduction to Biblical Interpretation* (1993, Word, USA) to which I am indebted for the following summary. It was Martin Luther (1483–1546) who laid down the principle of *Sola Scriptura*, that only the Bible is divinely authoritative for Christian belief and practice, and with it the affirmation that the Bible is its own best interpreter. Rejecting the medieval allegorical interpretation as 'empty speculation', Luther 'affirmed that Scripture had one simple meaning, its historical sense. This is discerned, Luther said, by applying the ordinary rules of grammar in the light of Scripture's original historical context. At the same time, Luther read the Bible through Christocentric glasses, claiming that the whole Bible – including the Old Testament – taught about Christ' (op. cit. p. 41). John Calvin (1509–64) added to Luther's conviction his own view that the 'inner witness of the Holy Spirit' within the individual Christian served to confirm the correctness of a right and valid interpretation of Scripture.

In brief, the Reformation represented a revolutionary break with the principles of Biblical interpretation formerly practiced. Whereas previous Bible scholarship had relied on church tradition and the interpretations of the church fathers, the Reformation leaned solely on the teachings of Scripture. If the past applied allegory to dig out Scripture's alleged many meanings, the Reformers opted for Scripture's plain, simple, literal sense. (op. cit. p. 41)

But why had the Church ever lost this essential biblical perspective? The roots of an allegorical approach to the Scriptures certainly go back as far as Philo (20 BC–54 AD), a Jewish scholar who lived and worked in Alexandria, where the Septuagint had been translated two centuries earlier. In that Greek context, Philo was impressed by Plato's philosophy that behind the 'forms' of reality perceived by the senses lay the 'ideas', which were the true reality. Applying this to the Old Testament, Philo began to look for a truer, deeper meaning than the plain, literal meaning of the text. Instead of drawing out from the text its clear significance, his method imposed on the text ideas which often owed more to Greek philosophy than to the Scriptures themselves. Culturally, this was an acceptable and popular method and it certainly influenced the leaders of the early Church, known as the apostolic fathers of the second century. As their influence grew, so their interpretations handed down gained the authority of apostolic tradition. A considerable school of biblical interpretation developed in Alexandria, committed to the allegorical approach, its main exponent being the famous scholar and apologist, Origen (185–254 AD). Eventually, a contrary school developed in Antioch, in which the literal sense of the text as a way to understanding its spiritual meaning was stressed. But in spite of attempts to reconcile the two views, it was the allegorical approach which dominated the Church, though not exclusively, through the Dark Ages. It was the influence of the thirteenth-century scholar Thomas Aquinas which started to pave the way for change, as he began to restore the insistence that the literal meaning of the text was the indispensable foundation for its understanding, at any level. The weakness of the allegorical method was its subjectivity, unsupportable from the biblical context, and once the tools of reason and logic were applied to it, large question marks appeared over its very validity. It was into that context that the Reformers' revolutionary approach exploded.

Among Bible-believing Christians, the basic principles of interpretation developed during the Reformation have been applied consistently over the past five hundred years. Foremost in their formulation was the dictum that Scripture must interpret Scripture: what has been called 'the analogy of faith'. This principle is a logical deduction from the recognition that the Bible alone constitutes God's self-revelation, and that the whole Bible is therefore an entity, having one author, the Holy Spirit, and a totally consistent revelation of Truth as a result. Because God is one and because the Bible is the product of the mind of God it demonstrates a consistency and coherence which guarantee that it cannot be contradictory. Since God's nature does not change, neither do his thoughts or purposes, and therefore what he once said in Scripture he is still saying. So no part of the Bible can be properly interpreted if it is held to be in conflict with what another part clearly teaches. It is a criterion which we would apply to any human thinker and author, and it should be applied so much more, with reverence and humility, to God's expression of his mind in Scripture.

In summary, then, we begin the process of understanding the biblical text by taking the natural meaning of the words in their relationship to one another, interpreting them according to the normal rules of grammar and syntax. We do this in the immediate context of the particular passage within its own book, but also in the wider context of the Bible as a whole, allowing the clearer parts of Scripture to illuminate the more obscure, with the recognition that the existence of coherence and consistency will validate our understanding. There is nothing of the 'magical mystery tour' in our interaction with the Bible. It is a unique book in its divine inspiration, but nouns are still nouns and verbs are still verbs. Sentences are still statements, questions or commands. Normal rules still apply. It may seem to be more exciting to work out the middle word of a long biblical sentence, chapter, or even book and say that its position indicates the kernel of the meaning, but it is a silly game of which we shall soon tire. It is equally foolish to treat the Bible as a lucky-dip, opening it at random, and, with closed eyes, putting a finger somewhere on the page, so as to determine what God is saying to us. There is an old story of the seeker who was 'given' by this method 'And Judas went out and hanged himself' (Matthew 27:5), only to follow up this unpropitious beginning with a second attempt, which yielded, 'Go and do thou likewise!' It's a healthy corrective to superstition and mysticism in our handling of God's Word.

But the 'hidden' meaning revealed only to the chosen élite, the *illuminati*, still exercises a powerful attraction to our human pride. Perhaps that is what lay behind the extraordinary best-seller of 1997, *The Bible Code* by Michael Drosnin. In that, and other subsequent books on the same theme, writers have claimed to discover predictions about events in world history, which occurred long after those books were written, including assassinations, scandals, bombings and the death of Princess Diana. All of these are said to be encoded in Bible texts and are only discovered by computer searches on the principle of the 'equidistant letter sequence'. In an article entitled 'A Cracked Code', published in *Christianity Today*, 12 July 1999, Professor Ben

Witherington of Asbury Theological Seminary had some telling criticisms to make of this approach. He noted that the 'researchers' read both right to left (Hebrew) and left to right to find the codes, that the 'universally accepted Hebrew text' they claimed to have used does not in fact exist, and that what Drosnin did use was a text with the added Hebrew vowels which would not have been in the original. For a while, however, in the media and the popular imagination, this novel way of discovering the Bible's 'secret messages' was the talk of the town. 'The reality,' Witherington comments, 'is that if you use the ELS method and apply it to any sufficiently long text, you can come up with names and messages of all sorts – you just need to keep trying different distances between letters and different directions until you get lucky.' There is nothing magical about the letters, sequence or form of words by which the Bible is constructed. Everything depends on what it actually says, and to that issue we must turn next.

To remind you

- Every form of human communication has to be interpreted, so it is vital to develop good practice based on sound principles. We need to distinguish between meaning and significance (pp. 96–8).
- We need to pursue the original, intended meaning of the writer, observing grammar, vocabulary and context (pp. 99–103).
- But this is not an arid, intellectual exercise. Through it we learn to listen to God and respond to him in a personal relationship of love and obedience, expressed in prayer and action (pp. 103–6).
- At the Reformation, Martin Luther re-affirmed the principle that the Bible is its own interpreter, challenging the allegorical interpretation of the past, which was essentially subjective (pp. 106–9).
- There is nothing magical about the Bible – its contents are plain for all to see (pp. 109–10).

Chapter 6

So How Do We Unpack the Old Testament?

CHRISTINE HAD TO admit it – against all the odds she was actually enjoying the weekly Bible study group with Alison at the church. She couldn't think why she had been so suspicious of it all at the beginning. 'I suppose I thought they'd try to brainwash me,' she explained to her husband, Dan, 'but it hasn't been like that at all. In fact, they really want you to ask questions and there's no pressure at all. It's all very relaxed! Oh, and by the way, they're having an evening in a couple of weeks' time when partners are invited to come too, so you will come, won't you? There will be a supper and . . .'

Dan grunted in a non-committal sort of way. He wasn't at all sure he approved of his wife getting so interested in 'religion'. You never knew what it might lead to. 'Hold on a minute!' he said. 'Do you mean to say you think you can really understand the Bible now? You don't want to believe all they tell you at the church, you know. Oh, I don't doubt that they're sincere enough in their way, but they can be sincerely wrong.'

Christine paused. She knew there was a lot she didn't understand at all yet, but then that didn't mean she had to doubt what she had begun to grasp. It all seemed to make so much sense. 'Well, of course, there's a huge amount I don't know anything about at all, but I love those stories in the Old Testament we're studying at present. The characters seem so real and normal, and I can identify so much with them,' she replied. 'Take Gideon, who we were reading about yester-day. He needed to be really sure that God was with him and was going to do what he had promised, because he was only a young farmer and God sent his angel to commission him to save Israel from her enemies.

So he asked God for a sign. One night he put a wool fleece out, and asked God to confirm his promises by dew being only on the fleece and all the ground around it being dry. And in the morning it was exactly so. The next night he asked for the opposite, the fleece dry and the ground covered with dew. And it happened again.'

'Yes,' Dan stirred, 'I think I do remember something about that from school, in the dim and distant. So what?'

'Well,' Alison said, 'we're just like Gideon and we can find out what God wants by "putting out a fleece". She told us about a young bloke at the church who had felt sure that God wanted him to be a missionary somewhere abroad, but he didn't know where. So, one day, he put out his "fleece" and said to God that the first place he brought to his notice that morning would be the place he should go to. Well, he went to buy his paper on the way to work, and there in the newsagent's was a big display of chocolate Brazils. So he knew where he had to go!'

Dan reflected, for only a second. 'Mmmm – just as well they weren't doing a promotion on Mars bars! Oh, come off it, Christine; you can't live your life like that! Just because it happened to some character in the Bible doesn't mean it's going to happen to you.'

Christine had to admit Dan had a point and she quietly stored the question away to ask next time round. How could you be sure that you'd really got the right message? How could the Bible's meaning be unpacked? She realised there was still a great deal to explore.

Our starting point is the realisation that the Bible is written in a wide variety of literary styles, or 'genres'. Among the different kinds of literary types within its covers are stories (narrative), poems, prophetic oracles, parables, allegories, logical argument, symbolism, proverbs, dramatic dialogue and letters. Each works in its own way, according to its own conventions, and if we want rightly to understand and interpret any part of the whole, we need to be aware of the broad principles which govern the composition of each of the major biblical genres.

Old Testament narratives

Let's start with the Old Testament and with 'narrative', or story-telling, since it has been calculated that this comprises over 40 per cent of the total. It also provides some of the most exciting and dramatically involving material, which has inspired generations of other story-tellers in music, the visual arts, drama and film. Many of us will recall the excitement of Bible stories from our childhood – Moses and Pharaoh, David and Goliath, Samson and Delilah. But do the stories exist at other levels for the adult reader of the Bible? When we have relished the unexpected turn in the plot, the shiver of excitement at the unpredicted outcome or the overturning of what seemed inevitable, what are we left with?

At this point, there are two favourite ways of dealing with the story, which suggest themselves readily enough and have a degree of plausibility, but which can actually hinder us from penetrating to its deeper meaning and grasping its full value. The first is moralising. This may owe something to the Victorian Sunday-school approach, devoted to regarding the Bible as a means of instilling social ethics into young people through force of example, good or bad. I'm sure that many Sunday schools did far more than that, but the tradition of learning improving moral lessons from Bible examples is still with us. 'Abraham did this and so should we' – but not in everything. Abraham is certainly the supreme example of faith in God's promises in the Old Testament. He is the man of faith *par excellence*, except when he isn't, which Genesis is honest enough to tell us was a considerable part of the time. 'We should be like David' – but not in every way. 'We must not be like Samson' – but does he have no redeeming features? The problem with a moralising approach is that it imposes an external framework on the passage in order to extract a 'meaning'. Of course, the actions of different Bible characters do provide us with examples of what obedience or disobedience to God looks like and its repercussions, but it is not always quite so easy to decide what is to be followed and what not, as Christine discovered in the matter of Gideon's fleece. The attraction of moralising is that it seems to bring us centre-stage in the story so that the matter of relevance is quickly established. Its danger is that its focus on us may actually destroy the primary (and therefore most significant) reason for the story's inclusion in the Bible at all.

The same is true of the other approach, which is psychologising. Here the interest focuses on the character(s) *per se* and on a psychological analysis of their actions, words and motivations. The attraction is that it brings the Bible within our contemporary cultural environment, shows us that Bible people were 'just like us' (as indeed they were), but then imposes the concerns of our world on to the text, in what usually has to be a highly speculative fashion. We know that we are losing the track when inferences are drawn, without any textual justification, about why a character acted in a particular way. For example, a whole strand of 'exposition' can be woven around the idea that David was the youngest son of his father Jesse. What that meant in terms of his brothers' attitude, his own psychology as he approached kingship, reasons for his later behaviour patterns towards his own children and so on: all this becomes the focus for 'understanding' the stories. But, again, its weakness is the importing of extra–biblical criteria, which are bound to be as arbitrary as the commentator's own judgments. They may resonate with our own psychologising culture, but that is no guarantee that we are listening to what God wants to say to us through the Bible. Rather, it may show how obsessed we are at listening to ourselves, and how skilled at screening out any voices that do not sound contemporary enough to us. The biblical narrative texts have considerable amounts of detailed information and description carefully integrated into the action of the story, and we must use all of it fully to understand their meaning.

However, 'reading between the lines' is always a dubious technique and its fruit will always be highly personalised and subjective. That may appeal to our 'reader response' contemporary values, but it will not help us to get to the timeless truths of God's self-revelation, which led the Holy Spirit to inspire these words through the original author. It is, in the end, a quick and easy approach, avoiding the 'given-ness' of the text, for a more attractive and superficially relevant agenda. Unfortunately, it doesn't bring the satisfaction of the deepening knowledge of God, which was the divine intention. Reading Old Testament narrative is designed to take the focus off me and my small concerns and to put it fairly and squarely on God, and on his majestic and universal purposes. Once I begin to get that right, I can return to my little world with much greater awareness of the resources of God's faithful mercy and providential care, with my vision clarified and my faith strengthened in a way that will not happen if the focus is always on me. In their excellent book *How to Read the Bible for All Its Worth* (1983, Scripture Union), two distinguished American scholars, Gordon Fee (New Testament) and Douglas Stuart (Old Testament), address the issue in their customary incisive way. 'No Bible narrative was written specifically about you,' they instruct us. 'You can always learn a great deal from these narratives, but you can never assume that God expects you to do exactly the same things that Bible characters did; or have the same things happen to you that happened to them' (p. 85). It is a healthy and much-needed corrective.

The first step towards a right reading of Old Testament narrative is to take seriously its historicity, because this is inseparably linked to its purpose. In Chapter 2 we argued that the whole Bible is the one story of God's loving plan to undo the effects of human rebellion against his rightful authority as creator and sustainer of his world. This he began through a man (Abraham), who became a family, which grew into a nation. That nation was entrusted with the commission of carrying God's light to all the nations of the earth, but its own sinfulness fatally flawed its character and mission. Eventually, in God's mercy, he came himself as the rescuer, focusing all his promises and their fulfilment in his own Son, who, having lived a perfect life, offered himself as the acceptable and atoning sacrifice for the sins of the whole world, through his death on the cross. In his resurrection, he proved the sufficiency of his sacrifice and his victory over all the hostile powers ranged against us, even death itself, and opened to all who trust him the privilege of a restored relationship with God the Creator, as a loving heavenly Father. This relationship begins here in this world through repentance and faith, receiving his forgiveness and submitting to his rule, and lasts for eternity. If this is the 'meta-narrative' of the Bible, then it will not be a surprise to recognise that all the constituent parts, the individual narratives, relate in some way to this big picture, and fit into their own specific place, along the chronological time-line of its development.

The historicity matters, because without it we have no guarantee that the contents have any more authority than wishful thinking. What I have written in the last paragraph would all be pious whimsy if the historical events on which it centres did not in fact occur in time and space. It might still be an interesting (more or less) way of explaining life and its meaning, a religious or philosophical viewpoint, but nothing more, for it would have no objectivity outside of the individual's mind. That is actually what most people assume Christian belief today to be. But the Bible's claims are far more radical than that. Old Testament narratives are not just stories about people and nations from the ancient Middle East; they are stories about God and how he acted in the ebb and flow of history, in and through, and even for, the lives of nations and individuals, to reveal himself authoritatively and without confusion or contradiction to all humanity. The history is essential; but the theological concerns which lie behind it control and dominate the narrative accounts. The historical and theological are therefore different but parallel approaches to the same revelatory events, each supplementing the other. Neither is dispensable and they are never contradictory. As Dr Francis Schaeffer stated in the early 1980s, 'It is essential for the truth of Christianity that the Bible relates truth about history and the cosmos, as well as about spiritual matters.' What we are concluding, then, is that the story itself, in the way it is told, together with its explanation, is the message, or meaning, for which we are looking.

God as the hero

If, as Fee and Stuart affirm, 'God is the hero of all Biblical narratives,' then his activity must be the key ingredient in every story-line. 'What does this story tell me about the character and purposes of God?' is an important foundation discovery to pursue in every narrative account, because that will provide both the clue to its central purpose and also the unifying principle around which its many different ingredients revolve. Of course, this information does not always sit on the surface of the story. The narrator may weave a tale of some subtlety, in which we have to be alert to follow the clues and draw the appropriate deductions. But those deductions must always be text-related and therefore capable of objective justification. However, as I observe the role of God in the story, I find it valuable to have in mind three separate 'levels' (or we might call them 'contexts') on which he is operating. They are closely inter-related, rather in the way that Russian dolls fit into one another. Largest and most significant is God working out his salvation-history plan for the whole human race, so I call that 'the big picture'. Next, because that plan focuses in the Old Testament on the nation of Israel, there will be a 'national level'. Israel is bound to God as her covenant lord, so in her community-life and relationship with him, much of God's character and purposes are revealed, as he makes and fulfils his promises. Third, within the covenant community there are individuals to whom God specifically relates, with whom he is particularly at work. I call this the individual, or personal, level of the story, dependent for its interpretation on understanding the first two levels properly. It is here that the temptation to put ourselves in the human figure's shoes is strongest, but we have to keep reminding ourselves that we are not Moses, for example, any more than we are Pharaoh. For which we may be thankful! We can learn from the observation of how the changeless character of God is revealed in relating with more or less sinful people, who are human like us, even though their uniqueness in circumstances or character does not directly apply to our very different context.

If these reflections help us to think about a story as a unit and to begin to explore its purpose in the scheme of the whole Bible, we need also to approach it as a literary construction and to give some thought to the ingredients of which it is made up. Story-telling is a universal art, and one in which the familiarity of technique does not make it at all threadbare. Children's stories are very instructive in this regard. What makes the three little pigs or Goldilocks and the three bears of huge delight to successive generations of children is the 'buzz' that comes when the third member of the trio bucks the trend and reverses what we have come to accept as the inevitable. It could be argued, surely legitimately, that the parables of the talents or the Good Samaritan work in exactly the same way. But every story has to build to a climax, frequently an unexpected turning-point, which is literally the reason for the story being told at all. This is especially true of story-telling in an oral, rather than written, form, which is how biblical narratives would have started their lives. Unlike modern written prose, which depends on a continuous and related flow of ideas, stated, explained, proved, by evidence, and always pressing on to its conclusion, biblical story-tellers have time to vary their pace, to give attention to relevant detail, to develop repeated phrases or ideas for emphasis, and so to lead up to the critical turning-point. Their approach is geared to the trained ear of the experienced listener, where every phrase or nuance is significant. Usually, at the heart of the story, though it may not be highlighted as such, there occurs a turning-point, or a central idea, around which, we come to recognise, the whole story revolves.

Turning points

That is what makes any story worth telling. Take a simple sentence – 'The book, which I really wanted, was on the top shelf.' The tension is built into this sentence, which might be the beginning of a story, in two ways – the need for the book is in conflict with its inaccessibility.

The story that follows will have to resolve that tension. The question that is sown in our minds is, 'How is the book to be obtained?' It might be resolved in a perfectly matter-of-fact, normal way. It could continue, '. . . so I moved the steps over to the shelves, climbed up and took it', or '. . . so I asked the librarian to fetch it for me, which she did'. That *is* a story, but hardly one worth the telling, because there is nothing unusual, dramatic, comic, or even tragic, about the resolution of the conflict. However, other alternatives will doubtless have come into your mind, which might include mounting an expedition of mountaineering proportions to scale the bookshelves and retreating with broken limbs, defeated. It may be only marginally more interesting, but at least it would be more of a story worth telling. The interest in story-telling and listening usually resides in how the conflict, or tension, at the narrative's heart comes to be resolved, and in biblical terms this is often the key to understanding the central meaning and ongoing significance of the story, to God's people, in every generation.

It may be helpful at this point to look at a specific example in order to see these principles working out. I have chosen a story which is very carefully and clearly constructed, and also one which is comparatively unknown, so that we do not bring too developed a prior understanding to it.

After Rehoboam's position as king was established and he had become strong, he and all Israel with him abandoned the law of the LORD. Because they had been unfaithful to the LORD, Shishak king of Egypt attacked Jerusalem in the fifth year of King Rehoboam. With twelve hundred chariots and sixty thousand horsemen and the innumerable troops of Libyans, Sukkites and Cushites that came with him from Egypt, he captured the fortified cities of Judah and came as far as Jerusalem. Then the prophet Shemaiah came to Rehoboam and to the leaders of Judah who had assembled in Jerusalem for fear of Shishak, and he said to them, 'This is what the LORD says: "You have abandoned me; therefore I now abandon you to Shishak."' The leaders of Israel and the king humbled themselves and said, 'The LORD is just.' When the LORD saw that they humbled themselves, this word of the LORD came to Shemaiah: 'Since they have humbled themselves, I will not destroy them but will soon give them deliverance. My wrath will not be poured out on Jerusalem through Shishak. They will, however, become subject to him, so that they may learn the difference between serving me and serving the kings of other lands.' When Shishak king of Egypt attacked Jerusalem, he carried off the treasures of the temple of the LORD and the treasures of the royal palace. He took everything, including the gold shields that Solomon had made. So King Rehoboam made bronze shields to replace them and assigned these to the commanders of the guard on duty at the entrance to the royal palace. Whenever the king went to the LORD's temple, the guards went with him, bearing the shields, and afterwards they returned them to the guard-room. Because Rehoboam humbled himself, the LORD's anger turned from him, and he was not totally destroyed. Indeed, there was some good in Judah. (2 Chronicles 12:1–12)

A contemporary reader might very well ask what meaning this historical narrative can possibly have for today. To answer the question we have to begin with an analysis of the way the story itself is constructed. It begins with an editorial, or narrator's comment, which explains the situation in Israel (Judah) at the time and provides the foundation on which the story is subsequently built. The tension is there from the outset. The king and all the people have 'abandoned the law of the LORD' (v. 1). What will happen? The answer lies in the attack of Shishak, king of Egypt. This is not accidental, or even coincidental, but is theologically attributed quite uncompromisingly to Israel's unfaithfulness (v. 2a). From verse 2b to verse 9 tells the story, in several scenes. An enormous Egyptian force, supplemented by his allies, led by Shishak, sweeps into Judah, mops up the fortified cities designed to block the aggressor's way to the capital, and presents itself at Jerusalem (v. 4). Surely the city must fall. That is how the tension of verse 1 will be resolved. But there is a sudden intervention, in the human form of the prophet, Shemaiah, although clearly its origin really lies with the Lord. He sends the prophet because he has given him the divine message, which seems one of hopeless judgment (v. 5) – 'I now abandon you to Shishak'. What looked as though it might provide a way out for Jerusalem, perhaps through a message of divine deliverance, has hit a brick wall. But then there is a second surprise reaction. Both the king and the leaders submit themselves to God's justice, humbling themselves before him (v. 6). This is quite unexpected (cf. v. 1), but it proves to be the turning point, the resolution, of the whole issue. Notice the causal connection in verse 7a, 'When the LORD saw that they humbled themselves . . .' Another prophetic message comes through Shemaiah (vv. 7–8) promising that Jerusalem will not be destroyed, but delivered. However, Judah will become Egypt's vassal, so that King Rehoboam and his people will 'learn the difference between serving me and serving the kings of other lands' (v. 8). That, of course, was the contention highlighted in verse 1. They did not want to have to serve the Lord. Shishak does attack; the temple is looted of all Solomon's gold treasures and Rehoboam is left to replace the royal shields with bronze, a constant reminder of his reduced state due to his rebellious disobedience. Matching the introduction of verse 1, verse 12 provides the narrator's summary conclusion, in which the theological significance of the narrative is driven home. 'Because Rehoboam humbled himself, the LORD's anger turned from him.'

The critical turning point is easy to identify. At the heart of the story lies the affirmation of previously rebellious people that the LORD (the covenant name – Yahweh) is just. They had previously abandoned his law because they did not find it 'just' or acceptable; they wanted to be free of the character of the God who had brought them into a covenant relationship with himself. But repentance (implied in their confession) and humble submission of themselves to God turned the tide of their circumstances. The seemingly inevitable destruction of the city did not occur, because the faithful covenant LORD delivered his people, when they cast themselves on his mercy. The key meaning of the story then, as Rehoboam doubtless recalled whenever he saw the bronze shields, is that God is just. He is faithful and dependable. He abandons those who abandon him, as he said he would, but he defends those who truly repent.

So, what of the three levels? On the 'big picture' time-line of God's salvation-history plan, we are at the beginning of the decline of the Davidic monarchy. The kingdom has already been divided and Rehoboam (Solomon's heir) is left with only Judah to rule over. Though for three years he walked in God's ways (2 Chronicles 11:17), yet, as verse 1 of the story shows, his comparatively established position quickly seduced him into an arrogant independence from God and his law. It is one of many reminders of the inadequacy of any human king to provide stability for the people of God, due to each individual's own inherent sinfulness. When Israel begged God for a king (1 Samuel 8) God revealed that at the root of their request was a rejection of him as their ruler, and we are being taught that only as they return to God's kingly rule can they be secure. In whole Bible terms, that kingly rule is fulfilled in Jesus Christ, and it is by submission to his authority that we enter into and enjoy all the benefits of the eternal kingdom of God. But the new covenant also contains its own requirements, and its grace never sanctions disobedience to God's instruction or development of our independence from him. These are issues of relevance to everyday life, for both the Church and the individual Christian. We have already slid into the national or covenant picture of the narrative. The lesson of attack and deprivation as a consequence of abandoning God, but that repentance secures God's mercy, is a constant biblical theme. Third, on the individual level, Rehoboam learns that though as king and representative of his people he has been made strong by God's goodness, if he is to continue to enjoy God's favour he must be obedient personally. The fact that he is the king does not exclude him from the responsibility of a personal life of devotion to, and dependence on, the LORD. The continuing message of the narrative is that we cannot play games with God. Heart-reality, demonstrated in faith and humble obedience, is his requirement for those who are in relationship with him. Our choices do determine the outcome of our lives, and perhaps in the emphasis on the bronze instead of gold, directly attributable to Rehoboam's rebellion, we are being given a warning that although God is gracious to forgive, we are not always spared the consequences of our foolish rebellion, so that we learn not to serve other masters.

This approach to Old Testament narrative accords with the emphases the Bible itself makes in its story-telling. One of its most extended and detailed is the story of Joseph, occupying most of chapters 37 to 50 of the book of Genesis. Undoubtedly, there is much that we can learn about God and the individual throughout the saga, but its aim is not primarily to encourage us to resist temptation, as Joseph did, or to bear adversity patiently, as Joseph did, or even to deal mercifully with those who have maltreated us, as Joseph did. For Joseph is not the hero of the story, but God is, and there are key verses which make that perspective abundantly clear. As Joseph reveals his identity as chief minister of Pharaoh to his bewildered, guilty brothers, he affirms, 'it was to save lives that God sent me ahead of you . . . to preserve for you a remnant on earth and to save your lives by a great deliverance. So then, it was not you who sent me here, but God' (Genesis 45:5–8). When those same brothers prostrate themselves before him as his slaves, he responds, 'Don't be afraid. Am I in the place of God? You intended to harm me, but God intended it for good to accomplish what is now being done, the saving of many lives' (Genesis 50:19–20). All the intricate details of Joseph's relations with his brothers are seen to be part of a greater salvation plan, mirrored in the preservation of the descendants of Abraham from starvation, through Joseph's wise work in Egypt, but coming to its fruition in their development as a great nation within that land and God's mighty exodus deliverance through his servant Moses, centuries later. The emphasis in Genesis is not that 'any dream will do' for a budding Joseph and that it will all come good in the end, but that God will work out his purposes in fulfilment of his promises and no force on earth will be able to hinder or divert him.

Such God-centredness matches the Christ-centredness of the New Testament's view of the Old, articulated by Jesus himself when he affirmed, 'These are the Scriptures that testify about me' (John 5:39). The same emphasis can be seen in the writer of the books of Samuel, reviewing the long biographical narratives of the life of King David, where the keys to understanding the significance of the narratives are all in God-centred terms. Following David's adultery with Bathsheba and the murder of her husband Uriah, a son is born, 'but the thing David had done displeased the LORD' (2 Samuel 11:27). The succeeding narrative of the almost total disintegration of David's family house is governed by God. Solomon is born and preserved as David's eventual heir because 'the LORD loved him' (2 Samuel 12:24–5). Although Absalom determines to overthrow his father and seize the throne, 'the LORD had determined to frustrate the good advice of Ahithophel in order to bring disaster on Absalom' (2 Samuel 17:14). So God is the chief player in the drama, and it is his will that is constantly being carried through. He is therefore the chief explainer of his actions, and when we are given such clear indications as to where the emphasis lies and what God's purposes are, we would be foolish to ignore them.

The power of poetry

From story-telling in narrative prose, we turn now to the second most common literary form in the Old Testament, which is poetry. 'Poetry' doubtless generates a wide variety of responses in our contemporary context. Much recent poetry written in the English language has a name for being opaque, intellectual, theoretical, deliberately confused and confusing. The lines seem to be of indeterminate length, rhyme no longer exists and the connections between ideas often seem inaccessible. That is certainly a widespread popular perception and it needs seriously to be taken into account, since many Bible readers are likely to import their negative presuppositions into their first encounters with the poetic text. Most readers do not come to poetry agog with expectation. Yet children love the intoxication of rhythm and rhyme, find it easy and delightful to memorise and enjoy revisiting the familiar favourites over and over again. The ability of verse, especially when coupled with music, to generate and give expression to the deepest human emotions is still a part of life, whether demonstrated in a love song or a football 'anthem', a pop concert or a choral symphony. If we can set aside any negative predisposition towards poetry and let the biblical material speak for itself, we shall find that it communicates at the deepest levels of our humanness still.

Hebrew poetry works in rhythm rather than rhyme. This is a help in translation, since if rhyme at the end of lines were the clinching factor it would be very difficult to translate. To most English ears, the rhyme at the end of a couplet completes and focuses the rhythmic pattern. Take, for example, the New International Version's translation of Psalm 19:9. It reads:

> The fear of the LORD is pure, enduring for ever,
> The ordinances of the LORD are sure and altogether righteous.

In this version we can detect something of the rhythmic structure of the two halves of the verse. Each begins with a statement in the same verbal pattern, 'The . . . of the LORD is . . .' and concludes with an explanatory phrase, indicating a further reason for the statement. But just a very small change to introduce a rhyme, to which English ears are attuned, helps us to pick up the rhythmic parallel much more clearly.

> The fear of the LORD is pure, enduring for ever,
> The ordinances of the LORD are sure and righteous altogether.

The rhyme binds the couplet together, to our ears, which is not the case in the first version. Of course, the translators have made their choice quite properly because the potential rhyme is an accident of English translation, not an intention of the Hebrew author, but the danger is that we miss the distinctive rhythmic effects of the original and drift into regarding the poetry as merely a slightly variant form of prose.

It is helpful, then, to note some of the key poetic devices of the biblical poets, of which parallelism is perhaps the chief characteristic. This is readily visible in our English Bibles where verse after verse is regularly printed in two sections, the second each time indented. The essence of parallelism is that there is a proposition first stated, which is then explained further, or perhaps contrasted, in the second half of the verse. The similarity in structure and form helps to drive home the point, but it is particularly to the differences that the focus of our attention is drawn. Parallelism is not mere repetition. Take, for example, Psalm 24:1.

> The earth is the LORD's, and everything in it,
> the world, and all who live in it

The second half of the verse deepens our understanding of the first proposition by focusing on ourselves as an integral part of the 'everything' that is owned by God. The implications are considerable, and the genius of the poetry is that it makes the point with a striking conciseness and penetration so that we are forced to take these implications on board and think them through as the poem develops. Two verses later, aware of the inevitable relationship with God which every human being has by virtue of our creation, we are asking with the psalmist, 'Who may ascend the hill of the LORD? Who may stand in his holy place?' – another powerful parallelism.

Although rhyme is not part of Hebrew poetry, assonance (a correspondence in sound) is. Points are often made by two words of similar sound, featuring in successive lines, in explanation of, or contrast with, one another. We are used to puns in English, which are points made by bringing together words which are alike or nearly alike in sound, but quite different in meaning. So Hebrew poetry will often make its point by juxtaposing two very similarly sounding words, but with very different meanings. A vivid example comes from Isaiah 5:7, where God compares his people, Israel, to a vineyard, planted, nourished and protected, but, instead of providing a crop of good grapes, yielding only bad fruit. His conclusion is expressed in the couplet:

> And he looked for justice, but saw bloodshed;
> for righteousness, but heard cries of distress.

A transliteration of the Hebrew text reads

> And he looked for *mishpat* and behold *mispach*
> for *tsedaqah* and behold *tse'aqah*.

Clearly the similarity of the sounds, coupled with the enormous contrast of meaning, combine poetically to make the point powerfully, and with much more penetration than our factual, but rather lame, English translations can achieve. It is difficult for us to pick up these nuances, though commentaries which work with reference to the Hebrew text are a great resource in helping us to get back into the position of the original hearers.

A poem exists as a single unit of expression, complete in itself. It may belong to a sequence of compositions, but it has its own life and structure, reflecting and conveying its own unique message. That separate unit, the poem, is also a totality and must be treated as such. Just as a prose paragraph of logical argument builds step by step to its conclusion, and none of those ingredients should be separated from its context or treated in isolation, so a poem is complete in itself, and none of its building blocks should be torn from the finished construction. To pick a verse out of a psalm, for example, and to deal with it on its own without relating it to the rest of the poem and understanding why it is there may make us guilty of taking the text out of its context to construct a pretext. Each poem is in itself its own context. This means that discovering the major purpose of its composition is an important exercise in coming to understand and appreciate its meaning today. For example, this treatment is often meted out to Psalm 46:10, 'Be still, and know that I am God.' Torn out of its context, it is used as a 'settling' verse in congregational worship. 'We have come from busy lives, lived in a frantic culture, into the presence of God, and now we just need to be still, to stop . . . listen to yourself breathe again, clear your mind of everything that clutters it, and in the emptiness and stillness know that God is God.' The verse has become part of the stock-in-trade of the 'worship' leader. Irrespective of the general truth or wisdom of the comments above, it is not what Psalm 46:10 means in its context. 'Be still' is not a gentle invitation but an imperious command. It means 'Stop fighting! Lay down your arms!' and the way you do that is by submitting to the Godness of God. The context is of a world in cataclysmic upheaval, both physically (earthquakes and tidal waves, vv. 2–3) and politically (nations in uproar, kingdoms falling, v. 6), yet through it all, in war, desolations (v. 8) and peace (v. 9), God is sovereign. He is God, exalted among the nations and in the earth. It is useless to fight against him, so lay down your arms, and submit, and in so doing you will find the Lord of hosts is your fortress and strength. It is the whole focus that provides us with the message, which, as always, is much deeper and stronger than our own little world of cosy comfort and self-indulgence, and which, rightly understood, nerves us to live with God, in the real world, with all its challenges, struggles and enigmas.

However, while it is true that the poem is a unit and must always be treated as such, the unit can be analysed and better understood as a whole by appreciating the individual ingredients and how they have been put together. In Psalm 46, which we have just looked at, the Hebrew word *selah* occurs on three occasions, in our English translations at the end of verses 3, 7 and 11. Clearly, it is a marker-post dividing up the thought-content of the poem. Its precise meaning is uncertain and its function may have been primarily musical, but it occurs over seventy times in the psalms and is one of the ways in which we can observe the poems' structures. The use of refrains, lines or phrases which recur, especially at the end of sections, is another way in which a poem can be divided up into segments or stanzas. For example, the question 'Why are you downcast, O my soul? Why so disturbed within me?' is asked in Psalms 42 and 43 on three occasions, and in the view of many scholars binds the two psalms together as originally one unit. Another poetic device (used in Psalms 9–10, 25, 34, 37, 111, 112, 119 and 145) is the acrostic, in which the first letters of each succeeding verse follow chronologically through the order of the Hebrew alphabet. In Psalm 119 (the longest of all the psalms) this is worked out section by section, and most English translations head the successive sections with the appropriate Hebrew letter. But perhaps the most common and effective device is what is known as the 'chiasm', where the point is made by contrast, through a reversed parallelism. A typical English example of this stylistic device could be, 'Do not live to eat, but eat to live.' Our attention is secured by the inversion of the order so that the emphasis falls on the second half. Psalm 33:6 provides a good example. The pattern of thought can be represented ab b, a,

       _____a_____   _____b_____
By the word of the LORD were the heavens made,
their starry host by the breath (spirit) of his mouth.
       _____b,___   _____a,_____

In a striking reference to the dawn of creation, the Word of God and the Spirit of God are identified as totally united in the command that made the heavens.

Using the psalms

Most Old Testament poetry is to be found in the prophetic oracles, which we shall consider as a genre in the next chapter, and in the psalms, to which we now need to turn our attention. They are, of course, very different from anything else in the Bible. Throughout this book, the concept that the Bible is the Word of God, spoken by him to people, has been central. We can see how that happens in propositional statements, narratives which reveal God's character and purposes, laws and commands, but the psalms are human words spoken (or sung) to God and to our fellow human beings. Fee and Stuart pose the challenge well when they ask, 'How do these words spoken *to* God function as a word *from* God to us?' (op. cit. p. 169). Their conclusion is that while the psalms' major purpose is to teach neither doctrine nor moral behaviour, they do provide an authoritative model both of reflection on God and his ways, and also of expression, by which we can learn how to relate the circumstances of our lives to God, in words. In similar vein, Eugene Peterson finds in the psalms the answer to his question, 'Where can we go to learn *our* language, as it develops into maturity, as it answers God?' (*Working the Angles*, 1993, Eerdmans). In the psalms and their divine inspiration, we have, then, God's authoritative model of the variety of ways in which we may rightly respond to him, corporately and individually, in praise and in prayer. The collection of 150 poems we call the Psalter, the book of Psalms, is rightly often referred to as the hymn book or the prayer book of Old Testament Israel, of Jesus and, through him, of the Church. As Athanasius is said to have expressed it, while most of Scripture speaks *to* us, the psalms also speak *for* us. They give us language by which we can answer God's initiating speech and enter into conversation, which deepens our relationship with him.

The types of response which individual psalms exemplify have led to a great deal of scholarly endeavour over the past century to categorise the different sorts of material, not according to author or general subject matter, but to the life situation which gave the poem birth. This is not an attempt to relate, say, each of the psalms of David to specific events recorded in the biblical histories of his life, but a recognition of dominant literary forms which were appropriate for response to God, in specific circumstances. So, there are psalms of individual and also national thanksgiving – for deliverance from sickness, enemies, antagonists, for victory in battle, for God's faithfulness to his covenant commitment. There are also general praise psalms, as for example the 'Hallelujah' sequence (145–150) with which the Psalter ends, the aim of which is to declare and celebrate the Lord's goodness, manifested both in the natural world and in the history of the covenant people. Private thanksgiving and communal praise unite together with a renewed invitation to the hearer to 'extol the Lord with all my heart' (Psalm 111:1). But there are also many psalms, categorised as 'laments', which provide words with which to come to God when the skies are black and life is threatening. A large number of these are individual, in which the psalmist turns to God in a situation of great need, or affliction. They are punctuated by urgent cries for help, specific prayers for deliverance, and contain the honest outpouring of the soul as the distressing circumstances are laid out before God. Sometimes the very description of distress is an implicit admission of guilt and preparation for penitence, as in Psalm 51, King David's prayer of repentance. But often the distress is that of unjust accusation, or undeserved suffering, where the problem is agonisingly dissected and explained, with resolution being found only in the dependable faithfulness of God, whatever the circumstances. Similarly, there are many national laments, prompted by defeat in war, plague, drought or other economic disasters, expressing repentance and calling on God for deliverance. Related to these are other psalms of confidence in which faith holds on to God's rescuing grace. The categorisation of psalms is a never-ending activity, but beyond the labels – royal psalms, messianic psalms, wisdom psalms, liturgical poems, canticles of Zion and many more – the right understanding and use of their content is what should govern our reading.

So how are we to go about things? First, we need to treat the particular poem as a literary unit, in its own right, and explore its content with the usual range of analytical questions. What is this psalm, or poetic oracle, about? What range of meaning exists in it, and where does the emphasis fall? It is often helpful to try to express the theme of the poem in a single sentence. Once we have grasped its main import or message, we can begin to benefit from its depth and subtlety by seeing how the details fit together. So we shall be asking how the points which flow together are related to each other and how they contribute to the main theme. This will prompt us to look at the pictures that are drawn, the metaphors that are employed, and how these work together, not just to produce an intellectual understanding of the subject-matter, but a personal and emotional involvement with it. For that is the genius of poetry. If we simply look at a psalm, abstract its cognitive content and express it in prose, we have destroyed the poetry. Our relationship with God is not simply one of cold doctrine, or of intellectual comprehension, but of personal interaction, of loving God with all our heart, soul, mind and strength, and the psalms provide us with a model for our affections and their expression. We must not destroy their warmth, their immediacy of relationship, their essential humanity, by putting them through a systematic theology mincing-machine and coming out with a depersonalised statement of propositional truth. God did not cause them to be written in that way.

Pointing to Jesus

There is one other important element to remember, so obvious, perhaps, that it appears to be frequently overlooked – namely, that the psalms belong to the era before Christ's coming. This means that they anticipate the fulfilment of God's purposes which the Messiah will bring, and that for us today, they must be interpreted in the light of the gospel. Indeed, Jesus applied the messianic predictions to himself and the apostles extended an ever wider range of references to Christ. There are three key psalms (2, 45 and 110) in which these concepts are focused and which can therefore serve as a summary for their significant interpretative insight. In Psalm 2, the rebellious world rulers are discovered plotting against God and 'his Anointed One' (v. 2) – the word is 'messiah'. The term refers to the separation by God of an individual to a holy status and resulting task. This is accompanied by a public act of anointing, indicating empowerment for the role, as in the case of a new king or high priest. So the anointed is also referred to by God as 'my King' (v. 6) and 'You are my Son; today I have become your Father' (v. 7). He is the one to whom rule over all the nations is given. There is a sense in which this was partially fulfilled by at least the godly kings in David's line, as they depended on God as Father and ruled invested with his authority, but their sinful, human nature meant that they could never adequately fulfil the image of the perfect Son, who would rule over all humanity. In Psalm 45, in the context of a royal wedding psalm, the king is addressed as 'God' ('Your throne, O God, will last for ever and ever' v. 6), though in the very next verse his subservience to God is also recognised ('Your God has set you above your companions by anointing you' v. 7). How can the two be reconciled? Finally, in Psalm 110, the king is seated at the LORD's right hand, as universal conqueror (v. 1) and further is invested with eternal priesthood, not in the line of Aaron and the Levites, but in the order of Melchizedek, the priest-king of Genesis 14:18ff, who blessed Abraham (v. 4). In these capacities the king will 'crush kings on the day of his wrath' and 'judge nations' (v. 5–6). Although these psalms use the language of earthly kingship in its Davidic, Jerusalem context, clearly no king of Israel began to fulfil these divine qualities, so that the psalms were increasingly attributed to the coming great King, great David's greater Son, the Messiah. It was in these terms that Jesus taught his disciples to see that he was spoken of. He is not only David's Son, but his Lord (Psalm 110 and Matthew 22:41–6). He is the one seated at God's right hand as ruler and judge of all, confirmed by his resurrection (Hebrews 1:3, 13). He is the firstborn who is worthy of worship even by the angels of heaven (Psalms 2, 45 and Hebrews 1:5, 8–9).

There are many other ways in which Jesus showed the fulfilment of everything that is written about him in the psalms (Luke 24:44), supremely in his crucifixion, where the details of his death foretold in Psalm 22 were amazingly fulfilled and where he identified himself as the rejected stone of Psalm 118:22–3 whom God has exalted to the position of capstone (Matthew 21:42ff). It is highly significant that Psalm 118 is itself the last of a sequence of psalms from 113 onward, known as the Egyptian Hallel, which celebrated the exodus and were sung at the end of the Passover feast. It was with these very words ringing in his ears that Jesus went out from the Upper Room to the Garden of Gethsemane, to his betrayal, passion and death, as the enactment of all that the psalmist had foreshadowed. That surely is Matthew's point when he tells us that following the inauguration of the new covenant in his blood, at the end of the last supper, with his disciples, 'When they had sung a hymn, they went out to the Mount of Olives' (Matthew 26:30). The psalms provide us with great resources for our Christian pilgrimage, in understanding God's faithful character and the majestic sweep of his eternal purposes more clearly, in seeing the glories of Christ, foreshadowed here, and shining from the pages of the gospels, in giving us perspective on the ups and downs of our human experience, 'the changing scenes of life', but especially in providing us with words with which to come to God ourselves, in all of life's circumstances. Calvin was right when he described them as 'an anatomy of all the parts of the soul'. God has given these words as authoritative patterns and examples for us, but it is as we take them into our hearts, making their praise the substance of our worship, their obedient submission the expression of our souls, their joyful acceptance of God's free grace and reliance on his faithful, steadfast love the fabric of our lives, that we know the happiness of the man who stands at the entrance to the Psalter, whose 'delight is in the law of the LORD [on which] he meditates day and night. He is like a tree planted by streams of water, which yields its fruit in season and whose leaf does not wither. Whatever he does prospers' (Psalm 1:2–3).

The wisdom literature

For life to prosper like that, in every area, is the goal of the wise man, which leads us to our third and last category of Old Testament literature in this chapter, which is usually designated 'wisdom'. This material is found in the 'writings' and particularly in the books of Job, Proverbs and Ecclesiastes. Of course, even in these three books there is a very wide range of literary styles, ranging from the dramatic dialogues of Job to the popular, pithy aphorisms of Proverbs and the extended reflective essay-form of Ecclesiastes. But wisdom material is also found in the historical sections of the Old Testament, as in the parables of Jotham (Judges 9:7–21) or Nathan (2 Samuel 12:1–12), in the prophets, as in the proverbial nature of passages like

Isaiah 28:23–9, and in the psalms, such as Psalm 49's reflection on the relative values of wealth and poverty in time and eternity, or Psalm 73's grappling with the riddle of the prosperity of the wicked. The genre of wisdom sayings and wise teachers is probably as old as writing itself. Certainly, it stretches back well into the second millennium BC in the cultures of Mesopotamia and Egypt. But the quality of biblical wisdom is very different in content, even though the material may be presented in a similar stylistic package. The difference, quite simply, is that of revelation. Hebrew wisdom writers are not groping after the good life; they are expounding it. 'For the LORD gives wisdom, and from his mouth come knowledge and understanding' (Proverbs 2:6).

At the heart of the wisdom literature, therefore, is the conviction that God has spoken to reveal his character and will, and that such knowledge is the foundation for life to be lived as a creature made in his image in the world he has created. 'The fear of the LORD is the beginning of knowledge, but fools despise wisdom and discipline' (Proverbs 1:7). So the world of human beings is divided into the wise and foolish, the righteous and the wicked. The former categories accept the world as God has made it, in all its 'givenness' and, with it, his self-revelation in the Torah. For them, this becomes the yard-stick of their values and life-style. The latter will not let God be God, either in their own lives or in the world. They spend their time fighting against the structures of reality, denying God's existence, ignoring their Maker's instructions and trying to construct their own independent pseudo-reality, barricaded against God. The distinctive of wisdom literature is that it applies the revelation of the Torah to the practical questions of everyday life in God's world, grappling with the seeming contradictions, and honestly facing the problems which living God's way can seem to generate. In short, wisdom consists in applying the Bible's teachings to every circumstance of daily life.

> I, wisdom, dwell together with prudence; I possess knowledge and discretion.
> To fear the LORD is to hate evil; I hate pride and arrogance, evil behaviour and perverse speech.
> Counsel and sound judgment are mine; I have understanding and power.

> By me kings reign and rulers make laws that are just; by me princes
> govern, and all nobles who rule on earth.
> I love those who love me, and those who seek me find me.
> With me are riches and honour, enduring wealth and prosperity.
> My fruit is better than fine gold; what I yield surpasses choice
> silver.
> I walk in the way of righteousness, along the paths of justice,
> bestowing wealth on those who love me and making their
> treasuries full. (Proverbs 8:12–21)

The great example of the wise king is Solomon, whose name is
inscribed at the entrance to the book of Proverbs. On his accession to
the throne, when invited by God to 'ask for whatever you want me to
give you', Solomon shows that he already has wisdom by asking for 'a
discerning heart to govern your people and to distinguish between
right and wrong' (1 Kings 3:4–14). God answers his request by
making him wiser than any other king, and from the outset of his
reign, the nation 'held the king in awe because they saw that he had
wisdom from God' (1 Kings 3:28). Solomon becomes the archetypal
'wise man', but the emphasis is constantly on this being God's gift,
not his natural ability. 'God gave Solomon wisdom and very great
insight, and a breadth of understanding as measureless as the sand on
the seashore' (1 Kings 4:29). This included three thousand proverbs
and a thousand and five songs, as well as extensive knowledge of plant
and animal life – a deep awareness and understanding of the whole
created order – as the next few verses show. But not only is covenant
Israel the beneficiary of such royal wisdom from God, his fame
spreads around the world and the Gentile nations begin to share in
these blessings to the children of Abraham. The classic example is the
visit of the Queen of Sheba, herself fabulously rich, to Solomon's
court to talk to him 'about all she had on her mind'. Her conclusion,
after all her questions have been answered by the king, is memorable.
'I did not believe these things until I came and saw with my own eyes.
Indeed, not even half was told me: in wisdom and wealth you have far
exceeded the report I heard' (1 Kings 10:1–9).

There is no doubt that this is to be seen as the highest point of the
monarchy in Israel. Solomon, 'in all his splendour', as Jesus described
him (Matthew 6:29), reigns over a united Israel, in great wealth, giving
his people rest from their enemies and receiving homage and

admiration from the kings of the earth. He recognises that all this is God's gracious gift and acknowledges, as the magnificent Jerusalem temple he has built is dedicated to the Lord, 'Not one word has failed of all the good promises [the LORD] gave through his servant Moses' (1 Kings 8:56). Things do not get any better for Old Testament Israel than this. Psalm 72, entitled 'Of Solomon', celebrates his reign as the climax of the second book of the Psalter. Intriguingly, it picks up the promise made by God to Abraham in Genesis 12:2–3 that 'all peoples on earth will be blessed through you', and affirms its fulfilment in King Solomon, concluding, 'All nations will be blessed through him, and they will call him blessed' (Psalm 72:17). But the sad reality is that not only was Solomon merely mortal, so he could never fulfil the eternal kingship role, but also he was sinful, and in spite of his enormous wisdom, the reign of splendour ended in tragedy. Having married many foreign wives, as Solomon grew old his heart was turned after their own pagan deities and a policy of syncretism began to creep into his religious practice. Although God had appeared to him twice, his heart turned away, and the greatness of the privilege he disregarded and even spurned required an equivalent severity of judgment to be pronounced:

> Since this is your attitude and you have not kept my covenant and my decrees, which I commanded you, I will most certainly tear the kingdom away from you and give it to one of your subordinates. Nevertheless, for the sake of David your father, I will not do it during your lifetime. I will tear it out of the hand of your son. (1 Kings 11:11–12)

The divided kingdom and the long, painful decline to the destruction of Israel and the exile of Judah is the agenda of the rest of the Old Testament.

What had happened that the 'wise king' erred so disastrously? The answer is that he was a fallen, sinful human being like anyone else. While he was totally dependent on God, he sailed the straight course of wisdom; but as soon as he began to rely on himself and to choose his own ways, perhaps through over-confidence, he drifted on to the rocks. Perhaps it is that very tragedy that gives the wisdom literature its urgency, for these issues are not just those facing a great king, they are the issues of life for every man and every woman. The monarchy, even at its peak, was no lasting solution for the problems of Israel's sinful heart, nor for the fallenness of the pagan nations, snared in the blindness of their idolatry. Something more was needed. It would require a king whose own character was perfectly obedient to God's revelation, flawless in righteousness, and so able to rule consistently in total wisdom. This king would be the seed of Abraham and a blessing to all the nations as he gathered a new international people of God, comprised of all who would receive his word and submit to his wisdom. And this fulfilment came when Jesus Christ declared, 'The Queen of the South will rise at the judgment with this generation and condemn it; for she came from the ends of the earth to listen to Solomon's wisdom, and now one greater than Solomon is here' (Matthew 12:42). It is wisdom to hear and obey him.

We can only sketch an outline of the three main wisdom books here, but, at the risk of over-simplification, it is perhaps helpful to think of them like this. The book of Proverbs is the basic wisdom text. It brings the whole of life into the presence of God and the Torah, to learn how to live according to his revealed will. Since this will be the way human beings function best, there is an unashamed appeal to the 'good life' emanating from wisdom. Obedience to God is always best. But this is not just a matter of social or personal expediency, it is because God is sovereign and because of his perfectly right character that living God's way (wisdom) works. However, it would be a mistake to absolutise the proverbs and turn them into promises which God is required to fulfil in every detail. Klein, Blomberg and Hubbard have a very helpful and pertinent paragraph, from which it is worth quoting.

[The Proverbs] point out patterns of conduct that, if followed, give one the best chance of success. In other words, they offer general principles for successful living rather than a comprehensive 'legal code for life'. Further, Proverbs place a higher premium on etching themselves on one's memory than on theoretical accuracy. That is, their primary goal is to state an important, simple truth about life in easy-to-remember terms. Hence, they do not intend to cover every imaginable circumstance. (op. cit. p. 315)

Their assertions help us to choose to go God's way, to decide the path we are going to follow and to do that on the basis of divine revelation, not merely human observation. They remind us that since the whole of life is lived under God's judgment, 'the fear of the LORD is the beginning of wisdom, and knowledge of the Holy One is understanding' (Proverbs 9:10).

Proverbs, then, is the basic wisdom text, but what about when its precepts do not seem to be working out? This is the struggle dramatised for us in the book of Job, which of all biblical texts can be most misunderstood if we do not read it carefully in its own context. The book begins with the portrayal of Job as the archetypal 'wise man', described by God himself as 'blameless and upright, a man who fears God and shuns evil' (Job 1:8). He is the head of a large family, a wealthy household, 'the greatest man among all the people of the East' (Job 1:3), but he loses it all. His flocks (the source of his wealth) are destroyed, his children are killed and he himself is afflicted 'with painful sores from the soles of his feet to the top of his head' (Job 2:7). Is this what wisdom brings? Is this the pay-off for godliness? That is the debate which stretches out through the book. It is conducted between Job and his three 'friends' or 'comforters' who come to share in his sufferings. In a sense, they take up a classic wisdom position. Actions lead to consequences, which is what it means to live in an ordered world. God is constantly meting out his judgment through the events of life. So for Job to be suffering so horrifically there must be some hidden cause, some heinous sin lurking beneath the outward persona of godliness he presents. The thesis is that what happens is a direct result of whether or not you have pleased God, so, in some way, Job deserves what he is getting. The idea was still current in Jesus' day, when, encountering a man blind from birth, the disciples immediately took this position. 'Rabbi,' they asked Jesus, 'who sinned, this man or his parents, that he was born blind?' Jesus' reply is direct and uncompromising and also provides a key to the book of Job. 'Neither this man nor his parents sinned, but this happened so that the work of God might be displayed in his life.' And Jesus gives the man his sight (John 9:1–7). The same thinking still lurks in our hearts whenever we find ourselves facing trouble and exclaiming, 'What have I done to deserve this?'

Throughout the book, Job protests his innocence. He is horrified at his suffering and its inexplicability. His argument that it is all grossly unfair is blasphemous to his pious friends. Eventually a fourth counsellor appears who adopts something of a mediating position, defending God's superior wisdom in ordering human affairs. Clearly, the start of the book shows us that God has given permission to the Satan to act in this way. He is neither powerless nor disinterested. Eventually, God himself answers Job, affirming his total sovereignty in the creation of the universe and its sustenance, 'Would you discredit my justice? Would you condemn me to justify yourself?' (40:8). Job is vindicated by God against his counsellors and their accusations, with their misrepresentations of God (42:7–9), and all that he had lost is doubly restored (42:10–15). The resolution of the book rests in a recognition that greater purposes of good, displaying the work of God, may lie behind human suffering. Life is not fair in a fallen world, but God is sovereign, righteous and just and his ways are higher than ours. It was that confidence which built, and, in spite of everything, sustained Job's wisdom.

Ecclesiastes also grapples with too mechanistic a view of life in God's moral world. The 'Teacher' (*Qoheleth*), who presents himself as its author, also challenges the over-simplified view of life that righteousness leads to wealth and wickedness to poverty. From simple observation, in which exceptions to the rule can easily be cited, he concludes that the seeming randomness of life and the inescapable finality of death combine to render life 'under the sun' as ultimately 'meaningless'. This view is expressed frequently, with great plausibility and passion, and it resonates more profoundly with our contemporary philosophies and world views than almost any other part of the Old Testament. 'Build your castle in life, but know that it is on the edge of the abyss and there is nothing beyond' is not an exclusively contemporary position. Ecclesiastes was there over two millennia ago.

But is that the real position of the book? And if so, what is it doing in the Bible? There is great debate as to whether the book's view is ultimately pessimistic or optimistic. For many commentators, its pessimism is realistic, when life is looked at simply from what Derek Kidner calls 'ground level'. Finite man can only be given meaning if there is an infinite reference point. Existentialism recognises that reality but then denies the existence of God as the reference point. Ecclesiastes recognises its realism but affirms the reality of God, and in that perspective finds a resolution of the tensions: 'Fear God and keep his commandments, for this is the whole duty of man' (12:13b). Moreover, there is existence beyond Sheol (death), 'for God will bring every deed into judgment, including every hidden thing, whether it is good or evil' (12:14). Those categories of moral values do apply, beyond this world as well as in it. There may not be a traceable action-to-consequence pattern in the circumstances of this life, but there is certainly a character-to-consequence pattern built into eternity. The 'righteous' and the 'wicked' will find their life-style materially affecting the circumstances of life in this world and, more importantly, determining their eternal destiny. Life at 'ground level' is too bad to be true. It drives us to look for meaning elsewhere. Such wisdom can only be found in God himself, as we submit to his rule and seek to obey his commandments. The wise man always lives in this world in the light of the world to come. 'Remember your Creator in the days of your youth before . . . the dust returns to the ground it came from, and the spirit returns to God who gave it' (12:1–7). That is wisdom.

To remind you

- The Bible is written in a variety of styles, of which story-telling is especially a feature of the Old Testament. We must neither moralise nor psychologise the stories, but recognise that the history contains the meaning (pp. 112–16).
- Taking God as the hero we see him work with his people Israel and with individuals, carrying out his great salvation-plan (pp. 116–17).
- Often Old Testament narratives focus on a turning point at the heart of the story (pp. 117–22).
- The power of poetry in the Old Testament lies in its rhythm and its characteristic parallelism where words and ideas are compared and contrasted (pp. 122–7).
- The Psalms provide us with words which speak for us to God, in all the changing circumstances of life (pp. 127–9).
- Many of them point forward to Christ and help us to see the fulfilment of the soul's longings in him alone (pp. 129–31).
- The wisdom literature seeks to apply propositional truth to all the practical areas of life in God's world. Proverbs, Job, and Ecclesiastes explore the enigma of life from God's revealed perspective (pp. 131–8).

Chapter 7

But How Does the Old Relate to the New?

'IT DOESN'T GET any easier, this understanding the Bible, does it?'
Andy had crashed out on the sofa and was idly thumbing his way
through the Bible he and Julia had bought last weekend and promised
themselves they would try to read. 'I mean, listen to this, Jule. "Know
and understand this: From the issuing of the decree to restore and
rebuild Jerusalem until the Anointed One, the ruler, comes, there will
be seven 'sevens' and sixty-two 'sevens' . . . He will confirm a covenant
with many for one 'seven'. In the middle of the 'seven' he will put an
end to sacrifice and offering. And on a wing of the temple he will set
up an abomination that causes desolation . . ." That's from Daniel,
chapter 9. I'm never going to be able to make head nor tail of this sort
of thing. It all seems so remote, so unreal. Makes you wonder what's
the point, really!'

'Well,' Julia took a deep breath, 'according to that bloke at the
church, the point is that it all points forward to Jesus, and that if you
use him as a sort of key to unlock it all, everything becomes clear . . .
well, eventually. He had a really good story about a jig-saw puzzle.'

'Oh, *did* he?' Andy tried not to express too clearly the cynicism
that was beginning to build in him.

Julia continued, apparently unperturbed. 'Yes . . . let's see, what
was it? Oh yes, I know. It was about a double-sided jig-saw. On one
side was a very complicated map of the world and on the other a
picture of a man. If you tried to do the world side first it would take
ages, but if you did the man first, it would be really simple. And he
said that the Bible was like that – big and complex and hard to put
together, but once you get Jesus, the man, right, you find the other

side has all fallen into shape too. Oh, and he said that you have to remember that the Old Testament is always pointing forward to the New. It was telling what was going to happen hundreds of years before Jesus came and the New Testament picks up lots of clues about the meaning of the Old, that we otherwise wouldn't be able to see. So it shows us how it all comes together in Christ and Christianity. I guess Daniel must be part of that.'

'I guess so,' Andy mused. 'I wish there wasn't this great gap between the two halves of the Bible. It's a pity somebody couldn't sort of build a bridge to help people travel between the two parts, so that we could make them fit together and see both sides of the story. Yes, a bridge is what we need, or maybe a Channel tunnel, or even a ferry . . . !'

Let's see what can be done! Our starting point will need to be another major genre of the Old Testament, which stands in a direct relationship to the New – prophecy. Klein, Blomberg and Hubbard in their *Introduction to Biblical Interpretation* (1993, Word) have the following encouragement for us. Quoting Martin Luther, the great leader of the Reformation, about the prophets, 'They have a queer way of talking, like people who, instead of proceeding in an orderly manner, ramble off from one thing to the next, so that you cannot make head or tail of them or see what they are getting at', their contemporary comment is, 'Probably no part of Scripture mystifies and frustrates readers more than the prophets. Indeed, Old Testament prophecy presents a veritable snake pit of interpretative problems' (op. cit. p. 302). Stay close!

The maze of prophecy

But why should prophecy be so daunting? One reason must be the extraordinarily bizarre interpretations put on some prophetic writing, reducing them more to the level of cosmic horoscopes, or the generalised doom-and-gloom predictions of an *Old Moore's Almanac*, or Nostradamus. Can this really be the Word of the living God? The answer is 'yes', but rightly understood and interpreted. So how should we go about it? If most people were asked to define 'prophecy', they would probably concentrate on its predictive content, the foretelling of the future, or as one Bible commentator summarised it, 'history, written in advance'. This is an unfortunate focus, because it generates a speculative interest about the unknown future, which does not reflect the original purposes of the prophetic writers. We are not dealing with impossibly secret messages which have to be decoded, not even in the symbolism of a book like Daniel. As in the rest of the Bible, we need to concentrate on the plain meaning of the text, and not import into it our own fanciful parallels from the contemporary world political situation. Our first level of understanding must always be that of the original hearers, and they were not specialists in the movements of the American fleet in the Persian Gulf or the 'no-fly' zones of Iraq! Nor should we seek to discover a mathematical symbolism, buried in the writings of the prophets, by which the date of the second coming of Christ and the end of the world can be predicted. Jesus himself warned us against such folly. 'No-one knows about that day or hour, not even the angels in heaven, nor the Son, but only the Father' (Mark 13:32). In fact, we should not be carried away by thinking that the predictive ingredient is predominant in the prophets. Fee and Stuart correct this false perception when they state that 'less than 2 per cent of Old Testament prophecy is Messianic. Less than 5 per cent specifically describes the New Covenant age. Less than 1 per cent concerns events yet to come, that is following the completion of the New Testament period' (op. cit. p. 158). So what is the purpose of the predictive content of biblical prophecy?

One of the most helpful explanations I have heard comes in the form of an illustration, though sadly I cannot remember its source. Supposing a large congregation is pouring out of a city-centre church on a Sunday morning, spilling out on to the pavements. As groups of friends are talking, individuals begin to edge off the pavement into the gutter and further into the road. If someone is standing too far into the road and his companion sees a car coming at speed, he may find that he is talking to a prophet. Certainly a warning would be in place and it may be phrased in predictive terms. 'Look out,' his friend alerts him. 'There's a car coming: you'll be run over!' That is a prophetic utterance, but of course its purpose is to correct behaviour in the present so that the prophesied future is actually avoided. If the person listens and moves back on to the pavement, the words have fulfilled their purpose. The car came, but he was not run over because he had taken action, while there was still time. The so-called 'prophet' will not be rejected as a liar and stoned (the penalty for false prophets in the Old Testament) because what he said would happen did not literally do so! But supposing no action was taken, and the unthinkable accident occurred so that the words were literally fulfilled, it would give the 'prophet' no satisfaction whatsoever, only the consolation that he had been right to warn his friend.

This illustrates the basic dynamic which operates in biblical prophecy. The prophets came to stir up lazy and complacent people, to disturb the comfortable, to warn of what the future outcome of their present behaviour will inevitably be. Their predictive message reminds the hearers that God is in control of his world and their lives, that he is working out his purposes through history, and he is moving everything towards its final goal in the return of Christ, the last judgment of everyone and the eternal states of heaven and hell. The prophets' work is to stimulate their hearers in the present to think rightly about the future, and so to live rightly here and now. So the prediction element reveals what will develop out of current events, or attitudes, if there is no amendment of life, no return to God, no change. The connection is temporal, but it is more importantly moral and spiritual.

The short Old Testament book of Jonah, the minor prophet, is an instructive example. It is a famous story of the disobedient prophet, told to go to Nineveh, the capital city of the ruthless world-wide Assyrian empire of his day, to prophesy God's judgment against it. Jonah's subsequent flight to Tarshish in the west, his shipwreck and the great fish which swallowed him are the details most often recalled. But that is only the first half of the book. Jonah is re-commissioned to go to proclaim God's message to Nineveh, which is, 'Forty more days and Nineveh will be overturned' (Jonah 3:4). It is a predictive message, which is designed to have a present effect, and it does. From the king downwards, a time of national repentance is proclaimed and enacted, in the hope that God's fierce anger will be averted, which is exactly what happens. 'When God saw what they did and how they turned from their evil ways, he had compassion and did not bring upon them the destruction he had threatened' (Jonah 3:10). Jonah's resulting anger is legendary. The last chapter reveals that he fled to Tarshish not because he was afraid to confront the heart of the mighty Assyrian war machine, but because he knew that God's nature was to be gracious and compassionate, and Jonah wanted pagan Nineveh to be destroyed. Instead, he has lost face because what he said would happen has not, and the pagans have got off the hook yet again. But God's response, with which the book ends, is a haunting question which takes us to the very heart of prophecy and of God. 'But Nineveh has more than a hundred and twenty thousand people who cannot tell their right hand from their left . . . Should I not be concerned about that great city?' (Jonah 4:11). In fact, Jonah is the most successful of prophets in this part of his ministry, for the message of judgment produced the desired effect and God showed his mercy. Ultimately, then, even the predictive elements in prophecy are a declaration of the character and purposes of God.

Preachers of covenant law

So, the prophets are preachers of the character of God in terms of their primary ministry, rather than foretellers of an already irrevocably decreed future. Fee and Stuart have a memorably helpful description, when they refer to the prophets as 'Covenant Enforcement Mediators' (op. cit. p. 151). Such a title reminds us that the ministry of the prophets was dependent on the Torah (law) already given and explained within the Pentateuch. They came to their generation, on the basis of what God had already said in the first five books, to remind, proclaim and apply that word into the current situation. In fact, the prophetic word and office themselves go right back to the time of Moses and his ministry. As the book of Deuteronomy draws to its end, along with Moses' life, the nation of Israel, about to enter the land of God's promise, is reminded of the stark choices they will have to make in Canaan. If they fully obey the Lord they will be blessed in every aspect of their lives, but disobedience will bring equivalent curses, 'confusion and rebuke in everything you put your hand to, until you are destroyed and come to sudden ruin' (Deuteronomy 28:20). The details of the two ways are spelt out and returned to many times later in the Old Testament, by the prophets, confirming God's faithfulness to what he said and spelling out the reasons for the consequences that are being suffered. In that sense, Moses is the first of the prophets, and all the later prophet-preachers follow in his footsteps. A little earlier in Deuteronomy the pattern had already been laid down.

The nations you will dispossess listen to those who practise sorcery or divination. But as for you, the LORD your God has not permitted you to do so. The LORD your God will raise up for you a prophet like me from among your own brothers. You must listen to him. For this is what you asked of the LORD your God at Horeb on the day of the assembly when you said, 'Let us not hear the voice of the LORD our God nor see this great fire any more, or we will die.' The LORD said to me: 'What they say is good. I will raise up for them a prophet like you from among their brothers; I will put my words in his mouth, and he will tell them everything I command him. If anyone does not listen to my words that the prophet speaks in my name, I myself will call him to account. But a prophet who presumes to speak in my name anything I have not commanded him to say, or a prophet who speaks in the name of other gods, must be put to death.' You may say to yourselves, 'How can we know when a message has not been spoken by the LORD?' If what a prophet proclaims in the name of the LORD does not take place or come true, that is a message the LORD has not spoken. That prophet has spoken presumptuously. Do not be afraid of him. (Deuteronomy 18:14–22)

Clearly, the provision of prophetic ministry is, in part, an antidote to sorcery. Ever since the law had been given at Sinai, Moses had fulfilled that function. He has been the means by which the Israelites have heard the word of God, particularly about their future in the land. Now, as Moses is nearing death, God is providing for the continuation of that process. Verses 18 and following indicate that this was fulfilled every time a prophet spoke in the Lord's name, which explains why the claim so to speak was so serious, and why the practical proof of the false prophet is that what he says does not take place. His words are not true; therefore he cannot be speaking on behalf of the God of Truth. But Moses was also a unique figure, superior to any of the other prophets, either at the time or afterwards. Numbers 12:6–8 explains it, in the Lord's own words. 'When a prophet of the LORD is among you, I reveal myself to him in visions, I speak to him in dreams. But this is not true of my servant Moses; he is faithful in all my house. With him I speak face to face, clearly and not in riddles; he sees the form of the LORD.' It therefore came to be believed that one day a prophet as great as Moses would be raised up. Possibly he would be the Messiah. Certainly the connection is made to Jesus in Acts 3:20 where the apostles, quoting Deuteronomy 18, see its fulfilment in 'the Christ who has been appointed for you – even Jesus'. Stephen, the first Christian martyr, quotes the same verse in Acts 7:37 and links Israel's refusal to obey Moses with his accusers' rejection of the

Righteous One (v. 52), 'You have betrayed and murdered him.'

Prophecy was the means by which God chose to visit and instruct his rebellious people down the centuries. Sometimes the prophets' ministry was directed to an individual, as when Samuel first anointed Saul as king and later challenged and rebuked his disobedience. Indeed, the withdrawal of communication from God to Saul was both the punishment of his rebellion and the cause of his future downfall. 'Saul died because he was unfaithful to the LORD; he did not keep the word of the LORD and even consulted a medium for guidance, and did not enquire of the LORD' (1 Chronicles 10:13–14). In the same way God sent the prophet Nathan to David to convict him of his guilt and bring him to repentance (2 Samuel 12; Psalm 51). It was treason and apostasy in the king of Israel for him to seek any other source of enlightenment or wisdom than the word of the Lord, as Ahaziah discovered when Elijah intercepted his courtiers as they went to consult Baal-Zebub, the god of Ekron, about Ahaziah's future (2 Kings 1:2–4). But as the Davidic monarchy descended into greater rebellion and chaos, the later prophets were sent directly to the people, to call them back to repentance and humility before God. This was to obviate the inevitable, predicted outcome of their apostasy, if it continued, which was their expulsion from the land, in national exile.

For this reason, the writing prophets of the Old Testament are located within a comparatively narrow time-band of three hundred years or so, approximately 760–460 BC. Beginning in the decades leading to the destruction of Samaria and the fall of the northern kingdom to the Assyrians, they move on through the century or more before the Babylonians similarly overthrew Jerusalem and Judah, and cover the period of the resulting exile, culminating in the return to the land and the decades of re-settlement. On a world scale, these were centuries of great upheaval, caused by the emergence of successive world empires – the Assyrians, Babylonians and Persians. National boundaries were overrun and even obliterated. There were great movements of people groups and shifts in population make-up. Israel and Judah felt the brunt of this politically and militarily, and therefore economically and socially, but, apart from a handful of notable exceptions, the response of both kings and people was to turn their backs on their covenant Lord, Yahweh, and to capitulate to the gods of the nations, in various forms of idolatry.

However, they were not dealing with wood or metal when they

related so faithlessly to the God who had created them as a nation and formed them to be his people. The ministry of the prophets reminds his recalcitrant people that Yahweh is the only living and true God, unlike the idols they have embraced in what amounted in reality to the worship of themselves. The Hebrew term for 'prophet' comes from the verb 'to call', reminding his people that it is God's grace which lays hold of a messenger, calls him, instructs him and gives him the word of the living God to speak. The message was frequently one which a rebellious nation did not want to hear and chose to reject, but God was being faithful to his covenant commitment. So the prophets came as God's mouthpieces, mediators of the covenant, sent by God to call his people back to repentance and a restored relationship with him. The edge to their message is the predictive element of warning and of promise, in which the hearers are challenged to make right decisions in their present in view of God's revealed plans about their future. This is what tears away the masks of self-deception and play-acting to reveal the corruption and rebellion which are gradually extinguishing the very life of the nation.

Applying the prophets today

But what does it all mean to us, in our very different circumstances, and how can we unpack its continuing significance for today? One of the advantages of studying the prophets is that their message to their own generation is almost as clear to us as it was to them. There may be place names we do not recognise and some allusions we find it hard to place, but the mainstream of their messages is strong and clear. Nor is it difficult for us to identify with their hearers' shortcomings, for their sins are our sins, too. It is not only God who is unchanging. Our sinful human nature shares that characteristic. So when we hear Amos, arraigning the leaders of Israel, declare, 'You hate the one who reproves in court and despise him who tells the truth. You trample on the poor and force him to give you grain . . . You oppress the righteous and take bribes and you deprive the poor of justice . . . Let justice roll on like a river, righteousness like a never-failing stream!' (Amos 5:10–11, 12, 24), we know that we live in the same world, guilty of the same sins. It is all too easy for the contemporary Christian, then, to apply these catalogues of sin to the secular society in which we live, and with them, the list of predicted judgments to which they inevitably lead. But that is to miss one very important consideration. It may be very comforting for cosy Christians to sit safe in their pews and listen to their preachers thunder 'prophetically' against the evils of this 'godless society' in which we find ourselves – comforting in the short run, but suicidal in the end. For who made up the prophets' target audience?

Of the three major and twelve minor prophets, only two focus on the pagan world around Israel. Jonah is sent to Nineveh, capital of Assyria, while Obadiah's single chapter is directed at Edom, one of Judah's neighbours. Certainly, Amos begins with a series of short oracles proclaiming imminent judgment on Israel's neighbours – Syria, Philistia, Tyre, Edom, Ammon, Moab, even Judah (1:3 – 2:5), but all the rest is directed to Israel. Similarly, Isaiah has a succession of chapters, 13–23, against Judah's neighbouring states and especially the super-powers, Assyria, Egypt and Babylon. But five-sixths of his total of sixty-six chapters are focused on Judah. God's prophetic words of warning and judgment are overwhelmingly directed to the people who are in covenant relationship with him. Of course, there is much that is true, and therefore urgently relevant, to all sinners, at all times and in all cultures, but we are not at liberty to draw a straight line from the theocratic covenant community of the Old Testament, whether Israel or Judah, across to a contemporary secular nation-state today, even if its name is Israel. For the people with whom God is in covenant relationship in the twenty-first century are those from every nation who have become rightly related to him through faith in the atoning death of his Son, Jesus Christ, on the cross, the shedding of whose blood has inaugurated the new covenant (Matthew 26:28) and rendered the old obsolete (Hebrews 8:13).

The primary impact of the Old Testament prophets must therefore be on the contemporary Church, and their warnings come to rouse us from our complacency and play-acting. It was Martin Luther who said that you may take the monk out of the world, but you cannot take the world out of the monk. The same is true of any Christian believer. We are involved in a daily struggle against the world, the flesh (or sinful nature) and the devil, and it is all too easy for us to opt for the easiest, most comfortable compromises, concentrating on outward conformity and ignoring the issues of the heart. That is why we need the message of the prophets in the Church. The same is true of our reading of the gospels, and especially the many detailed encounters and debates Jesus – the greatest prophet – had with the Pharisees.

They were the guardians of the covenant, in theory. Certainly, their doctrine of the authority of the Scriptures was impeccable and very highly developed. They were the biblical 'conservatives' of their day, but they had settled for an externalism, which preserved a veneer of respectable righteousness but concealed a heart of hypocrisy and bitterness. It is fatally easy for us to caricature them as the 'baddies' and to assure ourselves we would never do such things, while the supreme irony is that those very seeds of self-righteousness are growing in our hearts. Only when I realise that I have a Pharisee's heart do I begin to get the prophetic value of those gospel dialogue passages, and see how much I need to be corrected by God's Word. Else, I shall be like the Sunday-school teacher who had taught her children Jesus' parable of the Pharisee and the tax-collector in the temple at prayer (Luke 18:9–14). The Pharisee paraded his self-righteousness to God, while the tax collector could only beg God for mercy on him, as a self-confessed sinner. It was he who was made right with God. 'Well, children,' said the teacher, 'before we go home, let's just say a little prayer and thank God that we're not like the Pharisee'!

There is one other very important principle to bear in mind when dealing with Old Testament prophecy, which is that it all preceded the coming of Jesus, by about four hundred years at the least, and that through his coming everything has changed. We can only see and appreciate the light from the prophets as it is refracted through the prism that is Jesus. I find it helpful to keep this in mind by using an analogy from hill walking. Setting out on a walk, one may see three hill peaks which all seem comparatively close together. The distant view telescopes them together. But the reality of the walk reveals that the distances between them are considerably larger than one imagined and that there is a good deal of tramping down and up again before the final peak is reached. We can think of the three peaks as three points of reference or significance for the Old Testament prophecies. The first is what the prophecy meant in the prophet's own context to his own generation of original hearers or readers. We have to climb that peak first, since that is the plain, literal meaning of the text, and whatever significance it may have for us today, it will not be dissonant with that original purpose. The second peak is the fulfilment that is associated with the first coming of Christ in his life and ministry, death, resurrection and ascension. So much of the future blessing, promised by the prophets to those who repent, finds its fulfilment in the gospel of our Lord Jesus Christ. But there is a third and more distant peak, to which we are still climbing, and that is the second coming of Jesus, when he will come to judge the living and the dead and to inaugurate his eternal reign of glory in the new heavens and new earth. This will bring the ultimate fulfilment and completion of all God's promises.

This is not an imposition on the Old Testament's interpretation but the fruit of taking seriously that the two testaments are one Bible. 'The new is in the old contained; the old is by the new explained.' The pattern of the New Testament is overwhelmingly to interpret the fulfilment of prophecy, through the person and work of Christ, and in that way to demonstrate that he is the centre and theme of all that the prophets foretold. But while the kingdom of God has already broken into this present age and transformed it, in the coming of the King, the New Testament is also clear that there is a 'not yet' degree of total fulfilment, beyond the 'now' of present Christian experience. That awaits the 'third peak', when Christ returns, 'and every eye will see him' (Revelation 1:7), 'every knee should bow . . . and every tongue confess that Jesus Christ is Lord' (Philippians 2:10–11).

Let's end this section by taking an example from perhaps the greatest of all the writing prophets, Isaiah. The prophet has just predicted the exile of Judah from the land and the destruction of the city of Jerusalem at the hands of the Babylonians. It will look like the end of the line of David and the people of God (Isaiah 39:5–7). But immediately the exile has been announced, our attention is drawn to God's plans beyond that event, plans for a new exodus and a new covenant people, a great ruler and a universal kingdom. Chapter 40 is the overture to the second half of Isaiah's book.

Comfort, comfort my people, says your God. Speak tenderly to Jerusalem, and proclaim to her that her hard service has been completed, that her sin has been paid for, that she has received from the LORD's hand double for all her sins.

A voice of one calling: 'In the desert prepare the way for the LORD; make straight in the wilderness a highway for our God. Every valley shall be raised up, every mountain and hill made low; the rough ground shall become level, the rugged places a plain. And the glory of the LORD will be revealed, and all mankind together will see it. For the mouth of the LORD has spoken.'

A voice says, 'Cry out.' And I said, 'What shall I cry?' 'All men are like grass, and all their glory is like the flowers of the field. The grass withers and the flowers fall, because the breath of the LORD blows on them. Surely the people are grass. The grass withers and the flowers fall, but the word of our God stands for ever.'

You who bring good tidings to Zion, go up on a high mountain. You who bring good tidings to Jerusalem, lift up your voice with a shout, lift it up, do not be afraid; say to the towns of Judah, 'Here is your God!' See, the Sovereign LORD comes with power, and his arm rules for him. See, his reward is with him, and his recompense accompanies him. He tends his flock like a shepherd: He gathers the lambs in his arms and carries them close to his heart; he gently leads those that have young. (Isaiah 40:1–11)

When we think of the first peak (what did it mean to Isaiah's original hearers?) the answer is not hard to determine. Although the exile they have been warned about is clearly future (not during the reign of their present king, Hezekiah – see 39:8), they are now being told of a future restoration beyond the exile. A day of new beginnings will dawn for Jerusalem, when the price for her sinful rebellion has been fully paid (vv. 1–2). The remaining verses draw an exciting picture of God leading his people back from Babylon to the promised land, storming across the desert, or wilderness, with no physical features impeding his progress for one moment (vv. 3–4). He is sighted by watchmen, who relay the inspiring news of the LORD's return from hill-top to ruined city, until Jerusalem herself is presented with her king – 'Here is your God!' (v. 9). He comes as sovereign-shepherd, to rule his people and to care for his flock (vv. 10–11). At this level, the verses are full of promise for those of Isaiah's day who were prepared to listen to, and receive, God's word. They and the generations that followed, both before and during the exile, would have been strengthened in the knowledge that Babylon did not have the final word, that the great plan of salvation-history was not stalled, that a day of great restoration was coming. Historically, that was so when Babylon fell to the Medo-Persian ruler, Cyrus, and one of his earliest decrees permitted and encouraged the re-settlement in their own land of the captive peoples.

And yet . . . ! The degree of disappointingly inadequate fulfilment, which followed the return from exile, is the substance of the last section of the Old Testament. The difficulties of rebuilding the temple are described in the book of Ezra, and of completing the city walls and re-ordering the community in the book of Nehemiah, while the prophecies of Haggai, Zechariah and Malachi are all designed to challenge and motivate an increasingly demoralised, downcast people. Where was the glory Isaiah had predicted? Why did the Sovereign Lord not rule for his people, with his mighty arm? By way of answer, we have to journey to the second peak and the greater fulfilment of the prophecy in the coming of Jesus. When *did* the exile end? In Isaiah's understanding, when the 'voice of one calling' in the desert was heard, preparing the way for the LORD (v. 3). So it is this verse which Matthew quotes in his gospel (3:3), when, following the infancy and childhood narratives of Christ, he introduces John the Baptist as the forerunner of Jesus the shepherd, who is the king. In the beginning of Christ's ministry, the exile is ending and the new kingdom is breaking in, because the king has arrived. In the opening chapter of his gospel, John echoes the same note, picking up Isaiah's promise (v. 5) of God's glory revealed to all the world, when he affirms, 'The Word became flesh and made his dwelling among us. We have seen his glory, the glory of the One and Only, who came from the Father, full of grace and truth' (John 1:14). Constantly, in the gospel accounts, the Old Testament fulfilment motif stands out. The ministry of Jesus is primarily a declaration of the 'word of our God', which 'stands for ever' (Isaiah 40:8). As his words reveal his divine nature, so he declares, 'Heaven and earth will pass away, but my words will never pass away' (Mark 13:31). He comes to Jerusalem and to Zion, the temple mountain, to declare 'Here is your God.' His powerful arm is demonstrated in his sovereign authority over all kinds of sickness and evil, ruling over men and nature. His divine rule is witnessed also in his cleansing of the temple, overthrowing the tables of the money-changers and evicting the traders, who had turned his 'house of prayer for all nations' into 'a den of robbers' (Mark 11:15–18). At the same time his shepherd care is constantly exercised towards his flock, gathering the outcasts, caring for the weak and disadvantaged, protecting from the wolf, feeding with the truth of his Word and ultimately, as the good shepherd, 'laying down his life for the sheep' (John 10:15).

And yet . . . ! Wonderful as these fulfilments are in the first coming of Jesus, there is a third and further level, a last peak, to climb. For we do not yet see 'all mankind' humbled before the manifestation of God's glory, in Christ. We do not yet experience his sovereign arm ruling in unchallenged power, distributing his rewards and recompensing human beings for their actions, good and evil. That fulfilment awaits the last day of Christ's judgment, when the restoration will be completed and he will reign for ever. This realisation places Isaiah's oracle in a context of which we are all a part. To us, as its readers, it presents an obligation to adjust our lives to those coming realities. Our understanding of Isaiah's prophecy is totally transformed in the light of Christ's comings, both past and future. All our reading of Old Testament prophecy necessarily involves us in a journey between the three peaks, and to keep these focal points firmly in our sights will help us not to lose our way.

There is so much to be gained from this frequently ignored biblical genre of prophecy. We must not allow it to become the preserve of the bizarre and the eccentric. As the contemporary Church of Jesus Christ, we need the instruction it contains concerning God's faithfulness to his promises, his righteousness and judgment, as well as his mercy and grace. The world still needs to hear that it is on a journey to the throne of God's judgment, at the end of human history, that the passage of time and the pattern of history are linear, not circular, and that we are finite beings in a finite world. The message of the prophets, with its warnings now and its appeal to take remedial action in the light of God's stated future plans, needs to be recovered in our 'laid-back' generation. The prophetic books provide us with just such vital ingredients of a full-blooded, vital Christian faith. Because they are composed of collections of oracles, or addresses (we might call them sermons), they were not designed to be read through at a sitting, but to be listened to and assimilated as individual units. Often those with similar themes are grouped together in sections. It is also important to go for the major ideas and key points in each oracle and not to be side-tracked into excessive concentration on details. If we keep asking, '*Why* was this written?', its value to us as contemporary hearers will become much clearer. We shall then be able to appropriate its unchanging message, whether of encouragement or rebuke, warning or promise, to our changing lives in God's changing world.

Apocalyptic writing

Earlier in this chapter, we shared some of Andy's difficulties in trying to come to terms with the obscure meanings of symbols in the book of Daniel. This sort of writing represents a particular and rather specialised form of prophetic writing called 'apocalyptic', of which passages in Ezekiel (38–9), Joel (2–3), Zechariah (9–14) and especially Daniel (7–12) are the outstanding Old Testament examples. The most famous example in the New is the last book, Revelation, whose title is a translation of the Greek word *apokalypsis*. What marks out apocalyptic writing from mainstream prophecy is that it reveals or unveils the hidden realities of the spiritual world and future events in world history, usually associated with dramatic interventions of God in human affairs, especially focused on the end-times. The purpose of the unveiling is not to satisfy curiosity about the future, but to strengthen the people of God in the midst of hostile and difficult circumstances, such as the exile or national apostasy. Apocalyptic writing pulls back the curtain to reveal God at work behind the scenes, working out his ultimate purposes of justice and grace. These glimpses of the future are designed to give courage and confidence to God's people in their beleaguered present. The language is often symbolic, representing future realities by significant images – curious beasts with multiple horns, numbers which have symbolic meanings, mysterious terminology. Often the medium of revelation to the writer is that of dreams or visions, in which these strange realities appear.

Because space–fiction and video games tend to be our nearest cultural equivalent, there is a danger that we relegate apocalyptic writing to a fictional, mythological category in our thinking. 'Weird and wonderful' might be an appropriate label! But that would be a foolish and serious mistake. We must not be diverted or bemused by the detailed symbolism. As with all other genres of biblical literature, the basic interpretative questions and methods apply. What is the major message of a particular vision or dream? The passage in Daniel 9, which Andy found so daunting, clearly teaches that God will bring history to an end, which will result in the vindication and deliverance of his people. In fact, it is a central theme of the second part of Daniel that if God's people persevere through their present opposition and difficulties, with a firm trust that God's sovereign rule is the eternal reality, they will most certainly share in his everlasting kingdom. When it comes to the detail, images of beasts with horns indicate great energy focused at a single point. A charging rhinoceros with all its poundage concentrated in its horn is an apt picture of a powerful tyrant heading up a seemingly invincible national war-machine. The imagery is significant in terms of political realities. The numbers also have a conventional symbolic meaning, as, for example, 'seven' being the number of completeness or perfection, connected with the seventh day of creation when God rested from all his labours and found them 'very good'. This genre is difficult to interpret with certainty, but its central message is loud and clear. God will bring history to his conclusion, demonstrating his sovereign rule and overthrowing all the forces of evil. There will be a certain judgment, when those who are God's people and those who are his enemies will be infallibly revealed. All this is most clearly understood in the light of Christ's coming and expounded further in the book of Revelation. And we need to keep in mind that faithful perseverance rather than fanciful speculation is the purpose of its existence.

New Testament controls

In these ways, prophecy and apocalyptic help to build the bridge between the two testaments, because they prepare the way for the coming of Jesus Christ and provide a framework of reference in which to locate the gospel. If God's character is unchanging, then the principles on which he deals with human beings must also be unchanging, so that there will be a fundamental congruence between the two parts of the Bible, or, to change the metaphor, a balance of which Christ is the fulcrum. Once we see that the unity of the Bible is guaranteed by the oneness of the God who is its author and subject, it becomes obvious not only that we must interpret Scripture on its own terms, in its own context, but that we must also allow the later revelation (chronologically) to interpret and illuminate the earlier. It is a fact of history that God chose to reveal himself progressively over a long period of time, with the inevitable result that those at the end of the revelatory process are in a position to view, understand and connect the whole together in a way which those at earlier stages could not. This is not in any way to assert that the earlier revelation is at all inferior, primitive or deficient. The principle of unity leads us not to expect the later to contradict or correct the earlier texts. All truth is God's truth and it is all equally truthful. There is nothing lacking at any period in what God chose to reveal for that time. However, when

Jesus, for example, said about Abraham that he rejoiced to see Christ's day and was glad (John 8:56), he did not mean that Abraham saw, as in a futuristic vision, all the details of Christ's life and ministry which we now have recorded in the gospels. Rather, he was pointing to himself as the fulfilment of the promise to Abraham, that through his seed one would come who would bless all the nations of the world, by rescuing the human race and crushing the serpent's head (Genesis 12:1–3, 3:15). The point is finally clinched by the apostle Paul in Galatians 3:16, when he affirms, 'The promises were spoken to Abraham and to his seed. The Scripture does not say "and to seeds", meaning many people, but "and to your seed", meaning one person, who is Christ' (see Genesis 12:7, 13:15, 24:7). All this confirms that the New Testament must be allowed to interpret the Old, that the bridge-building starts on the New Testament side of the divide and leads us back, through Christ, to a proper (and Christian) understanding of all that came before.

Our best method, then, is to see what the New Testament has to say about the Old, in the avalanche of quotations and allusions which stream through its pages. Here is Paul, comparing Adam with Jesus Christ in his letter to the Romans. He sees both as federal heads of a race of people. Their actions affect all who are in contact with them. Adam's sin brought death to the whole human race, while Christ's obedience to death brings righteousness and life to all who trust him. The process is explained like this. 'Nevertheless, death reigned from the time of Adam to the time of Moses, even over those who did not sin by breaking a command, as did Adam, who was a *pattern* of the one to come' (Romans 5:14). The Greek word *typos* is translated 'type' rather than 'pattern' by the Revised Standard Version. What is being observed is a characteristic of Adam, which is shared by Christ ('the one to come'), namely that their representative actions have a profound effect on the destiny of humankind. It is this practice of comparison, which is called 'typology', which lies at the heart of the New Testament's interpretation of the Old.

There are other ways in which this interpretative bridge is described elsewhere in the New Testament. For example, in Galatians 4:24 Paul uses the Genesis story of Abraham's two sons, Isaac and Ishmael, borne respectively by his wife Sarah and his slave girl, Hagar, as an allegory, or, as the New International Version translates it, 'figuratively'. The parallel he discerns is between children of the slave woman and those who are in slavery to the law as a means by which to make themselves acceptable to God, contrasted with the children of the free woman, representing those who have found freedom through Christ, in the gospel. The observance of the pattern of similarity leads up to the conclusion, 'Get rid of the slave woman and her son' (v. 30) which is exactly the message Paul has for those who want to follow the Judaisers in the Galatian church and go back to the law.

But it is the letter to the Hebrews which provides the richest range of comparative models. The Old Testament tabernacle, or temple, with its repetitive system of sacrifices and offerings, is only a 'copy' or 'shadow' of the heavenly realities (8:5), simply an 'illustration' or symbol of what Christ has accomplished in the sacrifice of himself on the cross (9:9). The law is simply 'a shadow of the good things that are coming' (10:1). It is therefore second nature to New Testament authors to interpret the gospel in Old Testament terms and pictures. The exodus from the bondage of Egypt through the death of the passover lamb (Exodus 12) is paralleled in the death of Christ and our subsequent deliverance from sin (John 1:29; 1 Corinthians 5:7). The manna from heaven which provided the Israelites' daily diet and the water which flowed from the rock (Exodus 16 and 17) are paralleled by the sustenance given to his people by Jesus, on their pilgrimage from earth to heaven (Egypt to Canaan). So Jesus is the bread (John 6:33, 35) and the rock from whom the water flows (1 Corinthians 10:4; John 7:38). All the covenant promises to Abraham and David are fulfilled in Christ, whose son he is (Matthew 1:1). He is the new temple, the place where God and man can meet in fellowship (John 2:19–22) and his blood inaugurates the new agreement, or covenant, between them (Matthew 26:26–8).

The question naturally arises, however, as to how we assess whether or not such parallels are biblically intentional or arbitrarily imposed by the ingenuity of later readers. I am indebted to Dr John Goldingay for the substance of what follows as guidelines concerning the interpretative tool of 'typology' and how its validity can be determined. The material is found in his book *Approaches to Old Testament Interpretation* (1990, IVP, Apollos). Starting from the point that what can be said about Israel's relationship to God under the old covenant can be said about the Church ('the Israel of God' – Galatians 6:16) under the new, Goldingay stresses that the point of correspondence is in the saving acts of God, because of the consistency of his unchanging character. But the analogy is also combined with a degree of contrast, in that the New Testament parallels are always greater than the Old Testament originals. The language of fulfilment is always appropriate in this area, because we are never dealing merely with equivalents or repetitions of Old Testament events. There is always an element of intensification, or to use the characteristic terminology of the letter to the Hebrews, the new covenant is in every way 'better' than its predecessor. Added to this, there is a greater degree of clarity. 'The heightening is a matter of the New Testament making clearer or more explicit what was allusive or implicit in the Old Testament' (Goldingay, op. cit. p. 101). Further, we must recognise that metaphor and symbolism are built into some Old Testament foreshadowings which will have a more concrete, though spiritual, fulfilment in the gospel. The prophecy of Amos, for example, after eight chapters announcing God's judgment on Israel at the hands of the Assyrians, ends with a vision of ultimate restoration, in which 'David's fallen tent' is restored and the Gentile nations seek the Lord and bear his name (see Amos 9:11–12). Does this refer to the restoration of the state of Israel and the Gentile nations being converted to Old Testament Judaism? Not according to James, the leader of the Jerusalem church, who in Acts 15:14–18 relates the quote directly to the conversion of Gentiles to Christ, through the preaching of the gospel, as for example in the case of the Roman centurion Cornelius and his household in Caesarea, to whom Peter was sent (see Acts 10:9–48). That is what Amos was referring to in characteristically Old Testament language and symbols, and so that becomes the paradigm for interpreting other prophecies about the restoration of the kingdom and the blessings God will pour on his covenant people. As Paul expresses it in Ephesians 1:3, 'The God and Father of our Lord Jesus Christ . . . has blessed us in the heavenly realms with every spiritual blessing in Christ.'

How then can we separate typology from allegory? The one is expository and the other imposed. A typological interpretation still works with the plain, natural meaning of the text in its historical context, whereas allegory attributes from the outside a meaning which the original writer or readers could not possibly have been aware of. 'Typology studies events, while allegory is a method of interpreting words' (Goldingay, op. cit. p. 107). Typology is not therefore a systematic principle for Old Testament interpretation, but it can help us to a deeper and truly Christian understanding. We realise how much more wonderful in their fulfilment in Christ and the gospel are the prophecies of Israel's restoration after the exile, than the partial historical fulfilments in the fifth century BC. But that was always God's intention, stretching his people forward to the far horizon, increasing their expectations and hope, because the glories of his eternal kingdom far exceed anything that might be known in this world. And while it is true that in Christ and the gospel we have entered into that reality, in a measure, for the kingdom of God is among us, yet we too have great expectations of an eternal future of fulfilment beyond all that we might ask, or even imagine. In Goldingay's memorable summary, 'Old Testament prophecy calls people to look at the future, in the light of the past, so as to see how to live in the present' (op. cit. p. 122). Typology does just that for the New Testament Christian, on the certain basis of the perfect fulfilment of God's promises, in Christ.

In all of these ways, Andy's 'bridge' between the Old and the New is constructed by the Bible authors. It is time now for us to examine its solid foundations on the New Testament side and to see how the genres of gospel and epistle there clarify, interpret and focus the whole testimony of God's self-revelation.

To remind you

- Old Testament prophecy is not a secret code-book to reveal the hidden future. It is designed to change behaviour in the present, in the light of the future (pp. 140–3).
- The prophets recall the people of God to faith and obedience, in the light of the covenant, with its blessings and curses (pp. 143–6).
- Because their message is primarily to covenant people, the prophets' application is first to the Church, rather than the world. But their message must be viewed through the reality of Christ's coming and the gospel (pp. 146–9).
- We need to interpret Old Testament prophecy in the light of its eventual completion at his second coming, in God's everlasting kingdom (pp. 149–52).
- Apocalyptic prophecy reveals God at work behind the scenes of human history, bringing his universal and eternal plans to fruition (pp. 153–4).
- The New Testament provides the controls for our Christian understanding of the Old. Patterns of understanding begun in the Old are filled out and completed in the New (pp. 154–8).

Chapter 8

So How Do We Unpack the New Testament?

MATT COULD HARDLY believe it had happened. He'd completely blown it. He should never have been there in the first place. What was he doing at one of those Christian meetings? They were designed to convert people – he knew that. But he'd gone anyway. The visiting speaker had rather surprised him. Matt had expected a ranting tele-evangelist type, who would have been such an easy put-down, but this guy seemed very normal and he presented his 'sales pitch' very reasonably, pretty persuasively actually, he had to admit. 'And I should have left it there,' he exclaimed to himself as he flopped on to his bed. 'But no, I had to go and ask some clever, clever question and engage him in conversation, didn't I?' He went through it again in his mind, the speaker asking him whether he'd ever really examined the evidence of Jesus Christ, at first hand, in one of the gospels of the New Testament. He'd blurted out something about he never thought it was that important and then this guy was offering him that little book; it was still in his pocket – the gospel according to John. 'Come on,' he'd said, 'you've got nothing to lose but your prejudice.' Matt saw himself back away and then he heard that incredibly stupid thing he'd said; he could still hardly believe it. 'No thanks,' he'd said, 'because I know that if I read it, I'll be convinced.' The bloke had laughed, put it into his hand anyway and he'd dashed off at top speed. And now here he was in his own room, with this little book, which was supposed to be able to change his life. But how could it? It was only black dots on white paper, only words. It didn't have any sort of mystical powers, did it? Matt grinned to himself. 'Just matter: that's all it is and all I am,' he assured himself. 'So it can't do anything to you, can it? It can't change you, but it can't harm you.' Drawing it out of his pocket, he turned to the first page.

The message of the gospels

What was Matt about to experience as he opened the pages of that little book and encountered a text nearly two thousand years old, in a literary form like nothing we are familiar with today? Coming from their context in the first-century Græco-Roman world, the four 'gospels' of the New Testament have elements that are very much part of that culture, but also much that is innovatory and unique. Our nearest contemporary equivalent might seem to be the biography, but we must be careful not to import our standards of detailed accuracy, chronological order and independent documentation back into that first-century world. It will not do to reject the gospels because they do not read like a modern scholarly work. Chronology was less important than the moral lessons that might be learned from a great man. Details of events and circumstances mattered less than the exposition of character. We must also remember that central to the purpose of the four evangelists lay their theological perspective, which governed the content of their work. They selected, as every writer must, from a collection of material which might have been used, but the criteria they used were theological and evangelistic. 'Jesus did many other miraculous signs in the presence of his disciples, which are not recorded in this book. But these are written that you may believe that Jesus is the Christ, the Son of God, and that by believing you may have life in his name' (John 20:30–1). Far from that pointing to a biased presentation, based on pious fiction, it stresses the factuality of John's account and the reasonableness of his method. Here is evidence, pointing, in the end, to only one possible conclusion. The truth of the evidence is the driving-force of the argument. The evangelists, therefore, declare the gospel, without reservation or demur. Their material is ordered and carefully shaped, yet each one is distinctive in style and emphasis, so that together the four evangelists provide a portrait of Jesus of such depth and breadth as would have been impossible for a single author to produce.

The first three gospels are usually grouped together, since they contain a considerable body of common material. It has been calculated that 92 per cent of Mark is reproduced in Matthew. For this reason among others, Mark is usually considered to have been written first, probably from Rome in the early 60s AD, with Peter as its apostolic source. Matthew is much larger, and consequently includes a good deal of extra material, some of which is used also in Luke, though Luke also has a considerable amount that is unique to that gospel. John is usually thought to have been written after the synoptics, to provide different material and particularly a Jerusalem, rather than a Galilee, focus for the ministry of Jesus, so that much of its contents are unique to the fourth gospel. The comparison of the gospel accounts is an important exercise, not for the discovery of so-called discrepancies, which are anyway few in number and resolvable, but so that we can tune our ears to the distinctive emphasis of the gospel writer, in the portrait of Jesus which is being drawn. In *How to Read the Bible for All Its Worth* (1982, Scripture Union), Gordon Fee and Douglas Stuart describe this process as reading 'horizontally' across the pages of the New Testament, comparing gospel with gospel. This will alert us to the distinctiveness of each account. But then, in recognition that the Holy Spirit inspired four separate gospels and not one massive harmonisation, we must also read and think 'vertically', interpreting each unit as part of the larger structure of that particular gospel, understanding its contribution to the overall theological and evangelistic purposes of the author. Indeed, that should be our priority (op. cit. p. 110ff). With that in mind, we will briefly survey the major distinctives of the four accounts.

Mark

Mark, the shortest of the gospels, is a work of great vividness and movement. I like to think of it as the news-reel gospel, with the camera zooming in and out, the focus always shifting, the sound-bite assessment predominating. There are passages of more prolonged teaching and reflection, but Mark is action-packed. The first verse sets the agenda. 'The beginning of the gospel about Jesus Christ, the Son of God' (Mark 1:1). But the agenda is pursued in a gradual, revelatory way. Although it is all there 'up front' at the start – it's good news; it centres on a man who is both rescuer (Jesus) and Messiah (Christ); it's going to demonstrate to us that the very life of God is within him – nevertheless, the structure of the gospel is to build the evidence gradually to its climax on the lips of a Gentile centurion, 'Surely this man was the Son of God' (Mark 15:39). This is the conclusion to which the disciples have come in chapter 8, Peter's confession that Jesus is the Christ (8:29), providing something of a watershed in the gospel as a whole. The first half of the gospel explores the question, 'Who is this Jesus?', leading to the confession, 'He is the Messiah/Christ.' Immediately, the focus shifts and the question becomes 'What sort of Messiah is he?' or 'How will the Messiah carry out God's work?', leading to the recognition of the path of suffering leading to the cross, and only then on to the glory of the resurrection, a path which those who follow him are required to walk too. Each half of the gospel is introduced with a summary statement, in which the later ingredients are contained, waiting, as it were, to be unpacked.

'After John was put in prison, Jesus went into Galilee, proclaiming the good news of God. "The time has come," he said. "The kingdom of God is near. Repent and believe the good news!" ' (Mark 1:14–15). At a particular point in time and at a particular place on the face of the planet, the kingly rule of God breaks into human history. The 'good news', of which the whole book is the developed account (1:1), is a message that has a past. Already Mark has alerted us to the fulfilment of Isaiah's prophecy in the ministry of John the Baptist (1:2–8). The same prophet predicted Galilee as the focus of the Messiah's ministry (Isaiah 9:2) and summarised the message God had called him to deliver as 'Your God reigns' (Isaiah 40:10–11, 52:7). At last, the time of fulfilment has come. God's rule is presented in the person of God's ruler, Jesus, and his royal summons is to turn from sin and self to believe that Jesus is God's king and rescuer, to submit oneself to his authority and so to enter the kingdom of God. For where the king rules in people's lives, there is the kingdom of God on earth. Mark's continuing agenda until chapter 8 is to pile up the evidence of Jesus' kingly authority, and as he does so to keep nudging us with the question, 'Who is this man?' The early chapters are full of examples of his power and authority, which can only be accounted for in terms of the divine. He has authority over the forces of evil (1:25–8), over every sort of sickness and disease (1:29–34). He has the ability to forgive sins, a divine prerogative (2:1–12). He is lord of the Sabbath, a divine provision (2:23–8). He is master of the storm (4:35–41) and even the conqueror of death (5:35–43). And so a great debate develops concerning his identity (see 1:27, 4:41, 5:42, 6:56) to which various solutions are proposed. To the religious leaders, staggered by his claims, he is 'a blasphemer' (2:7), 'possessed by Beelzebub, the prince of demons' (3:22). To the people he is 'the carpenter . . . Mary's son'

(6:3), or perhaps 'John the Baptist . . . raised from the dead' (6:14), or Elijah (6:15), or 'a prophet, like one of the prophets of long ago' (6:15). Only twice is the right answer given, and on both occasions by evil spirits. 'I know who you are – the Holy One of God' (1:24). 'What do you want with me, Jesus, Son of the Most High God?' (5:7). For the disciples it is a long, slow road to understanding, but eventually they see enough to be able to confess that Jesus is the Christ (8:29).

'He then began to teach them that the Son of Man must suffer many things and be rejected by the elders, chief priests and teachers of the law, and that he must be killed and after three days rise again. He spoke plainly about this . . . "If anyone would come after me, he must deny himself and take up his cross and follow me" ' (8:31–4). Here is Mark's agenda for part two of his gospel, and it is equally startling. How will the Messiah accomplish God's great plan to rescue the human race? 'He *must* suffer.' What does it mean to be his disciple? 'He *must* deny himself and take up his cross.' Again, the disciples cannot understand it (9:32). They have been raised on the idea of Messiah as a triumphant king, ruling over the nations. How could a crucified Jesus fit with that picture? They were more interested in sitting with him in his glory, not drinking the cup of his suffering (10:35–40). Yet the shadow of the cross falls more deeply and with increasing inevitability over the pages of the gospel, with a persistent call to follow in his footsteps. 'All men will hate you because of me, but he who stands firm to the end will be saved' (13:13). That is how God's mighty plan is fulfilled and that is, effectively, how Mark's good news comes to its climax. At the death of Jesus, the temple curtain, which kept everyone out of the holiest place of all because of their sinfulness was torn down from top to bottom by the hand of God, as a demonstration that the way into relationship with a holy God is open to all the world, for those who repent and believe the good news. And in the very next verse, it is a Roman soldier, a pagan, who makes the first confession, 'Surely this man was the Son of God!' (15:37–9).

Matthew

By contrast, Matthew's focus is more distinctly Jewish. The beginning of his gospel establishes the genealogy of Jesus back through David to Abraham and sees him as the long-awaited fulfilment of God's covenant promises to those two great men (1:1). The wise men come to worship him, but as the one who is born 'king of the Jews' (2:2).

Incidentally, the appearance of Gentiles at the beginning of the gospel worshipping Jesus (2:11) and the commission of the risen Christ at the end of the gospel to 'make disciples of all nations' (28:19), together with many other references concerning Gentile inclusion in God's kingdom throughout the gospel, should prevent us from seeing too narrow or exclusive a Jewish focus in Matthew as a whole. This note of kingship strongly pervades Matthew's work. It is seen in his frequently used titles of Jesus as 'Son of God' and 'Son of David'. The former links with the kingly figure of the messianic psalms and the latter with the promised descendant of King David, whose throne will be eternal and whose kingdom will know no end. Through the crucifixion narrative, the phrase 'King of the Jews' runs like a motif.

Also derived from Matthew's Old Testament roots is the other dominant characteristic of Jesus as the Teacher, which features throughout the gospel. Isaiah had envisaged the Messianic age as a time when the Gentile nations would stream to Jerusalem to worship the LORD and be instructed by him. Those 'without the law' would now be brought within the sphere of this covenant blessing. 'He will teach us his ways, so that we may walk in his paths,' the Gentile nations say. 'The law will go out from Zion, the word of the LORD from Jerusalem' (Isaiah 2:3). Most commentators are agreed that Matthew has organised his gospel around five major blocks of teaching, which may be intended to be equivalent to the five pillars of the law in the books of the Old Testament Pentateuch. The units (chapters 5–7, 10, 13, 18 and 24–5) are each marked out with similar phraseology at the end, and clearly the first, which we call the Sermon on the Mount, is intended by its introduction to direct us back to God speaking to his people from the mountain at Sinai (5:1–2). In this teaching Jesus is summarising, defining and instructing a new covenant people, just as in his ministry he confronts the hypocrisy of the old religious order and gathers to himself a new 'remnant', who will become the building-blocks of the new Israel, including both Jews and Gentiles, who acknowledge Christ as king. I have dealt with this in detail in my survey of Matthew's gospel, *Taking Jesus Seriously* (1994, Christian Focus Publications). This also explains why Matthew contains so many references to the fulfilment of Old Testament Scriptures, in Christ. As suffering servant, as well as exalted king and conqueror, Jesus demonstrates himself to be the one who was to come. By his death he inaugurates a new covenant relationship and in effect institutes a new

Israel. It is Matthew's concern to provide Christ's teaching for the further expansion and development of that new covenant community.

Luke

Luke is himself a Gentile, a travelling companion of Paul and a medical doctor. His skilled observation and habits of detailed analysis are clearly evident in his two volumes, the gospel and the Acts of the Apostles. Of the three synoptics, Luke has the largest amount of material unique to him, and much of it indicates his essential interests. For Luke, Jesus is supremely the rescuer, or Saviour, the only hope of the lost world. Those of us who are Gentiles can especially appreciate that emphasis. As Paul reminds us in Ephesians 2:12, we were 'separate from Christ, excluded from citizenship in Israel and for-eigners to the covenants of the promise, without hope and without God in the world'. But Jesus has rescued pagans, who under the old covenant had no possible claim upon the grace and mercy of God, bringing us into his kingdom and adopting us into his family. It is not surprising, therefore, that Dr Luke is particularly interested in those from the outside who are brought into relationship with God, through Christ and the gospel. The note is sounded repeatedly from the opening chapter onwards (1:31, 47, 69, 71, 77) and finds its formal announcement in the message of the angel to the Bethlehem shepherds, 'I bring you good news of great joy that will be for all the people. Today in the town of David a Saviour has been born to you; he is Christ the Lord' (2:10–11). When Jesus begins his ministry in Luke 4:16–21, in the synagogue at Nazareth, he sets it firmly in the context of Isaiah's prophecy of rescue – good news for the poor, freedom for the prisoners, sight for the blind, release for the oppressed, the Lord's grace and favour (see Isaiah 61:1–2). 'Today,' says Jesus, 'this scripture is fulfilled in your hearing.' And just before his arrival at Jerusalem, with the inevitability of the cross ahead of him, at his last port of call, Jericho, it surfaces again as Jesus transforms the life of Zacchaeus, the tax-collector. 'Today salvation has come to this house, because this man, too, is a son of Abraham [i.e. an inheritor of the promise]. For the Son of Man came to seek and to save what was lost' (19:9–10).

Luke's focus is constantly on the lost whom Jesus is seeking and saving. What we discover is that they came from all the categories of life-style and strata of society which the pious religious Jews rejected. The clue is given as early as Mary's song (the Magnificat) in reflecting on the angel Gabriel's message that she is to be the mother of the Messiah. In celebrating the great things the Mighty One has done (and will do), she lists the upside-down nature of the kingdom which her baby will eventually inaugurate. 'He has scattered those who are proud in their inmost thoughts. He has brought down rulers from their thrones but has lifted up the humble. He has filled the hungry with good things but has sent the rich away empty' (1:51–3). In some ways, the gospel of Luke is a procession of fulfilment of that song. The shepherds are the first to receive the good news. Social rejects are found worshipping the king of heaven, but at a manger. Everything is being turned upside down. Many of Luke's notes and stories centre on the care and ministry of Jesus towards women, whom no rabbi would bother to teach. Mary herself, and later Anna, the prophetess, realise Christ's true identity at the very beginning (2:36–8). A sinful woman is forgiven and sent away in peace, as she shows her love for the rescuer by anointing his feet with perfume (7:36–50). At the home of the Bethany sisters, Mary sits at Jesus' feet listening to his word, while Martha is rebuked for not giving her attention to this one necessary thing (10:38–42). A crippled woman is healed on the Sabbath (13:10–13). Luke even lists the women who, with 'many others', played a supporting role financially in the ministry of Jesus and the apostles 'out of their own means' (8:1–3).

In 7:1–10, it is a Gentile centurion in Capernaum who is commended by Jesus, who is himself amazed at the man's faith. 'I tell you, I have not found such great faith even in Israel.' The outsiders are coming in; even Samaritans, the hated half-breed relics of the northern kingdom with whom the pure-bred Jews would have nothing to do. But it is Luke who records the parable of the Good Samaritan (10:25–37), who shows Jesus travelling through Samaria and rebuking his disciples' desire to call down fire from heaven to destroy them (9:51–6), and who tells the story of the healing of ten lepers, of whom only one returns to give thanks – 'and he was a Samaritan' (17:11–19). But perhaps the clearest focus of the theme is in Luke's fifteenth chapter with its famous three parables of the lost sheep, the lost coin and the lost son. The stories are told in response to a specific situation where Jesus is under fierce criticism from the Jewish religious leaders because as the tax-collectors and 'sinners' gathered round eager to hear his teaching, he not only welcomed them but actually ate with them (15:1–2). As the lost are sought and found, so those who think they are on the inside, because of their religious heritage or personal pedigree, are actually excluding themselves, by rejecting God's rescuer.

One other major theme of Luke is the power of the Word of God to do the work of God. At the start of the gospel, he describes Christians as 'servants of the word' (1:2), and at the end, Jesus commissions his disciples to be word-witnesses of all that they have seen and learned (24:48–9). But all the way through, it is the Word of God that accomplishes the will of God. Perhaps this emphasis was especially precious to Luke as it stressed the availability of the Word of God to those who had hitherto been without it. For him, the seed to be sown is always and only 'the word of God' (8:11) and it is only that seed, heard, retained and persevered in, with a noble and good heart, that can produce a crop, the harvest of eternal salvation (8:15, 21).

John

There is so much in John's gospel which is different from, and yet wonderfully complementary to, the portrait of Jesus painted for us by the synoptics. With a stronger background in Greek philosophy, yet combined with a profound understanding of the Old Testament, the apostle John presents us with a unique picture of the Lord Jesus. His famous prologue (1:1–14) in which Jesus is revealed as the *logos* made flesh, God's Word in human form, the incarnation of the mind and principle behind the whole universe, establishes from the beginning his deity and the fundamental unity between himself and the unseen 'Father'. John wants everyone to 'believe' (used over fifty times) and so 'see' this truth of who Jesus is, for he is the way to the Father, the key to knowing God and eternal life (John 14:6, 17:3). It is not seeing that leads to believing, for the post-apostolic disciple, but believing that leads to seeing. 'Blessed are those who have not seen and yet have believed,' Jesus tells Thomas (20:29), who should have believed the resurrection because of his fellow disciples' testimony, 'We have seen the Lord.'

As 'the Word made flesh', Jesus is naturally the subject of his own teaching. In a series of dialogues, first with individuals such as Nicodemus and the Samaritan woman, and then with the Jewish crowds and especially the religious leaders, Jesus constantly focuses attention on himself. This is centred on the seven 'I am' declarations and the seven signs of divine power with which they are interwoven.

168 • I BELIEVE IN THE BIBLE

Such revelation is always presented, however, in a context of challenge. Choices are to be made by every person, between faith and unbelief, and so between light and darkness, life and death. Again and again, the evidence is presented that Jesus is the revelation of the glory of God, the outshining in incarnated human life of the hidden inner nature and being of God. 'We have seen his glory,' John exclaims (1:14). Each of the miraculous signs demonstrates it. 'He thus revealed his glory, and the disciples put their faith in him' (2:11). His claims, using the Old Testament name of God ('I am') are all only explicable in terms of his deity. 'Anyone who has seen me has seen the Father' (14:9), he assures Philip. With the approach of the cross, the theme of God's glory revealed intensifies, and finds its locus in the 'lifting up' of Jesus to die. John's partiality for double meanings finds its full rein here as, in a number of references to the coming of 'the hour', we are led to understand that the glory of God will be seen in all its totality in the love of Christ's self-sacrifice, in the provision of atonement and mercy that flow from his broken body and poured-out blood. If, like Mark, we can divide John's gospel into two sections, we might express their content in this way. Chapters 1–12 concentrate on the revelation of the Word to the world, while 13–21 focus on his lifting-up (both as exalted king and as suffering servant) on the cross for the world. He is both the sacrificial lamb of God who bears away the world's sin (1:29) and the Good Shepherd-king whose love for his flock is seen in his voluntary laying down of his life for the sheep (10:11, 15, 17–18).

Jesus, the king

It will be clear that there are common, central themes running through all four gospels, in spite of their noted and valuable distinctives. Each of them places Christ at the centre of God's fulfilment of his long-promised blessings to all the world, through Abraham's seed. It was always true that the God of Israel was the universal sovereign, but now with the breaking in of the kingdom that is about to be fully demonstrated. The throne of David is occupied by the 'Son of Man' to whom is given authority, glory and sovereign power, over all people and nations, eternally and irrevocably. Jesus of Nazareth is that king. The old models of a renewed national Israel conquering the Gentiles are no longer valid. This king enters his city, not on a war-horse, but on a donkey, 'righteous and having salvation, gentle' and proclaiming peace to the nations, as Zechariah predicted (9:9–10), and as all the gospel writers record. For this kingdom is neither a geographical nor a political entity. Rather, it is a dynamic relationship, a covenant community, where each individual, submitting to the active rule of the king in mind and heart, finds forgiveness and peace through his atoning sacrifice, and newness of life in his resurrection. The kingdom, then, is present, here and now, but secretly. It is not recognised by many in this world, but wherever the king is ruling in an individual human life, there is the kingdom, 'within you' (Luke 17:21). And the kingdom is spreading, 'soul by soul and silently', as the good news is proclaimed through all the world and new believers are brought to see who Jesus is and to trust him. But the kingdom is 'not yet' experienced in the fulness which will be revealed, when the king personally returns to his world, in power and with great glory, to take this throne and set up his everlasting kingdom. That will be a day when the choices made, for or against him, will be finally revealed, a day of rejoicing like a great wedding banquet, but a day of judgment and exclusion too. It is the urgent, 'prophetic' appeal of the gospel writers to get ready for that day now, by repenting and believing the good news, and to enter into the present enjoyment of life with the king, even in this world.

Jesus, the teacher

We have investigated the great subject themes of the gospels, but we also need to give some thought to their literary styles and composition. In part, these are determined by the methods of Jesus' own ministry, which all the evangelists tell us was a blend of his wonderful words and his mighty acts. The teaching of Jesus took many different forms. Often he responded to questions or criticisms, enunciating key principles. He pronounced blessings and woes. Sometimes he taught by means of an extended dialogue, with either his disciples or his opponents. Frequently he used parables, especially with the crowds. The parables are among the most famous and popular of Jesus' teachings, because they are good stories, vividly recounted. Over the centuries, different interpretative methods have been applied to them. For a long time, they were seen as detailed allegories in which every ingredient had a hidden, symbolic meaning. The problem with that, as with all allegorical interpretation, is that ingenuity overcomes sense and meaning, until each exposition has a different gloss to put upon the story. In reaction, most modern interpreters have insisted that the story has one plain meaning and none of the details has symbolic significance. I remember being taught at school that a parable is 'an earthly story with a heavenly meaning'. That is probably sound advice in seeking to follow the main line through the story, but we should not ignore the vivid details which many parables contain, even though we do not deal with them allegorically. There are frequently nuances of understanding tucked into the details which reward careful investigation. Kenneth Bailey's works *Poet and Peasant* and *Through Peasant Eyes* (1983, Eerdman's) draw upon a lifetime of experience of living in Palestinian villages and are full of helpful allusions to deepen our understanding of the riches in the stories. While these things would have been obvious to Jesus' hearers, they are not to us in our culture, so that any help which enriches our understanding is to be valued. What we must not do is lose the vitality, colour and bite of the original story by reducing its 'lesson' to a piece of bland moralising or an abstract theological proposition. Parables are meant to surprise us, to stir us up to think, to challenge our preconceptions, and perhaps one of the most effective ways to make sure they are doing their work on us is to seek to re-express them in the cultural setting and dress of our own society.

Another key way in which Jesus taught was by what are sometimes called pronouncement stories, or what we might describe (less technically) as 'punch-lines'. An event occurs (such as a miracle) or a conversation is held in response to a question or criticism, or Jesus is in direct conflict with the religious authorities, but in each case the unit ends with a pay-off line, in which a key principle or important truth is expressed by Christ. This is usually related to the challenge his ministry brought to the complacency of traditional religion in his day. Further, it is important to realise that the miracle stories are used by the gospel writers as teaching tools. Their historicity is taken for granted, but their significance is the hard evidence they supply of Christ's divine power and nature, of which his own resurrection and ascension are the greatest example. However, they also reveal the quality of what he has come to achieve in his spiritual kingdom by demonstrating in the physical realm his sovereign authority and his compassionate grace. This does not mean that we are to 'spiritualise' the miracles in order to understand them. But we are to take encouragement, for example, from the fact that the Christ, who was able to open the eyes of a man born blind, is well able to give spiritual sight even to the most blind Pharisee, if only they were willing to admit their need (see John 9). Again, the punch-line makes the point. 'For judgment I have come into this world, so that the blind will see and those who see will become blind' (John 9:39).

Let us try to put these principles into practice by following a short sequence of events recorded in Luke, chapter 8.

'No-one lights a lamp and hides it in a jar or puts it under a bed. Instead, he puts it on a stand, so that those who come in can see the light. For there is nothing hidden that will not be disclosed, and nothing concealed that will not be known or brought out into the open. Therefore consider carefully how you listen. Whoever has will be given more; whoever does not have, even what he thinks he has will be taken from him.'

Now Jesus' mother and brothers came to see him, but they were not able to get near him because of the crowd. Someone told him, 'Your mother and brothers are standing outside, wanting to see you.' He replied, 'My mother and brothers are those who hear God's word and put it into practice.'

One day Jesus said to his disciples, 'Let's go over to the other side of the lake.' So they got into a boat and set out. As they sailed, he fell asleep. A squall came down on the lake, so that the boat was being swamped, and they were in great danger. The disciples went and woke him, saying, 'Master, Master, we're going to drown!' He got up and rebuked the wind and the raging waters; the storm subsided, and all was calm. 'Where is your faith?' he asked his disciples. In fear and amazement they asked one another, 'Who is this? He commands even the winds and the water, and they obey him.' (Luke 8:16–25)

The context (8:1–15) is that Jesus has just told what is usually called the parable of the sower, but might more accurately be the parable of the soils. He has explained its meaning to his disciples as indicating the various results of sowing the seed of God's Word. This parable comes at the end of a succession of events, in each of which the power of the simple word of Christ has been illustrated. At Jesus' word, Peter and his fishing companions let down their nets, after a fruitless night's work, and are so successful in the volume of fish they find that their nets begin to break and their boats start to sink (5:1–11). By a word, 'Be clean!' Jesus heals a leper (5:12–16). With a word, he forgives the sins of a paralysed man and then heals his body (5:17–26). By a word, 'Follow me!' Levi the tax-collector's life is transformed into discipleship (5:27–31). With a word a man's shrivelled hand is completely restored (6:10–11). A Roman centurion's servant is saved from death because of his master's faith in the power of Jesus' word. He did not even expect Jesus to come under his roof, but sent messengers to ask for the healing. 'Say the word and my servant will be healed,' and he was (7:1–10). With a word, Jesus can even raise the dead son of a widow woman in Nain, 'Young man, I say to you, get up!' (7:11–17). With such a growing confidence in the power of the word of God, it may well be that the disciples began to think nothing was beyond them, but Jesus wants them to be realists. On the one hand, he wants them to know that there is nothing deficient in the seed they are to sow. It can produce a yield a hundred times more than what was sown, far in excess of any yield a farmer might anticipate. But the seed will often be sown in hostile soils – hardened and compacted, rocky or infested with weeds. While some listen for a brief moment only, others believe for a while, and then fall away. Still others become diverted from Christ and the gospel by life's worries, riches and pleasures. The disciples are not to imagine that there is something wrong with the seed and start to look for an alternative message. It will always be that way. The challenge is to be good soil in oneself, and to keep sowing the good seed as widely as possible.

Our verses begin with the responsibility for disciples of diligent listening to Christ's word. 'Consider carefully *how* you listen' is the thrust of the first paragraph (vv. 16–18). Just as the purpose of a lamp is to give light to all, so the secret of the kingdom will not always be hidden; indeed, the disciples will be required to bring it out into the open and proclaim it far and wide. But the danger is that they themselves will not have received it as good soil. The implicit challenge to them is whether or not they are hearing, retaining and so producing a crop, or whether they are in fact losing that word, so that what they think they have turns out to have disappeared. One thinks of Judas Iscariot, who must have heard these words.

The next paragraph is concerned with a similar point (vv. 19–21). One might expect family loyalties to have first claim on Jesus' time and attention. His mother and brothers have made a special visit to see him, but instead of breaking off to talk with them, Jesus redefines what membership of his family actually involves. Those who are closest to him are those whose attitude to the heavenly Father is the same as his own. They are the ones who share with him the badge of membership of God's family, the only one that matters in eternity, and that is to 'hear God's word and put it into practice'. One can imagine that the disciples might well have been encouraged to see themselves in precisely that role. Had they not left everything to become his followers? But the danger is that unless that word is being retained and practised with perseverance, it will be lost, and so the third and last paragraph links it all together (vv. 22–5).

Jesus decides to show the disciples what sort of soil characterises their hearts by taking them out on the lake. Here we have a miracle story which is designed to strengthen the disciples' faith in the power of Christ's word. It is Jesus who initiates the trip and he seems to be the only one to fall asleep as they are crossing Lake Galilee. The sudden storm, not uncharacteristic of that lake, must have been of unusual ferocity for the experienced fishermen among the disciples to be afraid they were about to drown. Once awoken, Jesus first rebuked the wind and the waters. The immediacy of the total calm is testimony to the divine power of the creator at work, ruling over the natural forces of his world. But how does he do it? The answer is by his word. Shouldn't they have known it? This seems to be the point of his penetrating question, 'Where is your faith?' Do you have any? What are you putting it in? Here is a demonstration *in extremis* of the power of Christ's word to bring rescue from all the hostile forces beyond any sort of human control or even influence, totally and instantly. It is not a guarantee that his people will be 'air-lifted' out of all their difficulties, nor do we have to turn it into a glib spiritualised lesson, like the old song of my youth, 'With Christ in the vessel we can smile at the storm as we go sailing home!' The disciples did not smile at the storm. They thought they were about to drown. But they learned two lessons that day. First, that their hearts were not quite the unadulterated 'good soil' they seem to have taken them to be; but second, and much more important, that to put one's faith in the Word of God is to trust the most reliable and powerful authority in the cosmos. That is what it means to be 'good soil' and that is how they (and we) learn to put it into practice. As with the disciples, it is sometimes only in the most difficult and demanding circumstances of life that we really learn to believe in the Bible.

Acts and Revelation

Of the remaining twenty-three books of the Bible, twenty-one are letters and on these we must now focus, as the last of the biblical genres for us to examine. But first we must consider the two exceptions. The Acts of the Apostles is really the second volume of Dr Luke's gospel, and as such, much of what has been said about the gospel genre applies there as well. Although the apostolic ministry provides its contents, Luke is keen for his readers to understand what he describes as the continuation of 'all that Jesus began to do and to teach' (Acts 1:1). The spread of the gospel is the work of the risen Lord, carried out through his apostles. Luke's interest focuses, therefore, on the content of their message, with several of the early sermons carried in considerable detail, and then the impact of their mission, with the record of the founding of many churches in Asia Minor and Greece. Beginning in Jerusalem, the Church testifies to Jesus as Lord and Christ, spreading throughout Judea and Samaria, and on to the ends of the earth (Acts 1:8), so that at the conclusion of the book Paul is preaching the kingdom and teaching about the Lord Jesus Christ 'boldly and without hindrance', at the heart of the empire, in Rome (Acts 28:31).

The book of 'the revelation of Jesus Christ', with which the Bible ends, belongs to the genre of apocalyptic, which was discussed in Chapter 7. Its use of symbolism (the beasts with multiple heads and so on) would not seem as strange and unfamiliar to its original readers as it does to us. The opening paragraph spells out for us that it is also a 'testimony' or witness of Jesus Christ, a 'prophecy' interpreting God's sovereign rule of his world, in both the writer's present and throughout the future until the end of all things, and a 'letter' reminding us of its pastoral purpose which relates it to the historical setting of its recipients (1:2–4). The seven congregations specifically addressed, in chapters 2 and 3, were clearly undergoing many trials and suffering persecution for their testimony to Jesus as Lord. The interpretation of the book has produced shelves of volumes suggesting, at the two extremes, that it was exclusively a tract for that period of history (the end of the first century) or that its meaning will only be known by the generation on earth at the end of all things. Many commentators agree, however, that Revelation is built on a base of seven sevens, as follows: seven churches (1–3), seven seals (4:1 – 8:2), seven trumpets (8:3 – 11:18), seven visions (11:19 – 15:1), seven bowls

(15:2 – 18:24), seven last things (19:1 – 21:8) and the seventh day rest of the eternal sabbath (21:9–22). Some would see these sections as typical of successive stages of church history, though there is a considerable degree of subjectivity in such an approach. What is certain is that Revelation summarises the content of the Bible, as a whole. In a sense, it is an equal and opposite balance to the teaching of Genesis 1–11.

Throughout the book, the world continues its rebellion against God's rightful authority as creator and ruler. The heinousness of humanity's crimes against God and themselves inevitably generates God's righteous wrath and judgment of evil. But, in the midst of this maelstrom of human history, the book's 'revelation' is that heaven rules and that the throne of the universe is occupied by the lamb who was slain, now alive for evermore, that is Jesus Christ. It is to him that the future belongs, throughout time, and beyond, into eternity. His victory over all the hostile powers that may range themselves against him is total. What is revealed, then, is Jesus Christ reigning in unchallenged supremacy, a king of all kings and lord of all lords, with complete authority over all earthly rulers, power blocs, tyrants and ideologies, over the whole process of human history, and over the devil and all his agents. All of this reality, hidden at present, will be revealed in its totality when Jesus comes again, until which climactic conclusion of history, God's people must remain faithful and patient. They are to be committed to doing his will in every aspect of their lives, on a daily basis, as they wait for his purposes to be completed. The promises made to Abraham are now fulfilled in the numberless international community found around the throne of God, rejoicing in the salvation secured for them through the atoning sacrifice of Jesus, the lamb (see 5:9–12). As the book (and the Bible) ends, the people of God are found in the presence of God, under the rule of God, enjoying the restored relationship, which was lost in Eden, of unhindered fellowship and joy with their creator, who is now their redeemer. Is it any wonder that the Bible ends with a prayer, 'Come, Lord Jesus', and a promise, of his grace with his people until that great and glorious day (22:20–1)?

In the meantime, the great challenge to the churches, as to the individual believer, is to remain faithful in belief and behaviour, with the priorities Christ has taught us governing our lives in this world. 'Watch your life and doctrine closely,' Paul instructed his young colleague, Timothy (1 Timothy 4:16), and that crisp challenge could well provide an overall heading or summary of the purpose and contents of the New Testament epistles, or letters. Remarkably, thirteen of the twenty-one letters were written by the apostle Paul. Nine of these were to churches, and take their titles from their destination, the other four to individuals (Timothy twice, Titus and Philemon). Of the remaining eight letters, three are credited to John, two to Peter, one to James, one to Jude and the letter to the Hebrews is anonymous. The most obvious fact about the letters is that they arose to deal with questions, problems and potentially divisive issues in the churches to which they are addressed. They are not 'holiday postcard' communications, where the main reason for writing is to keep in touch, or reaffirm friendship. Although there is a personal ingredient in most of the letters, and in some a whole list of names of individuals who are to be 'greeted', much more serious purposes drive the author to put pen to paper. In interpreting these first-century letters for today, we need to keep this in mind and to do all we can to understand from within the letters themselves what was going on in the situation which provided the 'occasion' for the letter to be written. Here, as always in the Bible, a text which is not related to its context may degenerate into a pretext.

The letters of Paul

It is clear that this body of New Testament correspondence began during Paul's missionary journeys, in the earliest years of the 50s AD. A helpful way of dealing with the nine church-addressed letters is to see them in three groups of three, written over a period of a dozen or more years. The precise order is a matter of some dispute, but the three phases are fairly self-evident. The earliest letters are the two directed to the Thessalonians and the letter to the Galatians. These were churches founded by Paul's missionary endeavours, but already the target of false teachers. In Thessalonica, deceivers were claiming to have Paul's authority for saying 'that the day of the Lord has already come' (2 Thessalonians 2:2), while in Galatia the danger was of 'turning to a different gospel – which is really no gospel at all' (Galatians 1:6–7). As the letter develops it becomes clear that the infiltrators were Judaisers, who wanted to add the Jewish distinctives of circumcision and the ceremonial law to the gospel of salvation through faith in Christ alone. The letter expounds the nature of true

Christian freedom, received through faith in the crucified Christ and experienced through the powerful presence of the Holy Spirit in every individual believer. This raises an important interpretation point, which affects much of our understanding of the message of the epistles in our contemporary context. How do we move from the particularity of the problems addressed in the first-century world to bring the essential message of the teaching into our different cultural environment? After all, very few (if any) Christians are today under pressure from Jewish sources to be circumcised or to observe Jewish food laws or the ritual of the sacrifices and offerings.

Does that mean Galatians is irrelevant to the contemporary Church? Of course not. The precise clothing in which the problem appears will differ according to time and place, but the issue underneath remains a challenge to Christians in every generation, because it is based not in historical circumstances but in our sinful human nature. If we had to sum up the problem in Galatia, we might describe it as 'legalism', or 'the gospel plus . . .' The issue is that justification by God's grace alone, through faith in Christ's atoning sacrifice alone, is not sufficient ground for our acceptance with God, according to the legalist. Something else has to be added – extra beliefs, particular patterns of behaviour, unusual experiences – these are the things that will ensure you are really in the right with God. They will also ensure that you become a member of an élite club, more spiritual or more acceptable to God than the ordinary run-of-the-mill Christian, which Paul and the apostolic gospel seem to produce. The club may be marked by wealth and prosperity, super-spiritual experiences, keeping the letter of the law in the traditions of the elders or a whole range of additional ingredients to the New Testament gospel. They may sound extremely plausible and look very attractive. They will always prove very popular. But none of these are the criteria by which they should be assessed. That role belongs to the apostolic gospel alone. Anything which adds to Christ actually subtracts from him. He is no longer the fully sufficient rescuer and Lord. But not only is Christ dethroned by adherence to additional man-made rules and practices, the Christian who pays the club subscription is strait-jacketed by that commitment and ends up serving the new guru, rather than the risen Lord. That, of course, was precisely the reason the false teacher set up shop in the first place! So, far from being irrelevant, Galatians provides us with an indispensable tool by which to counteract legalism (a many-headed beast if ever there was one!) in all its attacks on the gospel of God's grace, without falling into the opposite error of libertarianism, or licence, on the other side of the narrow gospel pathway.

The middle group of letters, 1 and 2 Corinthians and Romans, come from the next phase of Paul's ministry. The church at Corinth, founded by his ministry, is facing a wide range of divisive issues. As a newly established church, in a city which was a by-word for its immorality and paganism, the Corinthian Christians were extremely vulnerable to teachers whose style and message presented a less radical challenge to their cultural habits than Paul's did. They wanted impressive speakers and leaders, inescapable demonstrations of spiritual power to 'out-glitz' the culture of their pagan city, for Christ. Paul's response is to regard them as 'mere infants in Christ', 'not yet ready for solid food' (1 Corinthians 3:1–2), their immaturity being evidenced by their obsession with the visibly impressive. As the correspondence proceeds, it becomes clear, especially in 2 Corinthians, that they have come under the spell of new teachers, pseudo or 'super-apostles', as Paul dubs them (2 Corinthians 12:11). But Paul wants to 'answer those who take pride in what is seen rather than what is in the heart' (2 Corinthians 5:12). His concern is with the heart, because that is the only guarantee that the gospel really is changing people's lives. Yet when he looks at the heart of the Corinthian church he finds gross immorality being tolerated (1 Corinthians 5), lawsuits between Christians (1 Corinthians 6), irregularities in marriage (1 Corinthians 7), improper behaviour in their meetings, divisions, excessive self-indulgence by some and deprivation of others (1 Corinthians 11). The most basic and essential of all Christian distinctives seems to be almost totally lacking from their corporate life – and that is love (1 Corinthians 13). And all this has happened because they are deserting the gospel of 'Jesus Christ and him crucified' (1 Corinthians 2:2) and his apostle, who demonstrates, in both his message and methods, the power of God made perfect in weakness (2 Corinthians 12:9).

That gospel becomes the great subject and theme of Paul's magisterial letter to the Romans, a church he had neither planted nor visited at the time. This is the nearest equivalent to a theological treatise in the whole of the body of Paul's letters and has been used by the Holy Spirit down the centuries to bring countless thousands to faith in Christ, and an assured discipleship. From its magnificent opening, the letter's one theme is the 'gospel of God . . . regarding his Son . . . Jesus Christ our Lord' (1:1–4). It is that message alone, promised in the Old Testament Scriptures, which now summons the Gentile nations, and so the whole world, to 'the obedience that comes from faith' which is the only way to 'belong to Jesus Christ' (1:5–6). Almost identical words are used at the very end of the letter, so that we are left in no doubt as to its contents and purpose. Paul ascribes glory to 'him who is able to establish you by my gospel, and the proclamation of Jesus Christ . . . now revealed and made known through the prophetic writings by the command of the eternal God, so that all nations might believe and obey him' (16:25–6).

Through the first eight chapters, Paul traces the story and development of God's great rescue-mission to the human race. In a masterly *tour de force*, he presents the whole human race, Gentiles and Jews, before God as guilty rebels, universally sinful and deserving nothing but his wrath and punishment (1:18 – 3:20). But into this scene of hopeless despair steps God himself to provide a 'righteousness from God . . . through faith in Jesus Christ to all who believe' (3:22). Paul explains how it can be possible for God to restore guilty sinners into a right relationship with their creator, through the work of the Lord Jesus (3:21 – 5:20). Chapters 6 to 8 deal with the realities of living as Christians with sinful natures in a fallen world, but rejoice in the provision to live differently in the present (although imperfectly) through the gift of the Holy Spirit and the expectation of transformation to perfection in the eternal kingdom, with its certain and complete salvation. Chapters 9 to 11 explore the relationship of the Jewish people to this gospel of their Messiah and to the Gentile churches it has produced. The remaining chapters (12 to 16) deal with the practical outworking of these gospel realities, in the offering of our whole selves 'as living sacrifices, holy and pleasing to God' (12:1) and in the loving and supportive relationships by which Christians authenticate the truth of the gospel's claims in the world and in the Church.

The final trio of Paul's church letters, Ephesians and Colossians (which are parallel letters in subject matter) together with Philippians, are usually dated to the early 60s AD and called the prison epistles. Each letter contains reference to Paul's imprisonment, for Christ and the gospel, yet his overall purpose is to keep the churches focused on the gospel and on their responsibility to live it and proclaim it faithfully. The Ephesian letter, which was probably circulated to several other churches in that city's hinterland, concentrates on the eternal plan of God 'to bring all things in heaven and on earth together under one head, even Christ' (1:10) and shows how the Church already is the prototype of that reality, in this world. Only the gospel could break down 'the dividing wall of hostility' between Jews and Gentiles, making a new unity out of the two, by reconciling both to God through the cross of Christ (2:14–16). For Christians living in Ephesus, in which all kinds of occult and magic practices thrived, it was of vital importance to know that no other power, however threatening, could have any authority over Christian believers who 'put on the full armour of God' in order to stand their ground (6:10–18). In the same way, Christians in Colosse need to continue to be rooted in Christ and not allow the alternative agenda of either legalism or licence to tempt them with a spurious claim of 'fulness', which they already genuinely had in Christ and in the faith they were taught (Colossians 2:6–10). For the Philippians, the challenge is to keep on 'holding on to the word of life' by 'holding it out' to others in a joyful, outgoing evangelism (Philippians 2:16). By this time the fires of persecution are beginning to be stoked, probably by Emperor Nero, and Paul is aware that he and his readers need not to retreat but to press on to know Christ better, with their eyes on the heavenly horizon, for only then will they be prepared to share in his sufferings (3:10–11). Similar themes surface in Paul's pastoral letters to Timothy (a pastor in Ephesus) and Titus (in Crete) as he urges them not to compromise the gospel or their faithful life-style of service to Christ whatever the cost may be.

Indeed, these concerns permeate the shorter and generally later letters at the end of the New Testament. Peter's focus is on the suffering congregations of Turkey, whose faith is being refined in the fires and who need neither to give up, nor to go low-profile, but to 'live such good lives among the pagans that . . . they may see your good deeds and glorify God' (1 Peter 2:12). John deals with churches from which there has been widespread apostasy, where the attacks of antichrist forces are already being experienced, and where the gospel values of light (truth) and love will be the only means by which they will be able to preserve themselves from idolatry. There is an urgency to these later letters, short though they are. As the generation of the apostles began to die, and the return of Christ had not yet occurred, it became clear that a church without the apostles was a coming reality.

That was why the written Scriptures had to be produced as an authoritative guide to apostolic teaching and practice, as derived from the Master himself. It also explains why the later letters are so full of urgent exhortation and application. The apostles' great twin concerns are to keep the churches faithful to the gospel (the truth, the whole truth and nothing but the truth) and active in propagating the gospel. The only way to hold on to the gospel is to give it away. Evangelism is always the way to a spiritually healthy church, but what is given away must be the pure gospel, and not a distortion by addition or subtraction, or any other corruption.

Finding the theme tune

In this brief survey, I have tried to indicate that the most important key to unlocking the huge relevance of the epistles for ourselves and our churches today is to find the theme tune, or what Dick Lucas has often called the 'melodic line' of each book. If we can travel back in time, through a really careful reading of the text, picking up the clues which it gives as to what was going on in the original situation, we shall begin to see how that same melody plays in our context. To quote Klein, Blomberg and Hubbard, 'Interpreters must reconstruct those original "occasions" and purposes as precisely as possible in order to separate timeless principles from situation-specific applications' (op. cit. p. 352). It is clear that the letters were largely written to churches and that their applications are often corporate. Paul expected the whole church to hear what he had written. 'I charge you before the Lord to have this letter read to all the brothers' (1 Thessalonians 5:27). The second person pronouns ('you', in English) are nearly always plural. Now, of course, it is true that the plural reality of a congregation is dependent on the individual Christians who comprise it and they all have individual responsibility for their choices, words and actions, just as they have an individual personal relationship with God to cultivate. But in our excessively individualised culture in the West, we can very easily lose, and then ignore, the corporate element of teaching and application which is built into the letters. When we read them, it is more like listening to a sermon, which will address both individuals and the congregation as a whole. It is the nearest we can come to sitting at the apostles' feet and hearing the teaching of Christ directly from them. It is worth remembering that the letters (like a sermon) were being prepared for the ear rather than the eye, and that the literary devices which are used are designed to aid the understanding and the memory. Repetition of phrases, patterns of words, specialist terminology, balanced sentence structures, debating with imaginary objectors, 'marker points' or 'book-ends' at the beginning and end of a specially important section using similar phraseology – all of these play their part in focusing the attention and driving home the point.

At one level, then, the New Testament epistles are much like any other letters of the Græco-Roman first-century world. They follow the commonly accepted structures, beginning with the author's name, the destination of the letter and a greeting. This often led on to an expression of good wishes for the well-being of the reader, which the apostles transform into a prayer and/or a thanksgiving for their readers' spiritual life and health. When this is absent (as in Galatians) it is highly significant, since it is a mark of Paul's urgency, expressing his distress and even anger at the current state of affairs. Where it is doubled (as in 1 Thessalonians) it is equally significant, though, of course, for the opposite reason. There then follows the main 'business' of the letter, laying out the arguments, together with evidences and proofs for the author's standpoint, and appealing with the reader to agree, to be convinced and to act accordingly. After this exhortation, there is often a closing summary of the main thrust before the farewell, which will frequently include greetings to other people known to both author and reader, and a closing wish, expressed as a prayer. But there are major differences in that the New Testament letters have a didactic authority implicit in their inspiration, which means that their teaching comprises a theology – a 'pattern of sound teaching' (2 Timothy 1:13), 'the faith that was once for all entrusted to the saints' (Jude v. 3). Therefore, our understanding will be greatly deepened by comparing Scripture with Scripture, by gathering together the major ideas and propositions, under a number of subject headings doctrinally, and by relating them to one another, identifying and describing a coherent theological position, which is systematic and biblical. This is why the epistles have become the major teaching materials of the Church and why so many theological issues turn on their exposition.

Now let's look at an example, to draw these principles together and work them out in practice.

It was necessary, then, for the copies of the heavenly things to be purified with these sacrifices, but the heavenly things themselves with better sacrifices than these. For Christ did not enter a man-made sanctuary that was only a copy of the true one; he entered heaven itself, now to appear for us in God's presence. Nor did he enter heaven to offer himself again and again, the way the high priest enters the Most Holy Place every year with blood that is not his own. Then Christ would have had to suffer many times since the creation of the world. But now he has appeared once for all at the end of the ages to do away with sin by the sacrifice of himself. Just as man is destined to die once, and after that to face judgment, so Christ was sacrificed once to take away the sins of many people; and he will appear a second time, not to bear sin, but to bring salvation to those who are waiting for him. (Hebrews 9:23–8)

First, we need to set this very rich paragraph within the historical context of the whole letter to the Hebrews. Its author is unknown, but as its title and contents make clear, it has Jewish Christians particularly in view, throughout what the writer describes, at the end, as 'my word of exhortation' . . . only a short letter' (13:22)! The letter is punctuated with a series of increasingly solemn warnings about the danger of 'drifting away' and ignoring 'such a great salvation' (2:1–3), hardening the heart through sin's deceitfulness and so falling short of God's promise of rest (3:7 – 4:11), 'falling away' and so 'crucifying the Son of God all over again' (6:4–12), 'trampling the Son of God underfoot', 'throwing away your confidence' and shrinking back to destruction (10:26–39). The 'occasion' is clear. These Hebrew Christians are being tempted to turn back to Judaism, probably because their Christian profession is exposing them to persecution. At first, the Roman empire was happy to regard Christianity as a variant of Judaism, a new sect within an established ethnic religion, such as was tolerated provided it was not politically subversive. But when the Jews became increasingly hostile towards the Christians, not least as a result of the mission to the Gentiles, the Roman authorities were alerted to the fact that this new belief did not sit comfortably under the umbrella of Judaism. It was in fact an illicit religion, and its creed 'Jesus is Lord' was exclusive, rather than pluralist. Its adherents would not declare 'Caesar is Lord' and so the wrath of the Roman machine was turned against the followers of the Way.

How tempting it would have been for Hebrew Christians quietly to drift back to their Judaism and to avoid all this trouble! Doubtless their families and friends were not slow to persuade them. They had already experienced public exposure to insult, persecution, prison and the confiscation of property (10:33–4). Why undergo any more? The letter sets out to answer that pressing question. In a nutshell, its argument is that such a retreat would be apostasy and that it would represent a movement from reality to shadow-land, from light to darkness. This is the argument which is coming to its climax in our passage. While the Jewish people claimed that they had received God's law spoken by angels (2:2), Christians know that God has spoken to us by his Son (1:2ff). While Judaism rightly took pride in the heroic grandeur of Moses and the priestly dignity of Aaron, they were but servants in God's house. Christ is the Son over the household (3:6) and the great high priest, not subject to an earthly temple and a mortal succession of priests, but eternally alive and active in the heavens (4:14), appointed by God as his eternal agent (5:10). While the temple with its sacrifices and the entrance of the high priest into the holy place, once a year, to atone for the sins of the people were marvellous pictures of God's grace, Christ has completed all they stood for and brought the reality of heaven to his people. 'This is an illustration for the present time, indicating that the gifts and sacrifices being offered were not able to clear the conscience of the worshipper. They are only a matter of food and drink and various ceremonial washings – external regulations applying until the time of the new order' (9:9–10). The new order, or covenant, is now explained, so that the readers see its amazing superiority to all that preceded it. This background is obviously essential for a proper understanding of the passage itself.

It is also essential to work at how the argument of the passage itself holds together. Verse 23 contains a contrast between the Old Testament sacrifices which served to purify the copies on earth of the heavenly realities and the heavenly things themselves. The blood of animals would serve for purification of the earthly copies in the tabernacle and temple, but they would be totally inapplicable to the sanctuary of heaven in which the divine majesty is enthroned. How could an earthly animal's blood possibly have any heavenly, eternal efficacy? The contrast continues in verse 24. The 'better' sacrifice can only be that of the Son of God, but it is so acceptable to God that Jesus, as the real and perfect high priest, has access into the very presence of God in heaven. Verses 25 and 26 present a further development of contrast, based on what we have just understood. This is between the high priest having to make atonement for the nation's sin year after year and Christ dealing with sins 'once for all at the end of the ages' (i.e. it is God's last major act in history before the end of everything). Furthermore, the high priest had to offer an animal's blood, but Christ sacrificed himself. In these two ways, his offering is immeasurably 'better'; in fact, the two bear no comparison. Verses 27 and 28 then present the final contrasts between man's one death leading to judgment and Christ's one death leading to salvation for those whose sins have been forgiven.

The method of contrast shows us then four ways in which Christ's sacrificial death, as both priest and offering, is immeasurably superior to ('better' than, in Hebrews vocabulary) all that went before in Jewish Old Testament belief and practice. Each of these constitutes another reason why it is impossible for any true Christian believer to countenance a return to Judaism, however personally demanding being a disciple of Christ may prove to be. To get the point of the passage it will be a help to list the points.

1 Christ has entered heaven itself to gain us access, not a shadow–land earthly tabernacle or temple.
2 Christ's sacrifice is sufficient and complete. Once for all, it never needs to be repeated, unlike the annual ritual of the Day of Atonement.
3 Christ offered his own blood, in his self-sacrificial death, not the blood of an animal, and so a full atonement is made.
4 Our death will lead to judgment, but Christ's death leads to salvation for those who belong to him.

There is, in addition, one last thread running through the passage, in the form of a verb, which occurs on three different occasions but binds the whole unit together. Each appearance is in a different tense, which enables us to see the spread of what is being taught, across past, present and future. The verb is 'to appear', and in each case Christ is the subject. In verse 26 'he has appeared' in the decisive once–for-all act of atonement on the cross, which was the very purpose of the incarnation. Having dealt with our sin by his sacrificial death, the risen Christ is able to be our trail–blazer into God's presence where he 'now appears' for us, as our intercessor and advocate (v. 24). Our acceptance with God depends on the certainty of sins forgiven through the finished work of Christ and his present session at the Father's right hand, where like the Israelite high priest he carries the names of his people on his hands and on his heart. That is what guarantees our future experience of this great salvation in its fulness. 'He will appear', not to deal with sin, which was the purpose of his first coming, culminating in the cross, but 'to bring salvation to those who are waiting for him' (v. 28). The qualification for receiving that full and final deliverance is that we live now, trusting in Christ's finished work on the cross and eagerly expecting the full experience of salvation, throughout eternity, in his presence. In the light of such realities, how could any true believer ever contemplate drifting away from such a great salvation? What could a return to the old system possibly offer?

The epistles of the New Testament provide an enormous reservoir of truth concerning Christ and his work for his people. They require careful reading, with attention to vocabulary and the way specialist terms are used within a particular letter, as well as an appreciation of how logical arguments build and the importance of connecting words, which relate ideas together, in parallel or contrast. It is always a good test to see whether we really understand the text's meaning by trying to express its ideas in vocabulary, images and metaphors of our own and relevant to our culture. The most important thing, as always, is to let the text speak, to encounter it with all its surprises and shocks, its questions and issues, and not to try to squeeze it into some preconceived theological grid, but to let it challenge and perhaps change our frameworks as we listen to God speak. It is to the question of the application of the Bible to our contemporary context that we must now turn in more detail.

To remind you

- The four gospels of the New Testament provide a rounded account not only of the life, death and resurrection of Jesus, but also of the reason why he came. They show us God's rescue-mission for humanity in action, each with its distinctive emphasis on particular aspects of the good news (pp. 160–8).
- Common to all the gospels is the conviction that Jesus is the long-awaited King, who will reign for ever, over everything (pp. 168–9).
- The teaching of Jesus explains the purpose and the meaning of his ministry. By a variety of approaches, he calls on his disciples to be

responsive and obedient hearers of his words, by putting them into practice (pp. 169–74).

- Of the rest of the New Testament, only two books are not letters. Acts tells the story of the spreading gospel, while Revelation generates faith in God's sovereign rule throughout history (pp. 174–6).

- Paul's letters represent the fullest theological understanding of the person and work of Christ and the impact of God's great salvation plan on the Church and the world (pp. 176–81).

- Interpreting the letters for today involves travelling back to the original purpose for their composition, and identifying the theme tunes which govern their contents (pp. 181–6).

Chapter 9

How Can I Hear God Speaking in the Bible?

As CHRISTINE SAT down to reflect on the past few months, she was amazed at the changes that had happened in her life. She smiled ruefully as she remembered how she'd bitten Alison's head off when she had come up to her, really politely (and incredibly nervously, as Christine now realised) and asked her to come to a mums' Bible study. It had seemed such a weird thing to do. She stirred her coffee, reflectively. And now, tonight, she and Dan were off to another couple's home to do just that together, in a group that had been really welcoming and non-judgmental. But it wasn't really the people – she had lots of good friends – it was that Book that had done it. She smiled again. The God behind the Book and in its pages might be a better way of explaining it. Through the Bible, God was changing their lives, and so much for the better. Of course, there was still a huge amount she didn't understand, but she'd come so far so quickly. It was such a relief to know that you didn't have to switch off your mind to be a Christian – quite the opposite, in fact. All that stuff she had trotted out about science disproving the Bible seemed so trivial now that she was understanding what the Bible actually said. And yet she had been so confident in what amounted to ignorance. She might never have opened a Bible, never have known about Jesus, never have found his forgiveness, peace and joy, never have seen how God intended marriages to work and how to bring the kids up positively in such a negative world, if Alison hadn't approached her at the school gate that afternoon. She glanced at the clock, swallowed her coffee and headed off to meet the kids. As she rushed out of the door, a thought crossed her mind. 'I wonder if Sarah down the road might be interested in a group to study the Bible . . .'

Matt couldn't believe where he was. The arch-atheist of his set, Mr Cool personified, he who could destroy a Christian at ten paces just by the curl of his lip, he, Matt, was standing at the front, in a students' Christian meeting, about to tell a roomful of fellow students how he had met God. But it was true, and he was so pleased about it! He told them about the guy who had 'forced' the John's gospel on him and told him that all he had to lose was his prejudice. That had really struck home to him. It was uncomfortably true. He really was totally prejudiced, not only against Christianity, but against anything else that didn't fit into his tidy little world, where he was king and everybody else was expected to bow down and worship. But it was that little book, John's gospel, which had got underneath his radar and exploded his cosy defence-systems. Actually, it was the person he had met in the book, who strode through its pages with such incredible authority yet blended with humility. His teaching was so obviously right and true. It was like a searchlight trained on to his life, exposing all his grubby compromise and petty self-seeking, penetrating even to the rats in the cellar, which he could still hardly bring himself to recognise were there. And yet he wasn't condemning or judgmental; there was such love and compassion in the way he dealt with people and put their fragmented lives back together again. He gave it to you straight, up-front, no nonsense. Heaven was a reality, so was hell. God is there; he is real and we're all going to meet him one day, but he's come in Jesus to meet us first, to offer us forgiveness and real freedom. Our part is to believe him, receive his rescue and follow his rule. Mind you, that wasn't an easy step. Matt had tried to find a way out for several days, but he knew that Jesus had 'cornered' him, with his truth and love, and he had to come home to God.

Andy and Julia had to admit that things were becoming clearer. When their relationship started to crack up, the last place they would have looked for help was the Bible. They knew nothing about it and they weren't religious types, anyway. But Julia's friend had given them one of those modern versions of the Bible which was surprisingly easy to read, and some help on which bits to look at to get started. What had surprised them was how much material there was about making relationships work. It was all in the context of marriage, of course, and that had made them think. Perhaps what was wrong was that they were really frightened of that sort of commitment. When they looked at the pattern of marriage and family life laid out in the Bible, it seemed to make a good deal of sense and, far from presenting them with a list of unwanted restrictions, it was quite liberating to see that what it advised actually matched in with their own deepest needs. But that was when they had hit the brick wall. How could anybody live that way? They had really tried, on and off anyway, but they just couldn't hack it. This unselfish love, putting your partner's needs above your own, building one another up – great when you're on the receiving end, but how would you ever be able to keep it going? Or want to?

Perhaps that was what Julia's friend had meant when she talked about the need for a 'heart transplant'. It sounded like one of those really weird phrases Christians use, but Andy and Julia were slowly coming to realise that some sort of change deep inside each of them was what was needed. If ever their relationship was going to be built on giving rather than getting, then somebody had to change. And they were rather beginning to suspect that only God could deal with something that big . . .

Getting to know God

In each of these scenarios, what is happening is a basic ingredient of every Christian's experience – people are coming to know God through his word, the Bible. The difference is between knowing about God and knowing him in a personal, relational way. Both sorts of knowing depend on the Bible. The first might be the substance of the religious studies syllabus at school. Different religions can be studied, their sacred texts, practices and rituals analysed and documented, what 'they believe' explained, without this content impacting the personal life of the student any more than a knowledge of the geography of Israel would. This is knowing about the world's religions and their 'gods', but in a clinical, detached and academic way. It can take you all the way to a research degree in theology. But knowing the God of the Bible as one's heavenly Father, living one's life in daily contact with him, experiencing his love and power, understanding his plans and purposes – that is knowledge of a different order altogether. Yet it is equally dependent on reading the Bible. As we noted in an earlier chapter, it is by the Word of God that the Spirit of God produces the people, or children, of God.

Everybody wants to know whether God has anything to say to us today. If he were to be advertised as giving a TV broadcast in the place of the nightly news, it is a fair guess that current record viewing figures would be shattered around the world. Even 'unbelievers' are curious. But very few people realise what is available through that familiar book, on sale in any bookstore, whenever it is opened and read seriously. The Bible is God speaking; what Scripture says, God says, and what he has said, he is still saying. Our problem is often with his method (a book that needs to be read, or listened to) or its content. But that does not invalidate the word God speaks, it simply deprives us of its benefits. Supposing a friend were to contact me about an urgent matter by leaving a message on my telephone answering machine, which I then choose not to listen to, because I say I haven't time. Does that invalidate my friend's communication? Of course not. I may ring him and berate him for not speaking to me, while all the time he has already spoken, but I have chosen to ignore it. That is not his fault, but mine. Yet that is precisely what so many of us do today, when we demand that if God exists he should address us personally, while all the time ignoring what he has already said in the Bible.

This is what is meant when Christians speak of the 'sufficiency' of Scripture. It does not imply that the answer to every question we might ask about life and the decisions we have to make is sitting there, waiting to be unearthed, in the pages of the Bible. It will not tell me whether to change my job this year, or next, or not at all. What it will tell me is how to do my work in a way that glorifies God and benefits others, and the sort of person I need to be whatever workplace I happen to be in. Similarly, it will not tell me whether to buy this house or that one, or to go on renting my present flat. What it will tell me is how Christians should use the material resources God has entrusted to them, as stewards in his world. It will warn me of the dangers of self-indulgent luxury and encourage me to use my home as a centre of God's love for my family, my neighbourhood and further afield. The reason the Bible works this way is that it has an agenda for personal change, deep in our characters and at the level of our motivation. That is where the real issues of life are and where we need to do business with God. But our agenda is usually for God to be changing our circumstances, not us. We tend to come to these issues with the presupposition that if our job was different, or if we lived in a different home or neighbourhood, we would be such excellent Christians. If only God would just arrange our circumstances the way we really want them, then we'd live for him, be fully committed to loving God and our neighbour. So wouldn't it be in God's interest just to tell us to do what we want to do, to legitimise that decision and take the weight of its responsibility for us?

It is not difficult to see why he doesn't play our games our way. We would remain hopelessly immature. The God who created us in his own image, to think and choose and love, is not going to short-cut the process by which we learn to think in line with his thoughts, which reflect his character, as revealed in his Word. He is not going to deprive us of the human dignity of making decisions, which use that knowledge and link it with the moral courage of doing what we believe to be right, as we choose how to live. When we submit to his authority, he doesn't turn us into zombies, programmed externally to carry out his plans, as though he was some bizarre inventor of robots. He puts his Word in our mind and heart (the biblical term means the control centre of the personality, where we make our decisions) and calls us to understand, trust and obey him. That is what the personal relationship at the centre of Christian experience means. God calls us to a life of faith and the object of that faith is himself, as he is infallibly revealed in the words that he has spoken. Our faith is that God is not deluding us, or playing games with us, when we give him our trust and try to obey him. It is a faith confirmed daily in the school of experience. It means that we do not have to read between the lines, or imagine that God may be giving us additional personal messages, without which we could not function as Christians. The Bible is God's sufficient Word, to bring us safely from earth to heaven, to guide every footstep of our life in this world and to tell us all that we need to know to enable us to trust him and obey him.

> His divine power has given us everything we need for life and godliness through our knowledge of him who called us by his own glory and goodness. Through these he has given us his very great and precious promises, so that through them you may participate in the divine nature and escape the corruption in the world caused by evil desires. (2 Peter 1:3–4)

Peter is convinced that in the 'divine power' and in the 'very great and precious promises' we have the total resources needed to know God, to live godly lives and to grow in holiness of character. The word translated 'power' is often used to describe the Holy Spirit, who is both the author and illuminator of Scripture, where the promises are to be found on every page. So in God's Word and through his Spirit, God has provided us with sufficient resources to be sufficient Christians in this world. There are many things we might like to know, but cannot. 'The secret things belong to the LORD our God, but the things revealed belong to us and to our children for ever, that we may follow all the words of this law' (Deuteronomy 29:29). The content God has revealed is totally sufficient to accomplish his purpose in our lives. Of course, God may use other secondary means to bring us into line with his will revealed in Scripture. He may 'speak' to us through a preacher, or a book, or a telephone call, or a group of friends who have been praying for us, or an unexpected contact, or an unlooked-for providence, or a sudden inspirational idea, or a subconscious memory. The list would be endless, if we tried to put one together, to adequately describe the variety of ways by which the living Spirit of God prompts and directs, checks and channels, rebukes and encourages God's children. But none of these means of God's grace needs to be written down and bound into the covers of the Bible, and all of them need to be checked and weighed against what is already written within those covers. All other communications, outside us or within, are necessarily subjective and fallible, but the sufficiency of Scripture is an expression of its unique authority and entire trustworthiness.

All Scripture is God-breathed and is useful for teaching, rebuking, correcting and training in righteousness, so that the man of God may be thoroughly equipped for every good work. (2 Tim 3:16–17)

Our next step is to realise that such sufficiency is only experienced by those who put into practice, in their lives, what they have understood from the biblical text. The proof of the pudding really is in the eating. The Bible itself is especially clear about this. Its purpose is always to promote action, never simply to provide knowledge. To know God is to love and obey him. This keynote is sounded loud and clear, as the people of Israel are about to enter the promised land. Summarising God's requirements, in the law, Moses concludes, 'Now what I am commanding you today is not too difficult for you or beyond your reach . . . No, the word is very near you; it is in your mouth and in your heart so that you may obey it' (Deuteronomy 30:11–14). Practical application is its purpose. At the other end of Israel's Old Testament pilgrimage, after they have returned from the Babylonian exile and completed the rebuilding of the temple and the walls of Jerusalem, the community itself was reconstructed by the reading of the law to all the people and its explanation by the Levites. 'They read from the Book of the Law of God, making it clear and giving the meaning so that the people could understand what was being read' (Nehemiah 8:8). As a result the whole community celebrated the Feast of Tabernacles, in obedience to what they heard, and re-dedicated themselves to God and to the covenant. Similarly, Jesus links the application of his word to the reality of a personal relationship with God. 'If anyone loves me, he will obey my teaching. My Father will love him, and we will come to him and make our home with him. He who does not love me will not obey my teaching. These words you hear are not my own; they belong to the Father who sent me' (John 14:23–4). By contrast, the greatest danger any Bible-hearer or Bible-reader can fall into is the hardening of the heart which comes by not acting on what has been understood. 'Today, if you hear his voice, do not harden your hearts', we are exhorted (Psalm 95:7–8). The reference is to Israel in the desert who saw God's deeds, such as providing water from the rock, and heard his words through Moses; but instead of trusting him, they tested and tried him. Their hearing was not combined with faith and so, through unbelief, they were unable to enter God's rest (see Hebrews 3:7 – 4:2).

Relating the Bible to our lives

Application, then, is all-important, but it depends upon a right understanding of the text first, and then the drawing of legitimate and appropriate lines from that context to our own. We have argued earlier that a biblical text has a fixed, intended meaning. Calling it a 'single' meaning can be misleading if it applies a reductionist approach to the limitless riches of God's word. But the text is not plastic; it cannot mean contradictory things. However, it may also have a wide variety of applications, built on that base. That is to say, the unchanging truth will have different significances to different readers. Sometimes these are cultural. Applying a particular text to life in a village in Papua New Guinea may produce a different significance from life in a Western mega-metropolis. Sometimes the differences are personal, to do with an individual's life situation, temperament or opportunities. The same meaning is applied in different ways. It is important to underline that this is not a charter for saying that the Bible means different things to different people. The text has one meaning, but the ways in which that meaning is worked out, in dependence on the illumination and enabling of the Holy Spirit, will be many and various.

What we need to discover are principles which can be used to keep us from making inappropriate or invalid applications. Otherwise, we may actually distort the meaning, which we originally rightly understood. This process properly begins with the general methods of interpreting the text we have already discussed and illustrated. As we set the text in its context, particularly the book of which it is a part, and see how its particular contents match with the book's theme tune, we begin to understand the purpose which the author had as its primary application. One of the key ways of hearing God speak through the Bible is to do our reading of Scripture with our antennae up, looking for the surprises, being prepared to ask questions. 'Why does he use *this* word? Why does he say it *that* way, and why at *this* point in the argument, or story?' It's especially helpful when we are stopped in our tracks and find ourselves recognising that we wouldn't have said it like that at all. All these investigative questions will find their answers within the larger textual context, including the overall purpose for it being written. Once we begin to see *why* the writer says what he says, in the way that he does, we shall begin to realise how the message gets under our twenty-first-century skin, as well. The more carefully we interpret the text in its context, the more likely we are to relate to its original applications, and the more likely we shall be able to recognise the common factors between the people being addressed and ourselves.

Let's take a short example from the teaching of Jesus on prayer in the Sermon on the Mount.

And when you pray, do not be like the hypocrites, for they love to pray standing in the synagogues and on the street corners to be seen by men. I tell you the truth, they have received their reward in full. But when you pray, go into your room, close the door and pray to your Father, who is unseen. Then your Father, who sees what is done in secret, will reward you. And when you pray, do not keep on babbling like pagans, for they think they will be heard because of their many words. (Matthew 6:5–7).

How does this apply to us? Obviously, the need for us to pray and to do so in a way that is acceptable to God is a common factor between the original hearers and ourselves. So it would be easy to see this simply as a straightforward teaching passage, which it clearly is, saying that the secrecy and sincerity of prayer are what matters most to God. That is fine, but it's not the whole story. After a while, simply to read the Bible 'on the flat' in that way will make it all rather predictable and even boring. Ask the bigger questions before you apply it. To whom does Jesus say this, and why? The sermon is directed to disciples (5:1–2), though doubtless many in the crowds listened in, too. But as we saw in our survey of Matthew, Jesus is gathering a new Israel, a new community of covenant people, and this is the manifesto of his kingdom, the statement of its citizens' life-style. Its cutting edge shows how following Jesus turns upside-down conventional ideas of religiosity, the exponents of which Jesus calls 'hypocrites' (6:5) and 'pagans' (6:7). This is not just information. The disciples would be perfectly familiar with the ostentatious prayers of the religious leaders and the mindless mantras of pagan religion. The one they might have admired; the other they would scorn. But they would not want to be called by either title. However, the direct instruction of verse 6 implies that they (and we) might very easily fall into either category. As soon as our confidence is removed from a child-like dependence on our heavenly Father, prayer will become either a point-scoring exercise of hypocrisy or a psychologically engineered exercise in self-persuasion. When we see that our hearts are by nature hypocritical and pagan, we begin to realise that the external form and practice of prayer means nothing unless it is accompanied by a right relationship with God, and that is the purpose of Jesus' sermon. The motivation to change comes from hearing Jesus describe my self-regarding religious formalism as hypocritical and pagan. That is a salutary shock to the system.

In the example we have just looked at, the transfer from the text's context to our own is not very difficult to make. We may not attend synagogues, and street-corner prayer is hardly in fashion, but prayer in public where our concern is more on the evaluation of its verbal quality by others than its honesty before God is a constant threat to our Christian meetings. Nor is it difficult to see that the strongest line of application will always be found by asking the question, 'What is God teaching us about God in this text?' As we have underlined already, that is why the Bible does not have to be made relevant.

Nothing matters more than that we should read, mark, learn and inwardly digest all that God is willing to reveal of his unchanging nature and his eternal purposes, in every part of Scripture. Nothing can be more relevant to every part of our human experience.

Diagnostic questions

But there are also other general questions which help us to draw valid lines of application from the Bible to ourselves. For example, 'What aspects of unchanging human nature do we find explained or illustrated by this passage?' Because God's rescue plan through Christ is clearly demonstrated in the Bible to be his last word to humankind before the end of all things, it can be reasonably assumed that we shall not see the effects of the fall reversed in human nature, this side of heaven. The gospel is going to be needed throughout human history, in each generation, and there is no alternative. If we take away the particular cultural clothing in which the individuals appear in their biblical context, what are the common human factors beneath, which we share with them? It is easy for us to sit in judgment on the Pharisees, in the gospels, for example, since we know they are the villains of the piece, but that would not have been at all evident in Jesus' day, when they were widely respected for their outward piety and their reverence for the Torah. It is only when I stop detaching myself from them and begin to identify the Pharisaical characteristics lurking in my own heart that the application of the gospel passages really start to bite and challenge, as they should.

Another application question would be, 'What can we learn from this passage about covenant people in their relationship with God?' This is one of the great values of the stories of Old Testament heroes. Chapter 1 of the book of Daniel tells the story of the Babylonians' siege of Jerusalem (597 BC) and the exile of the young Jewish élite to Babylon, of whom Daniel was one. Given Babylonian names and trained in the royal palace (equivalent to a top university education), Daniel and his friends are expected to assimilate to Babylonian culture and religion. This they refuse to do; yet at the end of the training period, they come out top of this intake. One of their 'rebellious' acts was to refuse the royal food and wine, and to request only vegetables to eat and water to drink. So is this a text to teach the values of vegetarianism and abstinence from alcohol? It might well be argued so and devotees of both today might well provide corroborative medical evidence, but there is no hint of that in the text. Daniel and his friends are not successful because of their diet. Their diet is an expression of their faith in their God. Three young men are in covenant relationship with the true and living God, and they want to prove to the pagan court that his power and ability are vastly superior to anything the wealth of Babylon, or its false idols, can be said to produce. The passage is not about diet but about God, and it all revolves around three statements about God and his covenant faithfulness, which leads us to its application. 'The Lord delivered Jehoiakim king of Judah into [Nebuchadnezzar's] hand' (Daniel 1:2) – the circumstances are entirely God's doing. 'Now God had caused the official to show favour and sympathy to Daniel' (v. 9) – he rules in the lives of those who do not even acknowledge him. 'To these four young men God gave knowledge and understanding of all kinds' (v. 17) – he honours covenant people who commit themselves to his faithful sovereignty. These are applications which we can immediately relate to our life in a world which is still opposed to God's rule, puts its confidence in its own idols and often wants to squeeze God's people into its mould. This process is what the American scholar, Walter Kaiser, calls 'principlization' in his stimulating book *Towards An Exegetical Theology* (1981, Baker Books, pp. 206ff). It can be expressed in terms of the question, 'What timeless principles does the author intend to stress?'

The most difficult parts of the Bible to apply tend to be the moral or spiritual exhortations of the New Testament, where it may be difficult to separate out the timeless truth from the specific cultural example. I well remember as a young minister having to deal with a middle-aged single gentleman who, a week or two after he arrived at our church, placed himself at the entrance door and planted a kiss on the cheek of any unaccompanied ladies of his own age or (particularly!) younger. This, we were told, was obedience to 1 Thessalonians 5:26, 'Greet all the brothers with a holy kiss.' Though one might have pointed out that the 'brothers' were conspicuously *not* those he was greeting, the wind was taken out of his sails when he protested that he meant nothing by doing it. The obvious retort was, 'Well, then, don't do it!' One modern British paraphrase renders the verse, 'A hearty handshake all round,' which is certainly safer and a more appropriate application of the principle, in a different cultural setting, even if it is somewhat redolent of the 'stiff upper lip' approach to life. As a rule, and it covers the great majority of New Testament cases, where the life situation or cultural context is directly parallel, or equally understandable, to our own culture, then the principle taught by the passage transcends the historical differences and needs to be translated straight across to our context. In debatable situations, we need to work from the foundation truths of the gospel outward to their ethical application and to consider whether other New Testament passages or similar issues help us to distinguish between the absolute principle and the culturally related application. There will always be applications about which equally sincere and biblically centred Christians disagree, and these can vary from generation to generation. Slavery was once such an issue, as were (and often still are) alcohol consumption, Sunday observance and tithing, to name but a few. In such situations, Christians should humbly understand and listen to one another's convictions and their biblical underpinning, recognising that after all is said and done they may need to 'agree to differ' on the application of these texts. There are larger issues at stake than everyone dotting their 'i's and crossing their 't's identically, where cultural factors are at work in application.

That is the burden of Romans 14, where Paul discusses two controversial issues of application in the early Church – should a person be a meat-eater or a vegetarian? (v. 2), and is one day more sacred than another, or is every day alike? (v. 5). Differences like this may be characterised as weaknesses and immaturity, but Paul's teaching is not to judge one's fellow Christian or look down on him because of such issues (v. 10). God is the only qualified judge (v. 11). Our responsibility is not to put any stumbling-block in a brother's pathway (v. 13), not to distress one another, but to act in love (v. 15). 'For the kingdom of God is not a matter of eating and drinking, but of righteousness, peace and joy in the Holy Spirit . . . Let us therefore make every effort to do what leads to peace and to mutual edification' (vv. 17, 19). The old motto, 'In all things charity', is one that needs to be followed when Christians disagree about their application of the Bible, and it can be, without any diminution of conviction. Remembering Jesus' warning that it is easier to concentrate on the speck of sawdust in one's brother's eye and miss the plank in one's own (Matthew 7:3–5), it is a wise position to be less dogmatic about disputed matters, and to cultivate a predisposition to question more vigorously one's own position when others disagree. That is especially the case when one's own reading blends in rather too readily with the prevailing cultural climate of one's own times. The Bible will always be at variance with the cultural norms of any generation, and we need to be especially vigilant not to nullify its counter-culturism by adapting its teaching to contemporary 'correctness', whether political, ethical or social. As soon as we start to argue that the Church had got this wrong until our generation appeared, all the warning lights should start to flash. It is highly unlikely that views which have been uniformly held as biblical and therefore binding on Christians down the centuries will now suddenly be revealed to be grounded in false exegesis or an unreliable text. It is much more likely that we find the application of Scripture too challenging for our own comfort and decide to soft-pedal, or even deny it, in the foolishly mistaken idea that it will somehow make the gospel more acceptable in the current climate. In over a century of such capitulation, it has never worked and it never will. The more the Bible challenges the ethical and cultural norms of a rebellious world, the more likely it is that we are encountering God's timeless truth, which demands not fashionable 'fudging', or cultural 'kow-towing', but radical obedience.

This is arguably the greatest challenge which the Christian Church faces as we enter the third millennium. Just as when the apostolic generation was dying out, the issue was whether it would be authentic, apostolic Christianity which their successors would hold on to and propagate, or a more dilute synthesis with the prevailing culture, so the challenge is for us to bring the Bible back to the churches and the churches back to the Bible. 'Do not conform any longer to the pattern of this world, but be transformed by the renewing of your mind', Paul exhorted his Roman readers (Romans 12:2a). The pressure of the culture around us will always squeeze us into its way of thinking, unless there is a daily counter-cultural pressure, illuminating and directing our thinking and behaviour. That power, or ability, is provided for the Christian by the Holy Spirit living within us, the life of God planted in the personalities of ordinary men and women, such as we are. But the channel which the Spirit has chosen and by which our minds are renewed is the Bible. If as individual Christians, and as churches, the Word of God is not constantly renewing our thinking, in a culture like ours, where the voices of the media, of commerce and of consumerism are so insistent and pervasive, we shall not stand the slightest chance of resisting being sucked into their vortex. Our 'Christianity' will become a thin veneer covering an idolatrous society, where the price of acceptance will be compromise to the prevailing norms, a 'dumbing down' of all that is biblically distinctive. That is why I so passionately 'believe in the Bible'. The practical issue is how we can ensure that our thinking is responsive to biblical teaching, on a daily basis and at every level of our lives. 'Then you will be able to test and approve what God's will is – his good, pleasing and perfect will' (Romans 12:2b).

Methods of Bible study

There are at least four ways in which most of us can ensure an increasing intake of healthy biblical truth in our everyday lives. They are a personal Bible study programme, reading the Bible with one other person, group Bible studies and listening to expository biblical preaching. First of all, it is helpful to settle on one translation of the Bible and to get to know it well, since the memorisation of key Bible verses is a very helpful practice and it is difficult to achieve across different translations. Probably the most widely used English translation today is the New International Version, which is published in a variety of editions, many with study guides and helps. Other popular translations are the New Revised Standard Version, the Good News Bible (with a simple vocabulary) and the King James (Authorised) Version of 1611, also available in an updated form. Each translation will have its pros and cons, since it is a translation, but accuracy and accessibility of language are criteria of great importance. In English, we have so many translations available that the choice can be bewildering. It is helpful to know that the spectrum of translations ranges from the literal, where sentence structures are as close to the original as possible and the translation is largely word for word, to the paraphrase, where contemporary language and thought forms are used to convey as accurately as possible the biblical ideas. At the literal end is the King James or Authorised Version and its Revised Version of the 1880s (especially valuable for a literal translation of Old Testament narrative and poetry), together with the New American Standard Bible. Moving across from the New Revised Standard Version, through the New International Version, to the New English Bible and the Jerusalem Bible (both about the middle point), the Good News Bible is the bridge towards the more free paraphrase approach, exemplified by J. B. Philips, the recently published *The Message* by Eugene Peterson, and the Living Bible. Every individual reader will have his or her own favourite version, and it is certainly worthwhile having more than one translation available for comparison and clarification. But for serious study purposes it is important to work with the more literal end of the spectrum so that we can be as close to the original as is possible in a translation.

Personal daily Bible reading is an essential ingredient of the healthy Christian life. Before the invention of printing and the widespread and comparatively cheap availability of books, this was impossible. But even then the rabbis (scribes and teachers of the law) would hold daily teaching sessions, and the office of the oral teacher was always of key significance in the Church, too. It has always been recognised that hearing God speak through his Word, to understand, learn and obey, is essential for a Christian's well-being. The irony is that in our generation, when we have more readily available Bible study aids, printed and visual, than at any other time in history, the practice of daily Bible reading is declining among Christian people. For many decades organisations such as Scripture Union, the Bible Reading Fellowship and the Crusade for World Revival have published daily notes, expounding and applying passages of the Bible, working through whole books consecutively, and systematically covering the whole Bible over a period of years. While it is possible to accept the pre-digested thoughts of others about the Bible and to end up reading the notes rather than the Scriptures, these programmes nevertheless have enormous value and ought to be more widely used. There used to be a popular phrase among Christians – 'No Bible, no breakfast'. But as I see all the advertisements for nutritious chewy bars to provide us with break-fast 'on the hoof', I realise that the demise of the British breakfast and the daily morning Bible reading have the same root cause. Life is too pressurised; we are too busy. It can't be fitted in.

There are two remedies for this. The first is to recognise that we all do, in fact, make time for the things we consider to be most important and the things we most enjoy. We are driven by the twin priorities of profit and pleasure. If we are convinced of the necessity of listening to God on a daily basis, then other things need to be fitted in around that. We shall need to plan the time into our routines, on a daily basis. While there is clearly great value in starting the day with God, for many another period of time is more productive, say in the middle of the day, or immediately after work. But the more one's appetite for the Bible grows, the less satisfying the 'quick snack' approach becomes. It needs therefore to be augmented with a longer period of personal Bible study, probably in a weekly schedule.

Our second remedy, then, is to make quality time for the luxury of some in-depth Bible study, understanding, applying and meditating on a book of the Bible. Set aside an hour a week, perhaps at the weekend, to soak yourself in God's Word, and see what a difference it will make. Persuade your spouse to take over the children, the phone, the dog or whatever for a whole hour, and give yourself in that time to listening to God. I would recommend that you choose a book of the Bible to work on over a period of weeks. Don't be too ambitious to start with. It is probably best to start with one of the shorter New Testament letters, such as Philippians, or 1 Peter, or 1 John. Perhaps the best Bible study aid you can acquire is a notebook in which to record your observations, what you have learned and how you are going to apply it to your life. Begin by reading the whole book through, carefully and attentively, two or three times, perhaps using a couple of translations. Try to get the big picture clear in your mind. What is it all about? What messages does the writer want most persistently and urgently to get across? What words or themes recur? What issues does he address? Then take the book, section by section, and work out what the heart of each paragraph is. What is being taught? Why does it matter? What are the surprises? Jot down your thoughts. Then take some time to reflect on its impact on your own life – personally, in the family or with friends, in the work place, in the church, in society at large. How ought your thinking to change, as a result? What actions do you need to take? How are you going to pursue with God the project of working what you have discovered into the fabric of your living this week? Write it down and pray it in. It is especially important to move from theory to practice, from knowledge to experience, so don't be afraid to be very practical in your resolves and in your prayer, for, as Jesus said, 'Apart from me you can do nothing' (John 15:5). The following little rhyme, which I learned as a child, has been a great stand-by all my adult life in studying the Bible, especially when I have felt spiritually dry and lethargic, as we all do from time to time. It can be applied to any passage of the Bible, and you will discover an answer to at least one of its questions, to get you started.

What have I learned about Jesus and God?
What have I learned to cause shame?

What have I learned about following good?
Is there a promise to claim?

Try it and see!

Another helpful method of Bible study is to read regularly with one other person. For many people newly starting out on the Christian life, this is the most helpful and positive way to get into the Bible, but every Christian can benefit from it, throughout life. There has to be commitment on both sides, since regularity is a key ingredient to its success. A more experienced Bible student may help a newcomer to the benefit of both, since the understanding and application of the text is the purpose of the exercise. A couple may do it together, or two colleagues at work. Sometimes a threesome can work well. The aim is to follow the sort of pattern I have outlined above, but with the added advantage of input from someone else. This will help to prevent an individual from being blinkered, or becoming 'rutted' in their study. It also provides accountability, not only for the study time itself, but also for the practical outworking of what has been learned and resolved, and fellowship and prayer to see it accomplished. It is probably best to commit to this style of Bible study on a fixed-term informal 'contract'. Agree to meet weekly for a month or two, or to complete the study of a particular book. Many people have found such arrangements developing into years and many different biblical books, which can be very valuable, but variety is also important, and no one should see such an arrangement as a life-sentence!

House groups

Studying the Bible in a group is an extension of the principle, which has become extremely popular in the last thirty years or so as many churches have inaugurated house groups or other types of small group ministry. In this type of study, everything depends upon competent leadership, which facilitates the growth in understanding of every group member. The yields can be very high in such a group, but it has to be admitted that for many the disappointments can be equivalently great. For, in this context, we are simply not dealing with the Bible but with the social phenomenon of group dynamics. Groups can be hijacked to the personal agendas of the most dominant member. They can develop a negative spirit of corrosive criticism. They can wallow in the quicksands of relativism, so that the Bible becomes a slippery, indeterminate collection of religious ideas, rather than the Word of God. The answer to all these, and the other problems which frequently beset house groups, is to have a clear, agreed agenda of the group's (united) purposes, combined with leadership which is well prepared and firm in moving the group to achieve its goals. Exegeting a Bible passage in a group where no one is adequately prepared is always a nightmare. So golden rule number one is, 'Don't let it happen!' Those who come to the group should agree that they will at least read through and consider the Bible passage before they attend the meeting. That means there needs to be a syllabus for the sequence of studies so that everybody knows which verses will be under consideration.

Groups should also contract together that they will use only one translation for their discussion. Many become bogged down in a meaningless comparison of English translations – meaningless because no one is competent enough in the original languages to be able to make a judgment, and so eventually agreement is reached (or not!) on 'what I like to think', or 'what appeals most to me'. In such a situation, 'I' have just usurped the Bible's authority. Nor should the group become a preaching session for the leader, or an opportunity for the display of biblical knowledge by the most experienced, or vocal, members. The aim of the group is to help one another to the intended meaning of the biblical text, and then to its varied applications in the particular contexts represented by the lives of the group members. Experience has shown that the most productive route to achieving these ends is the question method leading to open discussion and consolidation in agreement. In this, the leader's role is critical, and it has to be carried out in two different parts. The first is personal preparation, in which the leader works hard to understand the text so as to be able to facilitate the group's discovery of its meaning for themselves. The second is when the group meets and the fruit of this study guides the discussion, under the leader's chairmanship. A profitable Bible study occurs when these two ingredients come together and the group leaves understanding the passage and motivated to put it into action.

For the leader's preparation there are many aids. Various publishers produce outline materials suitable for group study and often with suggested questions to move the discussion to the heart of the matter. Outstanding among these is the growing collection from an Australian publisher, St Matthias Press. But no aid can be a substitute for time spent by the leader in careful, prayerful study of the Bible passage. A worthwhile group study cannot be prepared, on the back stroke, in a quarter of an hour snatched between supper and the members' arrival, by 'mugging up' somebody else's questions from a pre-packed outline. All such 'leadership' achieves is a progressive devaluation of the currency, with people drifting away often disillusioned with the Bible (they imagine) when their disillusionment is actually with the leader. Asking lots of good questions is the key to successful preparation. What does this passage say? Why was it written? Why does it occur here – in the book and in the Bible? Why are these particular words used? These 'what' and 'why' questions are an essential discipline for proper Bible study, at every level. The leader will be tempted to rush on to the application stage, as will the group when it meets, but thorough understanding is the only sure guard against misleading application. Only when the meaning is clear and can be expressed in the leader's own words should the application be considered, paying attention first to how the passage applies itself, and, second, considering how its principles relate to us today.

At this point, the leader is half-prepared. The meaning of the passage and some of its applications have become clear so that the overall content of the group's study is decided. This is not, of course, an arbitrary decision of the leader which is being imposed upon the group. It springs from the contents of the text and a right understanding of its meaning and significance. The leader is not deciding what to have the discussion about. The text has already decided that. But the leader is responsible for guiding the group towards the goal, and so careful thought must be given to the questions which will be most helpful in achieving that. It is best to divide the passage into sections and to prepare questions on each. Usually, these will be factual to begin with, simply encouraging the group members to take the text in and to recognise its contents. They need to be interestingly phrased and not to invite wooden answers, which are either monosyllabic or just involve reading the text back to the leader. From this basic comprehension, in which difficult vocabulary or technical terms will need to be explained, the group can be moved on to the meat of the study, discovering the meaning of the passage. This is where the 'how' and 'why' questions come into their own. They need not to be too complex, but to mirror the step-by-step process through which the leader came to understand the meaning, so that the group can share that experience. Of course, the leader needs to be creative enough not to insist that everyone follows along in his footsteps, and expansive enough to take a whole variety of suggested answers, value and sift them, but only to follow those which keep the group on the main road to understanding. Lastly, with the meaning established, the 'so what about us?' questions of application can be asked. They may be rather general at first, but as the group get to know one another better the discussion will become more personal and the degree of support and empathy among them will deepen. The leader also needs to think hard about the questions the group may want to ask, and be as ready as possible to field them. All the time, in the questions that are planned and throughout the discussion, the movement must be into the Bible text and what it is actually saying, not away from it, either into other passages which may be easier to understand, or into mere speculation.

The spin-off benefits of well-run groups are numerous. They become a focus for fellowship, support and mutual prayer. They can develop particular evangelistic and service projects within the community and perhaps support work further afield in international missions and relief schemes. But it is the quality of the Bible input which will largely determine the effectiveness of the group's existence. It is especially in the area of application that such groups are strong, because of the life-experience of their members. When I was minister of a city-centre congregation, which had over forty groups meeting regularly all over the city, I remember that some of the most effective study series we ran linked the mid-week group meeting with the Sunday preaching/teaching programme. It was my custom to preach my way through whole books of the Bible on a systematic, consecutive, expository basis, but in a single sermon and with a large congregation representing a wide cross-section of the city's population, as well as all age groups, it was always difficult to do more than sketch in the outlines of how we might apply the text to our lives. From time to time, however, we synchronised house groups with the teaching programme and invited members to reconsider the passage which had been preached the previous Sunday, especially with a view to more detailed discussion of the application. Another way to ensure maximum benefit in the group can be for a ten-minute taped introduction to be produced, by the minister or one of the Bible teachers in the congregation, copied and circulated to each leader so as to give an introduction common to all the groups, before the discussion. The tape can deal with more difficult or contentious points of exegesis and so free the way for the discussion to be profitable in areas of mutual need and experience.

The importance of biblical teaching

This leads me to the last great provision by which the Bible can consistently change our thinking and impact our behaviour, and that is the regular preaching and teaching ministry of the local church. One of the most devastating blows to the vitality of the churches, over the past half century, has been the gradual decline and virtual disappearance of a regular biblical preaching ministry in many local congregations. This is not the place to argue the case for biblical preaching to be restored to its rightful place at the very heart of the life of the local church. I have done that, in company with others, in the volume entitled *When God's Voice Is Heard* (edited by Christopher Green and the present author, and published in 1995 by Inter-Varsity Press). But if you are serious about believing in the Bible, do all that you can to persuade the leader of your local church that what must be central to the meetings of the congregation is the clear, authoritative and applied preaching of the whole counsel of God to the whole people of God. Whatever else may happen, if the seed which is the Word of God is not being regularly sown, there can be no lasting harvest. There is no alternative product.

One of the books I have most profited from reading in recent years is John Piper's work, *The Supremacy of God in Preaching* (1990, Baker Books). In the course of its stirring call to biblical preaching, the author quotes the words of Cotton Mather, one of the New England Puritan preachers of three hundred years ago. 'The great design and intention of the office of a Christian preacher,' he declared, 'is to restore the throne and dominion of God in the souls of men.' Piper points out that the quotation is taken from a sermon Mather preached on Romans 10:14–15, one of the great New Testament texts on preaching.

How, then, can they call on the one they have not believed in? And how can they believe in the one of whom they have not heard? And how can they hear without someone preaching to them? And how can they preach unless they are sent? As it is written, 'How beautiful are the feet of those who bring good news!'

The word translated 'preaching' at the end of verse 14 means to herald, to make a public proclamation. This work is to be done by those who are sent (v. 15a). The word is the same root as gives us our word 'apostles'. The content of the commissioned herald's proclamation is 'good news' (v. 15b), the gospel. And the detail of the message is contained in the original context of the quotation from Isaiah 52:7 with which verse 15 ends. It is that 'your God reigns'. That is why God sends out preachers of the Bible, to restore his throne and dominion through the gospel. It follows, then, that if that work is ignored and if God's own methodology is spurned, it will not be done by any other alternative method. It will not happen. And all around us we see the proof of that, in the Church and in the world.

The problem is that so many have given up on preaching, but for all the wrong reasons. As John Stott has commented, for many congregations the only sort of preaching they have ever known consists of three types of sermon: 'the dull, the duller and the inconceivably dull'. Yet the answer to bad preaching is not less preaching, but better preaching. For Jesus Christ, this was the focus of his whole earthly ministry. As the crowds wanted to detain him in Capernaum, pressing in on him and demanding more and more healing miracles, it is striking how he responded. 'I must preach the good news of the kingdom of God to the other towns also, because that is why I was sent.' And Luke adds, 'And he kept on preaching in the synagogues of Judea' (Luke 4:43–4). Clearly the same priority lay at the heart of the ministry of the apostles, too. The Great Commission instructed them to make disciples of all nations, 'teaching them to obey everything I have commanded you' (Matthew 28:19–20). Two passages from the writings of Paul show how his preaching of the Word of God was absolutely central to his apostolic ministry. Indeed, it would not be an exaggeration to say that the key ministry the New Testament recognises and wants to develop for the future well-being of the Church is the ministry of the Word.

I have become its [the Church's] servant by the commission God gave me to present to you the word of God in its fulness – the mystery that has been kept hidden for ages and generations, but is now disclosed to the saints. To them God has chosen to make known among the Gentiles the glorious riches of this mystery, which is Christ in you, the hope of glory. We proclaim him, admonishing and teaching everyone with all wisdom, so that we may present everyone perfect in Christ. To this end I labour, struggling with all his energy, which so powerfully works in me. (Colossians 1:25–9)

In the presence of God and of Christ Jesus, who will judge the living and the dead, and in view of his appearing and his kingdom, I give you this charge: Preach the Word; be prepared in season and out of season; correct, rebuke and encourage – with great patience and careful instruction. For the time will come when men will not put up with sound doctrine. Instead, to suit their own desires, they will gather around them a great number of teachers to say what their itching ears want to hear. They will turn their ears away from the truth and turn aside to myths. But you, keep your head in all situations, endure hardship, do the work of an evangelist, discharge all the duties of your ministry. (2 Timothy 4:1–5)

The apostles knew that the regular declaration and exposition of the Word of God was the only way to counter false teaching and to promote authentic discipleship. The pastoral letters are full of such references (1 Timothy 1:3, 2:7, 3:2, 4:1, 6, 13, 5:17; 2 Timothy 1:13–14, 2:2, 4–6, 14–15, 24–6, 3:14–17, 4:1–5; Titus 1:9–11, 2:1, 7–8, 15, 3:8) as are the later, more general epistles (e.g. 2 Peter 1:12–15, 2:1–2; 2 John 9–10; Jude 3, 20). There is a body of divinely revealed truth to be conveyed and believed, from one generation to the next, and it is central to God's purpose that this should be done by teaching.

I am sometimes asked whether a distinction should be made between teaching and preaching. I would not wish to push the point too far, but I think it is true to say that all good preaching is teaching (at least as a major part of its composition), while not all teaching is preaching. It would be possible to give a teaching lecture on a biblical theme or text, in which information was relayed truthfully and accurately but without any appeal to the hearers to act upon it, simply to acknowledge or learn its content. But preaching cannot remain at that level. What may be appropriate to the lecture room is inadequate for either the pulpit or the market-place. Biblical preaching teaches God's truth with a view to life-change, with a summons to action. It is therefore never merely cerebral. It begins by engaging the mind with the truth God has revealed, but then proceeds to apply this to the heart, the seat of the affections and the locus of our decision-making, in order to activate the will. 'Do not merely listen to the word, and so deceive yourselves. Do what it says . . . The man who looks intently into the perfect law that gives freedom, and continues to do this, not forgetting what he has heard, but doing it – he will be blessed in what he does' (James 1:22–5).

Bad preaching, which is sadly so prevalent, is bad not because of incompetence of technique or style, but because of its paucity of biblical content (and therefore of true spiritual authority) and its absence of heart–felt passion for change. If all I got for going to church was a ten-minute reverie on what has been happening in the news this past week and what we think of it in the vicarage, or a kebab-stick of half-cooked, disconnected moral platitudes, or a parading of intel-lectual doubts about the basic doctrines or the moral absolutes of the faith, of course I wouldn't bother to go back next week – if ever! That is what has emptied churches for the last hundred years or more and is still doing so. But what produces joyful, confident, yet humble, and gracious, godly people is the hearing and receiving of the living and enduring Word of God, Sunday by Sunday, year in, year out. Last year, I preached at a guest service in a parish where a friend of mine had recently become the rector. Over coffee afterwards, I got talking to a middle-aged lecturer at the local university, who had regularly attended church for many years, since his youth in fact, but who, in his words, had never really understood what the Bible was all about. 'But do you know what our new rector is doing?' he asked me. 'Well, when he goes into the pulpit each Sunday, he just opens the Bible and starts to explain it, so that we can all understand what it means. And,' he added, 'what's more, it's changing my life!' Biblical preaching always does.

Those of us who really do believe in the Bible must therefore do all we can to encourage our ministers and lay preachers to preach the Word and to make it their priority. Good preaching takes time in preparation and prayer, but it yields great dividends. In a church which is regularly taught the Bible, a great deal of preventive pastoral care is accomplished through the preaching. It is good to establish a consecutive programme, expounding either whole books or sections of them over a series of sermons. If a team of preachers is involved, this brings consistency to the teaching and ensures that all the expo-nents are seen to be under the same divine authority. It also means that the balance of biblical truth dictates the subject matter, rather than the bees that are currently buzzing in the preacher's bonnet. Over a period of years, a theme or doctrine which is frequently treated in the Bible will have to be covered with corresponding frequency in the preaching, whereas one may have to wait a while for something rarely mentioned to be preached on, however dear it may be to the preacher's heart. It also ensures that the hard passages are not 'dodged' and that the favourite pastures are not worn out by too-frequent trampling. Best of all, the Bible sets the agenda, rather than the preachers. The same effect can be obtained partially by preaching through a lectionary, but continuity is often a problem and the range is more restricted. If we take seriously the way God has given us the Bible, book by book, then our preaching programmes should reflect our submission to his wisdom, in recognition that he knows better than we do what will help us most. So do encourage your preachers by expressing your appreciation when you are taught the Bible. It can be a lonely and discouraging business, and very easy to decide that other higher-profile activities are more significant than time spent in study and in prayer, preparing to feed the flock with a good, nourishing biblical diet. Yet the absence of that diet is perhaps the greatest single cause of the Church's present anaemia.

Some years ago, a cartoon was published in *Leadership* magazine. It showed a harassed, exhausted minister sitting at his desk with an in tray either side of him, piled high with paper. His wife, or secretary, is coming in with yet another huge pile, and as she enters she is saying, 'Cheer up! God loves you – and everybody else has a wonderful plan for your life!' It is not only ministers who know that feeling, of course, but it is fatally easy, in a self-employed work situation, where there is no direct supervision or accountability and where one's own choice determines where one's energy is spent, to be diverted into a hundred and one useful things but to miss out on what is the most important of all – 'Preach the Word' (2 Timothy 4:2). I do not think many ministers are lazy; most work enormously long hours, for very little earthly remuneration, dealing with complex and resistant human problems. The likelihood is not that they will not work hard, but that they may not work 'smart', and so they may find little lasting success for their labours. The 'smart' way to do ministry is God's way and the Bible is clearly the pattern book for anyone who is willing to search it out and put it into practice.

If you cannot find a church with a biblical teaching programme, one of the great blessings of the modern age is the existence of audio-tapes and videos of excellent Bible exposition from large conventions and conferences, and from a number of biblical preachers and pulpits. Certainly, I know of a number of Christians who keep their minds fed with God's truth by listening regularly to teaching tapes on their car journeys to and from work, even though where they live seems to be a land of famine. There are also many printed commentaries and studies on Biblical books and themes readily obtainable from Christian bookstores, as well as reference and background books which will greatly enrich one's biblical understanding. The best list I know of such excellent resources is an annotated bibliography at the end of *Introduction to Biblical Interpretation* by Klein, Blomberg and Hubbard (op. cit. pp. 459–91). This is as valuable as it is detailed and provides much information for further study. The Scriptures are an inexhaust-ible treasure-house, by which God continues to speak to his twenty-first-century people with as much truth, clarity, relevance and urgency as he has always done. 'He who has ears to hear, let him hear' (Matthew 13:9).

To remind you

- The Bible is the primary means of getting to understand and know God, because all of its contents communicate his mind and constitute his Word (pp. 190–4).
- In relating the Bible to our own lives, understanding the purpose of the original writing will help us to see the application (pp. 194–7).
- Other diagnostic questions need to be asked about the character of God, the picture of human nature and the relationship between the two. The cultural setting may be very different today, but the timeless truths and principles need to be carried over into our world and applied (pp. 197–201).
- Bible study needs to be a priority in the Christian's programme, whether this is individual, with one other person, in a group or by being taught through preaching. There are skills to be developed in each of these areas (pp. 201–4).
- House groups have great potential but need skilled leadership. Good questions that lead group members into the biblical text need to be carefully prepared (pp. 204–8).
- Clear and careful explanation of the Bible, through preaching which is related and applied to life, is one of the greatest needs of the con-

temporary Church. The heart of all ministry in the New Testament is
ministry of the Word, and ministers need to make this their priority
(pp. 208–13).

Chapter 10

Is There Anybody Out There Listening?

IN THE AUTUMN of 1995, a letter was circulated to all Anglican clergy in the English diocese of Chelmsford, proposing 'an alternative Bible'. It was written by one of their number, a parish vicar, who suggested, 'Having now an Alternative Prayer Book in the Church of England, it is possible to contemplate an Alternative Bible to stand alongside it.' This new publication would remove considerable parts of the Old Testament on the grounds of the material being 'unclear', 'virtually obsolete' or 'repetitive'. It would include 'inspired' writings from the centuries since the canon of Scripture was completed, and especially 'adequate guidance and teaching on many of today's moral problems: e.g. capital punishment, euthanasia, birth control, homosexuality, divorce and re-marriage'. Contemporary writers 'of recognised spiritual authority' would be commissioned to compose works for inclusion, 'in prayer and obedience to the will of God'. Publication was scheduled for the year 2000, but there is no word as to its progress at the time of writing.

The proposal is a fascinating document, not least for the presuppositions which it uncovers about God, about the Bible and about 'us'. It all sounds so eminently reasonable and contemporary; indeed, it is unmistakably positioned in the culture of the 1990s. The Bible is an artefact, the product of human workmanship, described in the proposal as 'an extremely valuable collection of sacred writings'. To such thinking, its origin is human, its contents are dispensable, its authority entirely dependent on our authorisation. What it may say to us is only relevant in so far as it is 'helpful' to us. It is a book over which 'we' (the Church, or presumably the individual) have ultimate control, and if we decide that it isn't up to the job we want it to do, we can substitute it with a better, more up-to-date alternative. We have almost all grown up in a culture where that attitude to the Bible is taken for granted, in our schools and universities, in the media, in the public forum of debate and in the market-square of commerce. It is a little unnerving, however, to see how deeply this presuppositional virus has penetrated even the Church's bloodstream.

The challenge ahead

I use this example because it seems to me to express so well the challenge all those of us who want to affirm that we 'believe in the Bible' face, in this new century. The Bible goes on being translated, published and sold in vast quantities around the world, but is there anybody out there listening? Sometimes it seems, at least in the 'post-Christian' West, as though there are very few prepared to let the Bible speak for itself, or to listen with any sort of serious attention. What is the future of the Bible, as we enter the twenty-first century? Christian believers will immediately (and rightly) want to affirm the words of our Lord Jesus Christ, 'Heaven and earth will pass away, but my words will never pass away' (Mark 13:31). Yet the same Lord also asked that poignantly haunting question, 'When the Son of Man comes, will he find faith on the earth?' (Luke 18:8). Again, we can affirm with confidence that there will always be a Church on earth in every generation, not least the last (see Matthew 16:18, 24:30-1), but its existence is not guaranteed in any specific location, or within any nation, at any point in history. The challenge for Bible-believing Christians in the West is to let the Bible loose, to let it be our mouthpiece in all the cultural debates in which we engage, to make it the substance of our proclamation and teaching, to build our own lives on its truth, in faith and obedience.

In the course of this book, we have examined the evidence and arguments for accepting the inspiration and authority of the whole Bible, as the living Word of the living God. There is a vast literature supportive of this position, of course, dealing with many of the issues raised in much more detail, linguistically, philosophically and technically. In addition, we have sought to take the Bible seriously in its description of itself and its internal methods of interpretation and use, so as to develop handling-skills of coherence and integrity for those who want to derive true value from the text. But in this final chapter, I want to think through some of the challenges which Bible believers currently face, and endeavour to sketch an outline strategy by which we might work together for a fresh recognition of the Bible's truth and power, and therefore a fresh encounter with the God who is still speaking, in a way that will impact our time. If we believe in the Bible, we can be content to work and pray for nothing less.

First, it will be helpful to draw a map of where we are with regard to our culture's perception of the Bible. I have found great help in this area from an extended essay entitled *Scripture and Authority Today* written by Professor Richard Bauckham of St Andrew's University and published in Cambridge in 1999, in the Grove Biblical Booklets Series, No. 12. Professor Bauckham's thesis is that the traditional concept of the Bible's authority is a combination of both 'extrinsic' and 'intrinsic' elements. The first was attacked by the Enlightenment thinking known as 'modernity', and the second by the contemporary movement we call 'post-modernity'. The 'extrinsic' claim is that the Bible is the Word of God and has divine authority, because God has authority to say it and has done so. It is therefore both to be believed and obeyed. To this, modernity replied, in the famous quotation of Immanuel Kant, 'Have the courage to use your own intelligence.' Elevating the principle of autonomous reason, one should accept only what can be demonstrated from first principles in a universally accessible way. This broadside led theologians to construct a 'modernist' theology, based on what seemed reasonable because it was independently verifiable, but evacuating the Bible of much of its supernatural content and consequent authority. The 'intrinsic' claim is that the same Holy Spirit who inspired Bible authors to write inspires Bible readers to understand and accept it as God's Word. Nor is this simply an intellectual perception, for as we put into practice what the Bible says, we find it works. Biblical truth is realised, in our experience, and so proves to be self-authenticating. To this, post-modernity replies, 'I must be free to believe my own truth.' Any claim to a universal truth is simply a power ploy, an attempt to dominate me by the so-called knowledge of a particular élite. Christianity is, of course, a prime 'offender' here; but once all truth claims are shown to be simply the expression of personal preference, its hold is broken and we are set free to live in an unrestricted pluralism. As with modernism, so with its successor: the danger will be that Christian thinkers will accommodate the faith to the premises of post-modernism and capitulate to a privatised form of religion. That is an area in which the range of acceptability tolerated by the prevailing culture is constantly shrinking.

These are real and powerful challenges at a variety of levels. While it may be argued that the philosophical issues of deconstructionism are the interests of the academic world, their trickle-down effect in society as a whole is already plain to see. When a public leader, on oath, declares that he has not lied, he does not mean by that that he has spoken the truth. For what is 'the truth'? It is many-sided and no one can perceive its entirety, so what he has said represents what he believes to be his personal perception of what happened. In such a world you cannot lie, since truth no longer exists. When a businessman reneges on a deal on which he gave his word, all that word implied was a readiness to act in accordance with the terms of the contract as he interprets them now or at any time in the future. And if that should be tried in a court of law, the aim will not be to establish the truth, because such a thing does not exist, but to convince the arbiters of the validity of his own 'reading'. At the popular level, this translates into a pluralistic culture where the only position that will not be tolerated is intolerance. We are already seeing the disintegration of many of the structures which have given our society its cohesion and stability, not least the family unit, and with it the inevitable isolation of the individual. A generation free to believe its own truth is also a generation desperate for deep and lasting relationships. But they require 'commitment', and in a world without ultimate values, other than myself, such a commodity is in short supply. These challenges are real and pervasive, but they also represent great opportunities and potential openness to a voice from outside. Whether that 'voice' will be another round of totalitarian tyrants (which will always be attractive to a disintegrating society) or that of the living God may depend, in human terms at least, on how committed to the Bible's message his people are.

In facing the intellectual challenge of the contemporary situation, Professor Brian D. Ingraffia of Biola University, California, has produced a volume entitled *Postmodern Theory and Biblical Theology* (1995, Cambridge University Press) which is full of good things. First, it is helpful to realise that there is 'nothing new under the sun' and that these issues have confronted Christians in many different contexts. The apostle Paul himself faced them, in Athens, Corinth and when writing to the church at Colosse. For the common denominator in both first- and twenty-first-century attacks on the Bible's authority is that they all start with human philosophising and proceed from there to the deconstruction of the Bible. But all that is actually rejected, or deconstructed, is what Ingraffia calls 'theology based upon human imaginings about God' (op. cit. p. 241), for which the current technical term is 'onto-theology'.

This was precisely the problem Paul encountered in Athens when he delivered his famous speech at the meeting of the Areopagus.

Men of Athens! I see that in every way you are very religious. For as I walked around and looked carefully at your objects of worship, I even found an altar with this inscription: TO AN UNKNOWN GOD. Now what you worship as something unknown I am going to proclaim to you. The God who made the world and everything in it is the Lord of heaven and earth and does not live in temples built by hands. And he is not served by human hands, as if he needed anything, because he himself gives all men life and breath and everything else. From one man he made every nation of men, that they should inhabit the whole earth; and he determined the times set for them and the exact places where they should live. God did this so that men would seek him and perhaps reach out for him and find him, though he is not far from each one of us. For in him we live and move and have our being. As some of your own poets have said, 'We are his offspring.' Therefore since we are God's offspring, we should not think that the divine being is like gold or silver or stone – an image made by man's design and skill. In the past God overlooked such ignorance, but now he commands all people everywhere to repent. For he has set a day when he will judge the world with justice by the man he has appointed. He has given proof of this to all men by raising him from the dead. (Acts 17:22b–31)

The very description 'To An Unknown God' illustrates both how dependent on revelation human beings inevitably are, for no real god could be 'known' in any other way, and how fundamentally insecure such ignorance makes us feel. We ought to put up an altar so as not to offend, to cover off all possible options. If we are starting from a human base that will always be the problem. So Paul 'reveals' the nature of the Creator God, 'Lord of heaven and earth' (v. 24) in terms of three negatives which expose the emptiness and folly of all human-based religious constructions. The real God 'does *not* live in temples built by hands' (v. 24), 'is *not* served by human hands' (v. 25) and 'is *not* far from each one of us' (v. 27). Far from needing humans to construct a shrine for him to live in, the living God made the earth for them to live in. Far from needing humans to serve him, by bringing food offerings or looking after his shrine and image, the living God served them by giving them life itself and all that is needed to sustain it. Far from being static in one place and needing to be visited for worship, the living God is everywhere, constantly available to anyone who will reach out to find him.

So what is the categorical mistake which human beings will always make whenever they start with themselves as the basis of their understanding about God? Verse 29 is the crunch verse. 'We are God's offspring'; he is not the projection of our desires, or the construct of our finite minds. Therefore, 'we should not think that the divine being is like gold or silver or stone – an image made by man's design and skill'. But that is precisely what we humans always do think, whenever our imaginings become the ground of our belief-systems. Paul calls it 'ignorance', not knowing. Agnosticism is a more polite synonym, but it lacks the bite, because not knowing is no longer excusable. The reason is that God has revealed himself, in Jesus Christ, raised from the dead, the coming judge of all, and on that basis he 'commands all people everywhere to repent' (vv. 30–1). Whenever we try to formulate a human understanding of God rather than receiving the divine revelation of God in Jesus Christ, crucified and risen, mediated to us through the Scriptures, we shall produce a 'god' who is merely a figment of the human imagination and inevitably a distortion of the divine reality, which can only be known by revelation. In the same way, atheism is equally onto-theological, since it affirms from its own base that we are able to know, of ourselves, that the idea of God is an illusion. It is this false base which Paul attacked in Athens, and which is still there in post-modernist critics of the Christian faith. As Ingraffia expresses it, 'We *should*, therefore, vanquish god's shadow (a phrase of Nietzsche's), the shadow god created by human reason's imagination, that we might seek the revelation of the living God in the cross of Christ' (op. cit. p. 241).

It is the cross which becomes the focus in the similar argument which Paul conducts with the Corinthians at the opening of his first letter to them. In a pagan city, surrounded by idol temples and immoral practices, the Christians were tempted to compromise the message of the gospel with a much more culturally acceptable presentation of rhetorical wisdom and miraculous powers. Paul is by no means anti-intellectual. He himself had a first-class mind, as his writings show. But he is not prepared to allow a philosophy built from human origins with human wisdom, which is in the end mere speculation, to overthrow the revelation of God's unique historical intervention in his world, in the cross and resurrection of his Son, Jesus Christ. The following argument makes the point with great clarity.

Where is the wise man? Where is the scholar? Where is the philosopher of this age? Has not God made foolish the wisdom of the world? For since in the wisdom of God the world through its wisdom did not know him, God was pleased through the foolishness of what was preached to save those who believe. Jews demand miraculous signs and Greeks look for wisdom, but we preach Christ crucified: a stumbling-block to Jews and foolishness to Gentiles, but to those whom God has called, both Jews and Greeks, Christ the power of God and the wisdom of God. For the foolishness of God is wiser than man's wisdom, and the weakness of God is stronger than man's strength. (1 Corinthians 1:20–5)

The next chapter goes on to point out that there is a 'message of wisdom' which Paul does preach, but it is the otherwise hidden wisdom of God's rescue plan for humanity accomplished through the self-emptying of Jesus, crucified for the world, and revealed only by the Holy Spirit (see 1 Corinthians 2:6–10). Again, the point is made that Christianity is not a ladder by which to climb up to God. That may be a feature of all other religious beliefs, with their systems and disciplines, self-denials and offerings by which to make one acceptable to God. Each of them provides a ladder to climb, but it is not the God of the Bible who is at the top, but rather a product of our own imaginations. For the God of the Bible comes down the ladder to us, to rescue us when we are helpless and hopeless, and the way in which he conquers evil is to surrender himself to the death of the cross. 'The theology of the cross pronounces an either/or: either biblical revelation or philosophical speculation. The same either/or must be proclaimed to the present age: either biblical theology or post-modern theory. Only as a theology of the cross will Christianity recover its prophetic voice' (op. cit. p. 241).

Two other New Testament examples underline the point still further. The churches in Colosse and Philippi were in danger from false teachers, whose message reflected the amalgamation of Jewish and Greek thinking which characterised much first-century religion. Greek thought was always dualistic, separating body and spirit, earth and heaven, the material and the spiritual. Sometimes this showed itself in asceticism, where the body was denied, even denigrated, and sometimes in libertinism, where the pure spirit was thought to be so superior to the flesh that any behaviour could be indulged in the body with impunity. There are signs of the first in Colosse and the second at Philippi. In Colosse, some want to bring the young Christians under ascetic rules ('Do not handle! Do not taste! Do not touch!' 2:21), but Paul says 'such regulations indeed have an appearance of wisdom, with their . . . harsh treatment of the body, but they lack any value in restraining sensual indulgence' (2:23). The answer is in the cross, realising that there 'you died with Christ to the basic principles of this world' (2:20). The Colossian mistake is that they are working from the ground up, 'taking the earthly situations as their starting point from which by their own efforts and techniques they will ascend into the heavenlies. Paul moves in the reverse direction, since he sees the starting point and source of the believer's life in the resurrected Christ in heaven, from where it works itself out, into earthly life (3:5ff)' (Andrew T. Lincoln in *Paradise Now and Not Yet*, 1991, Baker Books, quoted by B. D. Ingraffia, op. cit. p. 75).

In Philippi, the stress is on liberty, not just from legalistic rules but from most moral constraints, it seems. Earthly life was being devalued as meaningless, because only the life of the soul in the world beyond really mattered. Again, Paul turns to the theology of the cross to refute this error. Our citizenship is in heaven (3:20), but the Christ who once came to earth, emptying himself even to death on a cross (2:5–8) will come again to earth to redeem and transform our physical bodies (3:21). This is what gives meaning and significance to life on earth. Again, the movement is from heaven to earth, in divine revelation and redemption, not from earth to heaven, in human speculation and imagination. This is where we need the Bible's own emphasis on revelation to engage in the debate with post-modernism. Its theories may well have deconstructed the gods of human imagination, whoever their builders may have been, but they are human constructs, not the God of the Bible. We need to be set free from these false gods, because they have so frequently been a reflection of current ideologies, masquerading as the God of the Bible. In Brian Ingraffia's words, 'Christian thought must not let postmodern theory guide its critique: it should be guided by a hermeneutic of faith, which in turn must be guided by biblical revelation' (op. cit. p. 238).

Living the Bible's story

The rise of post-modern thinking and attitudes, therefore, presents Christians with a moment of great opportunity. If 'I must be free to believe my own truth', then the Bible must be free to tell me its truth, to present to me its story. Or, more significant still, I, as a Christian, am free to tell you 'my' truth, 'my' story, which happens to be the Bible's. For while the essence of being *post*-modern is that the old over-arching stories or 'narratives', as ways of explaining reality, are no longer legitimate, so that any so-called 'meta-narrative' is rejected automatically, nevertheless what might be called local, or personal, narratives continue to thrive. We all sense the need to own models or paradigms which describe our identity and give definition to our existence. Again, this is not new. A large percentage of confessing Christians today who were converted to their faith, rather than growing up in it, would bear testimony to the fact that the biggest single factor in their conversion was seeing the gospel work out in the life-story of someone they knew well. I recently heard of a middle-aged Christian woman who came to faith in Christ while holding a senior management position in a city firm. What was it that got her thinking about Christianity in her mid-thirties? The change in beha-viour of a man in her office was the key. He was a well-known womaniser, always sailing close to the wind in terms of sexual in-nuendo and offensive behaviour, and suddenly it all stopped. He announced that he had become a follower of Jesus Christ, and he was instantly different and gradually transformed. It was when she heard his 'local' narrative that she began to be interested in the 'meta-narrative' which lay behind it. Eventually, she too became Christ's disciple.

Of course, we do have to get to the 'meta-narrative', for that is the heart of God's revelation, the gospel, which constantly needs to be proclaimed. It will not do just to share our story, since it may strike very few chords with those who listen, particularly if their age, background or other characteristics are different from our own. The reaction will frequently be, 'Well, I'm very pleased for you, but I'm a very different person, so please don't ask me to accept your outlook and please don't try to force your religion down my throat!' Personal testimony alone will always be working from a merely human base, and if it remains at the level of 'I found this works. Why don't you give it a try?', people will come to regard the gospel as just another remedy on the shelves of the ideological supermarket, for which they have neither need nor interest. But the quality of life Christians live, and especially the expression of genuine Christian love, can open doors for the gospel which would otherwise remain firmly shut. It is important to remind ourselves that though the Bible is a book containing timeless truths and moral principles, it is not presented in that format. As we saw at the start, it is a story, stretching from creation to the new creation and embracing the meaning of all reality within its compass. As Richard Bauckham sees it, becoming a Christian is making the Bible's story (or meta-narrative) our own. He writes,

> To accept the authority of the story is to enter it and inhabit it. It is to live in the world as the world is portrayed in this story. It is to let this story define our identity and our relationship to God and to others. It is to read the narratives of our own lives and of the societies in which we live as narratives which take their meaning from this meta-narrative that overarches them all. (op. cit. p. 10)

The fascinating fact is that when the Bible's story of God's self-revelation is actually heard, it subscribes to none of the stereotypical categories by which post-modernist thinking would seek to dismiss it. Far from it being the tool of a knowledgeable élite who would use it to exercise power over others, the gospel is the greatest agent of personal liberation the world has ever witnessed. 'If the Son sets you free, you will be free indeed' (John 8:36). For the gospel's central motif is not one of demand from a remote and autocratic deity. That is the product of onto-theology, as we have seen. The revelation of Scripture is of a God of grace, who demonstrates his incredible love and mercy through Jesus and the cross, and invites from me a free response of love, expressed in faith and repentance. The movement is from heaven to earth. As Bill Hybels has often said, 'Religion may be spelt "Do" but Christianity is spelt "Done".' Or, in the apostle Paul's memorable words, 'God demonstrates his own love for us in this: while we were still sinners, Christ died for us' (Romans 5:8). All the way through the biblical meta-narrative, the pattern is the same. God chooses to take the initiative, to bring rebellious human beings back into a right relationship with himself, but there is always the necessity for personal response, the call to faith. The gift of God's grace is constantly presented first, preceding all requirement of response. Indeed, it is only because of this unmerited favour and compassionate mercy of God that we ever could respond to him, or be brought into relationship with him. So Abraham was given great and gracious promises by the Lord at the very beginning of salvation history, promises of a great name and a great nation, a great land and a great blessing, but there was a response of faith required. He had to leave his country and go. 'So Abram left, as the LORD had told him' (Genesis 12:4). Yet as he travelled on with God he found, not a set of arbitrary rules and impossible demands, but a relationship of covenanted faithfulness in which God's generous gifts of grace were lavished on him and his wonderful promises increasingly fulfilled. No wonder he was the man who believed God.

Faith like that is the use of the freedom God's grace brings to obey God freely from the heart. The Bible's story is full of examples by which the love of God reaches out to transform human lives. At the heart of its self-revelation lies the understanding of God as a trinity in unity, three persons in one divine being, co-equal in nature and status, yet different in function and role. One of the clearest and deepest statements in the whole Bible about the nature of this triune God is that made twice by John in his first letter, 'God is love' (1 John 4:8, 16). It is not just that God loves, but that he is, by nature, love. Relating this to the concept of the trinity, we can see that at the heart of God, the very essence of his divine being, there exists a dynamic interaction of constant love between the three persons. The Father loves the Son, the Son loves the Father, the Spirit loves the Son, and so on, in constant, eternal activity. And humankind are made in the image of God, to love God and our neighbour. 'There is no commandment greater than these' (Mark 12:31). But love must be a free response, an act of the will. The one thing it cannot be is coerced, or it ceases to be love. How, then, will God freely win the response of love from sinful human beings who continue to rebel against him? John has the answer.

> This is how God showed his love among us: He sent his one and only Son into the world that we might live through him. This is love: not that we loved God, but that he loved us and sent his Son as an atoning sacrifice for our sins. Dear friends, since God so loved us, we also ought to love one another . . . And we have seen and testify that the Father has sent his Son to be the Saviour of the world. If anyone acknowledges that Jesus is the Son of God, God lives in him and he in God. And so we know and rely on the love God has for us. God is love. Whoever lives in love lives in God, and God in him. (1 John 4:9–11, 14–16)

The Bible's story is validated by the transformation which occurs in the life of the Christian, in gratitude for such amazing grace. That is how it impacts the world still, irrespective of whatever philosophies may come into, or go out of, fashion. There is no argument against a life transformed, from the inside out, by God's grace, turned around from serving self to loving God and loving people. The Bible's story of God's transforming love and power, through Christ crucified and risen, is the only dynamic by which alienated people can be reconciled and a broken world restored. It is not true because it works; but it works because it is true.

The bigger picture
However, the Bible's impact must be wider than our personal acts of love, essential though they are to God's great plan. Our individual part in the 'big story' is infinitesimally small alongside the massive scope of the story itself, so we must never be content with the small canvas of our individual lives alone. The 'meta-narrative', which is the Bible's story-line, encompasses time and eternity, the universe and everything within it. This is not separate from our local, personal stories: they are an integral part of it, but its scope is immeasurably vast. We noted the pattern in the opening chapters of Genesis and its three distinctive movements, or stages in creation, fall and rescue, or redemption, as the rest of the Bible calls it. In the beginning, God brings into being, by his sovereign will executed through his word, a created order of perfection. At its apex is a creature made in his own

image, with God-like abilities to know him, love him and relate to him in trust and dependence. But the creation of a being with potential for such free response inevitably implies the possibility of wrong choices, of using this autonomy to usurp the creator's rightful place. This was realised in the fall. 'Your eyes will be opened, and you will be like God, knowing good and evil' (Genesis 3:5). This act of rebellion fractures the perfection of God's creation and alienates humankind from the creator. The Bible shows us that this is not some localised event, with significance only for Adam and Eve, but one with cosmic consequences. As a result of human sin, the ground is cursed (Genesis 3:17) and the whole creation is 'in bondage to decay' (Romans 8:21). This does not mean that God has rejected his creation. Its structure remains and God is committed to its sustenance and continuance. 'For everything God created is good, and nothing is to be rejected if it is received with thanksgiving' (1 Timothy 4:4). But the direction of the whole created order is one of distortion and perversion because of the arrival of evil, in the fall of humankind. A. M. Wolters makes the point cogently:

> Anything in creation can be directed either toward or away from God – that is, directed either in obedience or disobedience to his law. This double direction applies not only to individual human beings but also to such cultural phenomena as technology, art, and scholarship, to such societal institutions as labor unions, schools, and corporations, and to such human functions as emotionality, sexuality, and rationality. To the degree that these realities fail to live up to God's creational design for them, they are misdirected, abnormal, distorted. To the degree that they still conform to God's design, they are in the grip of a countervailing force that curbs or counteracts the distortion. (*Creation Regained*, 1986, Inter-Varsity Press, p. 49)

Into this situation God steps, in his intervening grace. We see it in his rescuing mercy to Noah and his family, brought through the judgment of the flood to the new world beyond, by the provision of the ark. But bound up with Noah and his family in the floating zoo are 'two of all living creatures' (Genesis 6:19). The animal creation shares both in the judgment that falls on humanity's sin, but also in the rescue that comes through God's grace. So the covenant which God makes, following the flood, in which he promises, 'Never again will all life be cut off by the waters of a flood; never again will there be a flood to destroy the earth' (Genesis 9:11), is directed not only to humanity, but to 'every living creature'. The redemption and restoration which God brings extend as widely as the effects of the fall, to all the created order. This is supremely the case in the greatest rescue mission of all, the atoning death of Jesus Christ, for the sins of the world, on the cross. Paul reminds us that God's purpose was fulfilled through Christ, 'to reconcile to himself all things, whether things on earth or things in heaven, by making peace through his blood, shed on the cross' (Colossians 1:20). As the cause of all evil is dealt with at that cross, the possibility of restoration exists in every area infected by mankind's fall. But that will be part of the progression towards the eternal city, not a return to a primitivism, in a forlorn attempt to recover Eden. Christians are not Luddites or antiquarians, wanting to put the clock back to an age that is past. Much of the development of the creation mandate has been good and valuable, although inevitably always tainted by sin and distorted in many ways. To talk of restoration is not to look backwards to a day before antibiotics or computers and to yearn to return to a 'golden age', which actually never existed. Rather, it is to look forward to the restoration of everything in the new heavens and the new earth where righteousness will dwell, to the heavenly Jerusalem where Christ's kingly rule in righteousness will be unchallenged and unending, and where at last his people will be, as he intended, in unbroken relationship with him. Christians are not looking to 'build Jerusalem, in England's green and pleasant land', or anywhere else for that matter, as though some earthly Utopia was the goal of the gospel. We know that perfection can only be in heaven, and that the only way we 'build Jerusalem', the eternal city, is by spreading the gospel throughout the world, so that, through faith in Christ, multitudes may become members of that community.

So what is our present role? On the basis of what we have seen of the totality of the pattern of creation, fall and restoration, all cosmic in their scope, we put our energies and skills, our time and talents into fighting the spiritual battle for the kingdom of our God and of his Christ, here in this world, as citizens of the heavenly Jerusalem. 'For our struggle is not against flesh and blood, but against the rulers, against the authorities, against the powers of this dark world and against the spiritual forces of evil in the heavenly realms' (Ephesians

6:12). To accomplish that battle, God has given us the armour of the gospel 'and the sword of the Spirit, which is the word of God' (Ephesians 6:13–17).

Every Christian is aware of this at the personal level, within our own minds and hearts. We are not yet sinlessly perfect, not yet what one day, by God's grace, we will be. To imagine we are is to delude ourselves, and usually depends on moving God's goal posts. We rejoice in the power of the Holy Spirit, living within us, to enable us to resist temptation and to produce the fruits of his character within us, as we depend upon him. But we know, from bitter experience, what a daily battle that will be, and that, in spite of the words of the Victorian hymn, the option is not open for us 'to float to heaven, on flowery beds of ease'! Rather, we are involved in spiritual warfare against the world, the flesh (our sinful nature) and behind them the devil, who uses both to pursue his destructive ends. The battle will have different dimensions and contours in each individual life. Temperament, background, genetic inheritance, early life experience – these and many other factors combine to make us the people we are, who are called to become progressively what God intended us to be, through God's great restoration plan. For God's grace restores nature, and the new directions we receive through the gospel redeem the whole person, as God made us. The image of God, marred but not totally destroyed through sin, is being restored, as we grow into the likeness of Christ, in the process we call sanctification. Of course, all that is a gift of God in the gospel.

Our progress in godly living is entirely dependent on God's grace to us, through Christ's sacrifice, mediated to us by the Holy Spirit within. On the one hand, we know the sharpness of the battle, identifying with the apostle Paul when he writes, 'So I find this law at work: When I want to do good, evil is right there with me . . . So then, I myself in my mind am a slave to God's law, but in the sinful nature a slave to the law of sin' (Romans 7:21–5). We know, as Romans 8 tells us, that the power of the Spirit is given to keep us fighting in the battle all our life long, not to air-lift us out of the conflict into a super-spiritual state of near perfection. We know that it is only in heaven that we shall experience the full redemption and restoration Christ has accomplished, when our mortal bodies are redeemed and we share in his glory. That is future. 'For in this hope we were saved. But hope that is seen is no hope at all. Who hopes for what he already

has? But if we hope for what we do not yet have, we wait for it patiently'
(Romans 8:24–5). Yet, on the other hand, we have wonderful experiences of God's transforming grace, here and now, through the work
of his Spirit within us. The more we respond to his Word, the more
we depend on him in prayer and the clearer our focus on Christ is, the
more we shall experience the freedom of liberation from our old sinful
agendas, with their destructive self-centredness, and the inflow of
God's strength and ability to live differently, a redeemed and restored
life. For 'we, who with unveiled faces all reflect [or contemplate] the
Lord's glory, are being transformed into his likeness with ever-
increasing glory, which comes from the Lord, who is the Spirit'
(2 Corinthians 3:18).

It is a critical and central ingredient of our Christian living to fight
the good fight of the faith and take hold of the eternal life to which we
are called (1 Timothy 6:12). The Bible is the great resource God has
provided to enable us to know how to live, and the Spirit is the great
energiser within, to motivate our will and empower our actions. There
is no part of a Christian's human experience which is outside of these
influences. Our thinking, our feelings, our sexuality, our relationships,
our work, our leisure, our material resources – all of these are elements
of our life in God's world as God's created beings. 'The directional
battle does not take place on a spiritual plane above creaturely reality
but rather occurs *in* and *for* the concrete reality of the earthly creation'
(A. M. Wolters, op. cit. p. 73). Realisation of this will have a profound
effect upon our thinking. It means that our lives are whole entities in
God's sight, and that there can be no division between the sacred and
the secular. We do not take parts of our lives (church, prayer, Bible
study, evangelism, works of mercy, etc.) and pack them off to a separate
upstairs level, labelled 'spiritual', leaving work, home, family, leisure,
etc., downstairs, labelled 'secular', or, still worse, 'the real world'. This
is an error of devastating proportions and consequences. It will lead
us to restrict God's interest, and therefore ours if we are to follow
him, to the spiritual realm alone, and everything else will matter far
less to God, and so to us. That in turn commits us to a 'privatised'
religion, in which no word of God is ever spoken in the public forum
or the market-place. The result is a very damaging sort of spiritual
schizophrenia. It leads one to suppose that only 'spiritual' work
matters to God – activities such as mission, evangelism, Bible study –
so that spending one's time in a so-called 'secular' occupation is

always and inevitably to be second-best. This in turn distorts the Bible's view of priorities, putting emphasis on what I do rather than on who I am, and so defining myself in terms of my activity, rather than my relationship with God. Such a view must in the end produce ghettoised Christians, in a marginalised Church, which is seen as clinging to a life-negating message by an increasingly alienated society.

Impacting our culture

The remedy lies in a more radically biblical approach to our involvement in every area of life. It has been said that what the gospel needs as we enter the new century is not so much more salesmen, but more free samples. The climate is such that intellectual theorising may cut very little ice, but a life which embodies and exemplifies its belief and value systems is always going to have a magnetic attraction. Wasn't it Nietzsche who said that if ever he was to become a Christian, the Christians would have to look a lot more like Jesus Christ than they did? So one of the greatest contributions any of us can make to the spread of biblical understanding and gospel credibility is our personal godliness. That begins with our marriages and family lives, where the Bible's values need not simply to be accepted, but to become the building-blocks of how we relate to one another. Our practice and our proclamation need to go hand-in-hand here, if either is to be credible to a sceptical culture. Marriage is not merely a human construct, a dispensable social structure, the Bible tells us. Marriage is God's idea (Genesis 2:24), both as the context for our sexuality and also as the foundation blocks of a stable society. But it will not do to preach the virtues of marriage, if Christian marriages do not demonstrate the fragrance of Christ. The critical issue is whether we allow our direction of the structure to be shaped by Scripture or by culture. If it is the latter, then we should expect to see a drift away from both faithfulness within marriage and celibacy outside it. In fact, of course, we are aware of a landslide in this area which threatens to engulf our social structures in the culture at large. The danger is that the more Christians accommodate to that trend, the greater will be its penetration in the Church, until in this key area of human life the one is indistinguishable from the other. The only counter-force is the Bible's clear teaching. God's design is for a man and woman to live together in monogamous marriage until death parts them. Adultery is always wrong. Sex outside of marriages is always contrary to God's will.

Such sentiments will never be popular with *Newsnight* or the icons of popular culture, but that is nothing new. What is new is the capitulation of so many churchmen and Christians to the spirit of the age. That must stem from a deep lack of confidence in the Bible's truth and lead to a version of Christianity bereft of any real moral authority. In this area of life, the Bible has a great deal to say, but unless Christians demonstrate marriages that are dependent upon God's grace and living testimony to the power of his Spirit, in spite of all their human fallibility and weakness, it will not be heard.

Extending beyond the circles of the nuclear family and friends, we need also to consider the impact of the Bible in the life of God's wider family, the Church, at both the local and national levels. Archbishop William Temple was not being cynical when he commented that the biggest hindrance to the spread of the Christian Church is the Christian Church. For unless the people who claim the authority of Scripture demonstrate its credibility in their corporate life, what reality does it actually have? Throughout this book we have recognised the primacy of Scripture over the Church. It is not that the Bible was 'invented' by the Church, but that the Church exists because of the Bible. The Reformers were always keen to underline that the mark of the reformed Church is that it is constantly being reformed, by the word of truth in the gospel. However, our current danger is that the Church, of any and every association or denomination, is seen as an autonomous corporation and run in rather the same way. The local minister is seen as a jack-of-all-trades, with the inevitable consequence. His training is often a mish-mash of various theological influences, coupled with add-ons from sociology, business management, media studies, and so on. Because there is little understanding of the (biblical) priorities of his role, the practice tends to be unfocused and often unsatisfactory. If, however, we believe that we stand in the apostolic tradition of Christ and the gospel, from which all truly Christian ministry must derive, ought we not radically to review by those criteria what is happening in our churches? The direction a local church takes will largely depend on its leadership, and if there is confusion over its aims and goals, even sometimes its *raison d'être*, there will certainly be no clarity over its priorities and subsequent programmes.

But local churches are made up of individual Christians, however confused or confusing the context may be, and they constitute the greatest resources at the Church's disposal. This is where the cutting edge of the gospel is experienced, and it is enormously encouraging to see so many congregations keen to move out with the good news into their community. Once again, the Bible is the spearhead. What a joy and privilege it would be to belong to a church where new believers in Christ were being added on a daily basis. That was the situation in Jerusalem described in Acts 2:47, after the Day of Pentecost. But before Luke tells us that, he paints a pen-picture of what that congregation looked like.

> They devoted themselves to the apostles' teaching and to the fellowship, to the breaking of bread and to prayer. Everyone was filled with awe, and many wonders and miraculous signs were done by the apostles. All the believers were together and had everything in common. Selling their possessions and goods, they gave to anyone as he had need. Every day they continued to meet together in the temple courts. They broke bread in their homes and ate together with glad and sincere hearts, praising God and enjoying the favour of all the people. And the Lord added to their number daily those who were being saved. (Acts 2:42–7)

We cannot put the clock back, and any attempt to re-live the times of the early Church is doomed to failure. We are not in their situation, for which we may be grateful when we think of the lions in the arena! But we are surely right to see in Luke's account strong pointers to the sort of church God delights to honour, and it would be a useful exercise, at least, to measure our own contemporary experience of church against theirs. Where do we need to be more biblical in our life together as God's covenant people?

We should make a start in the area of greater unity among those Christians who really do 'believe in the Bible'. I am not pleading for a revival of the wilting structures of ecumenism. Such a plan contained two fatal weaknesses. It would have to be imposed hierarchically, working from the top down in the already existing denominational structures, rather than from the grass roots out. Also, it was institutional and organisational, rather than vibrant and confessional. It was always going to falter on the rocks of divergences over the basic content of the gospel, reflecting the fundamentally different value placed on Scripture by different groups and individuals. Bible

Christians will always anathematise those who preach a gospel other than that of the apostles, contained in the pages of the New Testament, as the apostles Paul (Galatians 1:8–9) and John (2 John 9–11) did. However, a truly radical biblicism should want to take our present denominational and local church structures back to Scripture as their judge, and to be submissive to its teaching. Let me exemplify this from both ends of the denominational spectrum. If the ancient system of parish boundaries means that some areas of the country are actually prevented from hearing the gospel message and seeing it lived out in community, because the local church building is closed or has lost its congregation, ought not that system to be reformed, so as to allow gospel work to be re-planted in those locations? If an independent, nonconformist church allows its independency to degenerate into isolationism from other Christians in the same location who clearly believe and preach the same biblical gospel, so that it only ploughs its lone furrow, ought not that system to be reformed to embrace the biblical priority of gospel unity, in practice as well as theory? God is not just interested in 'you in your small corner and I in his', as the cynic put it! Jesus was passionate about the unity of all who believe in him through his message, which he saw as powerfully evangelistic (John 17:20–1).

This is where Bible Christians can have a real impact in our culture. When we can begin to demonstrate that we are prepared to give up our secondary differences in order to unite around the greater and vastly more important truth of the gospel and getting it out into the world, perhaps more people will be interested in listening. One of the persistent warnings of the New Testament letters is against that club mentality that so easily develops and takes over when we start to add something else to Jesus Christ, crucified and risen. It can be a particular system of church government (episcopal, presbyterian or congregational), a particular view of baptism or holy communion, views on prophecy or eschatology, spiritual experiences and charismatic gifts, or a myriad other issues, but not one of them is as important as the gospel. Why, then, do we drive the gospel down the agenda by elevating these issues as the required ground of our fellowship and unity, and failing to work together for what matters most of all? Local churches are not fast-food franchises working a neighbourhood in cut-throat competition. We are 'all one in Christ Jesus' (Galatians 3:28), and we need to demonstrate that reality to the watching world.

Lastly, there is a vast agenda of need in seeking to bring the Bible back into our public life and the decision-making centres of our culture. We can be thankful that there are several excellent Christian agencies which are dedicated to doing exactly that and are very active in bringing biblical perspectives and principles to bear on current social and political issues. They need more support by prayer, finance and personal involvement. Committed biblical Christians in high-profile national positions have a unique opportunity to bring the Bible to bear on matters of public debate. They need the support and encouragement of their fellow-Christians in their demanding and sometimes vulnerable positions. But while only a few may be capable and called to such national responsibilities, all of us can have a biblical influence in the communities in which we live. It is not our role to provide glib and easy 'proof text' answers to what are often complex and almost intractable problems. What we can do is to present God's values, as revealed in Scripture, and seek to apply them not only to the problem and its solution, but also to the process and the people involved in it. To take seriously the pattern of creation, fall and restoration, and to seek to relate these to the structures of which we are a part and the directions in which they are moving, is to fulfil, at least in part, Christ's intended role for us as 'the salt of the earth' (Matthew 5:13). It provides a 'narrative' by which the confusing cross-currents of modern life can be mapped and understood. It does not short-circuit the hard work of careful observation and analysis, but it does provide a coherent foundation on which moral decisions can be made and a consistent world view by which alternatives can be evaluated. Those who 'believe in the Bible' are always needed as active participants across the spheres of influence that make up our culture, and their presence will be more important, not less, in the coming decades. Thankfully, many are already there, but they need courage to speak up and perseverance to keep going, and many others to come and share the load. So whether it is in the classroom or the board room, the operating theatre or the department store, on the factory floor or at the office desk, there are great opportunities for God's Word to be heard and exemplified, through articulate, humble and gracious Christians who are prepared to stand up for their convictions. Wherever there is human life and activity, there the Word of God needs to be known and heard.

This is the immensely challenging and exciting agenda that

presents itself to those who believe in the Bible at the dawn of the twenty-first century. I am deeply thankful to be among them, as we give gratitude to God for the Word he has spoken, for the privilege of unrestricted access to it and for freedom to believe and proclaim it. The Bible is God's gift to us. It will be so, as long as the world endures, far beyond our time and on into eternity. There is nothing more precious we can give our children, or they can give their children, than the opportunity of hearing the living and enduring Word of God, which is 'able to make you wise for salvation through faith in Christ Jesus' (2 Timothy 3:15). But that is God's gift, too. Our responsibility is to be good stewards of what he has given us, so that we shall not need to be ashamed at his appearing. What better way to affirm 'I believe in the Bible' than by letting it loose to speak its own truth?

'For my thoughts are not your thoughts, neither are your ways my ways,' declares the LORD. 'As the heavens are higher than the earth, so are my ways higher than your ways and my thoughts than your thoughts. As the rain and the snow come down from heaven, and do not return to it without watering the earth and making it bud and flourish, so that it yields seed for the sower and bread for the eater, so is my word that goes out from my mouth: It will not return to me empty, but will accomplish what I desire and achieve the purpose for which I sent it.' (Isaiah 55:8–11)

Now that you have purified yourselves by obeying the truth so that you have sincere love for your brothers, love one another deeply, from the heart. For you have been born again, not of perishable seed, but of imperishable, through the living and enduring word of God. For, 'All men are like grass, and all their glory is like the flowers of the field; the grass withers and the flowers fall, but the word of the Lord stands for ever.' (1 Peter 1:22–5)

Your word, O LORD, is eternal; it stands firm in the heavens. Your faithfulness continues through all generations; you established the earth, and it endures. Your laws endure to this day, for all things serve you. (Psalm 119:89–91)

Oh, how I love your law! I meditate on it all day long. Your commands make me wiser than my enemies, for they are ever with me. (vv. 97–8)

How sweet are your words to my taste, sweeter than honey to my mouth! I gain understanding from your precepts; therefore I hate every wrong path. Your word is a lamp to my feet and a light for my path. (vv. 103–5)

'Let the prophet who has a dream tell his dream, but let the one who has my word speak it faithfully. For what has straw to do with grain?' declares the LORD. 'Is not my word like fire,' declares the LORD, 'and like a hammer that breaks a rock in pieces?' (Jeremiah 23:28–9)

Heaven and earth will pass away, but my words will never pass away. (Mark 13:31)

To remind you

- The contemporary believer in the Bible faces many challenges ahead from the culture – relativism, pluralism and post-modernism (pp. 215–18).
- However, much of the New Testament was written in a precisely similar context. Letters to Corinth, to the Colossians and Philippians, all deal with cultural challenges which threatened to distort or obscure the good news (pp. 218–23).
- In a post-modern society, living the Bible's story of love for God, issuing in obedience to his will because of his great love for us, is a powerful dynamic for change (pp. 223–6).
- Every individual life matters because we all affect the bigger picture in which society is moving either nearer to God, in obedience to Scripture, or further away from him (pp. 226–31).
- We need a more radical biblical approach to our involvement in everyday life – in the family, Church and nation. In each of these contexts, Scripture's priorities need to be recognised, believed and practised (pp. 231–5).
- The way to affirm our belief in the Bible is to let it loose in our own lives, and through them in the world at large, to declare and demonstrate its eternal truth (pp. 235–7).

Bibliography for further reading and study

The Bible's 'Big Picture'

Clowney, Edmund P. *The Unfolding Mystery – Discovering Christ in the Old Testament.* Colorado Springs: Nav Press, 1988.

Gibson, R. J. (ed.) *Interpreting God's Plan.* Carlisle: Paternoster, 1997.

Goldsworthy, Graeme *Gospel and Kingdom – a Christian interpretation of the Old Testament.* Exeter: Paternoster, 1981.

Strom, Mark *Days are Coming.* Sydney: Hodder & Stoughton, 1989.

Old Testament Books and Themes

Dumbrell, William J. *The Faith of Israel – Its Expression in the Books of the Old Testament.* Leicester: Inter-Varsity Press, 1989.

Martens, Elmer A. *God's Design – A Focus on Old Testament Theology.* Leicester: Inter-Varsity Press, 1994.

Motyer, J. Alec *A Scenic Route Through the Old Testament.* Leicester: Inter-Varsity Press, 1994.

Motyer, J. Alec *Look to the Rock – An Old Testament Background to our Understanding of Christ.* Leicester: Inter-Varsity Press, 1996.

New Testament Books and Themes

Barnett, Paul — *Bethlehem to Patmos – The New Testament Story*. Sydney: Hodder & Stoughton, 1989.

Gundry, Robert H. — *A Survey of the New Testament*, third edition. Carlisle: Paternoster, 1994.

Holwerda, David E. — *Jesus and Israel – One Covenant or Two?* Leicester: Inter-Varsity Press, 1995.

Ladd, George Eldon — *A Theology of the New Testament*. Guildford: Lutterworth Press, 1975.

Interpreting the Bible

Fee, Gordon D. and Stuart, Douglas — *How to Read the Bible for All Its Worth*. London: Scripture Union, 1993.

Klein, William W., Blomberg, Craig L. and Hubbard, Robert L. Jr — *Introduction to Biblical Interpretation*. Dallas: Word, 1994.

McCartney, Dan and Clayton, Charles — *Let the Reader Understand – A Guide to Interpreting and Applying the Bible*. Wheaton: Victor Books, 1994.

Reid, Andrew — *Postcard from Palestine – A Hands-on Guide to Reading and Using the Bible*. Kingsford: St Matthias Press, 1989.

The Bible's Reliability

Bruce, F. F. — *The New Testament Documents – Are They Reliable?* fifth edition. London: Inter-Varsity Press, 1960.

Carson, D. A. and Woodbridge, John. D. (ed.) — *Scripture and Truth*. Leicester: Inter-Varsity Press, 1983.

Packer, J. I. — *God Has Spoken*. London: Hodder & Stoughton, 1965.

Stott, John R. W.   *The Bible: Book for Today*. Leicester: Inter-Varsity Press, 1983.

The Bible's Message
Boice, J. Montgomery *Foundations of the Christian Faith*. Leicester: Inter-Varsity Press, 1986.

Guthrie, D. and   *The New Bible Commentary – 21st Century*
Motyer, J. A. (ed.) *Edition*. Leicester: Inter-Varsity Press, 1998.

Jensen, Peter   *At the Heart of the Universe – What Christians Believe*. Leicester: Inter-Varsity Press, 1991.

Milne, Bruce   *Know the Truth – A Handbook of Christian Belief*, second edition. Leicester: Inter-Varsity Press, 1998.